Watching War

Watching War

Jan Mieszkowski

Stanford University Press
Stanford, California

Stanford University Press
Stanford, California

Printed in the United States of America on acid-free,
archival-quality paper.

Library of Congress Cataloging-in-Publication Data

Mieszkowski, Jan, author.
    Watching war / Jan Mieszkowski.
        pages cm
    Includes bibliographical references and index.
    ISBN 978-0-8047-8239-5 (cloth : alk. paper) —
    ISBN 978-0-8047-8240-1 (pbk. : alk. paper)
    1. War in literature.   2. War in mass media.   3. Mass media—
Audiences.   I. Title.
    PN56.W3M54 2012
    303.6′609—dc23
                                                        2012005968

Typeset by Westchester Book Group in 10.9/13 Adobe Garamond

To Sarah

Contents

Illustrations

Acknowledgments

Many people have offered important advice and criticism at various stages of this project. I am particularly grateful to Benjamin David, David Ferris, Patrick Greaney, Werner Hamacher, Hugh Hochman, Jocelyn Holland, Edgar Landgraf, Jacques Lezra, Michael Mirabile, Haun Saussy, and Rei Terada. I would also like to thank the participants of the 2006 Bloomington Eighteenth-Century Studies Workshop at Indiana University, the editorial board of *PMLA*, who oversaw its October 2009 special issue on war, and the audiences at lectures I delivered at the University of Colorado at Boulder and the University of California at Santa Barbara. Completion of the manuscript was supported by a fellowship from the National Endowment for the Humanities, whom I thank for sharing their anonymous reports on my research. I finished the book while a Visiting Scholar at the Clark Library at UCLA, where Kirstie McClure and Sianne Ngai extended me warm hospitality. Final work on the text was guided by the insightful suggestions of Rebecca Comay and Paul K. Saint-Amour in their readers' reports. At Stanford University Press, Emily-Jane Cohen, Sarah Crane Newman, and the entire staff brought their considerable wisdom and expertise to bear throughout the editorial and production process. For her creativity, candid commentary, and support with all facets of the project, I am indebted to Sarah Roff, who will hopefully always have something better than war to occupy her discerning gaze.

Introduction

Watching War

At the opening of Michelangelo Antonioni's 1975 *The Passenger*, journalist David Locke is pursuing fieldwork in the deserts of Chad for a documentary about a guerrilla war. Locke follows combat as a professional observer, someone paid to convey news from the Third World to the First. Speaking for a moment as a viewer of the film rather than an actor in it, Jack Nicholson, who plays Locke, describes the scene succinctly: "This is the place where a war is taking place. This is a reporter trying to find it."[1] If human history is any guide, Locke should have no concerns about job security; there will always be a wealth of conflicts to cover. In this case, however, the desert is vast, his tips from local informants prove unreliable, and when his vehicle becomes stuck in the sand, he gives up. He has failed, in Nicholson's words, "to find the war upon which he is reporting— this is kind of Antonioni's sense of humor, you know, kind of a very dry joke."[2] The thesis of this book is that since the turn of the nineteenth century, we have all been in the same boat as Locke, trying—and failing— to find the war. The "dry joke" that has been played out time and again is that as armed conflicts have assumed unimaginable proportions and we have all become potential spectators to the destruction, the greatest show on earth of modern militarism has failed to meet its audiences' expectations by consistently underperforming as entertainment or shock or even as a forum that can reveal something essential about the human condition.

The spectatorial dynamic that has organized the experience of warfare over the past two centuries took shape in Napoleonic Europe, as military conflict acquired its unique status as a performance that everyone needed to follow. As early as 1789, Edmund Burke, a harsh critic of efforts to overthrow the House of Bourbon, offered his famous account of what it meant for the rest of Europe to be observing a civil war unfolding in a neighboring land: "As to us here our thoughts of everything at home are suspended, by our astonishment at the wonderful Spectacle which is exhibited in a Neighboring and rival Country—what Spectators, and what Actors! England gazing with astonishment at a French struggle for Liberty and not knowing whether to blame or to applaud!"[3] In Burke's view, even if we do not know whether to celebrate or disparage the "French struggle for liberty," we can still rejoice in the sight of it. The audience in this theater of world history was as aware of its own importance as a collective viewing entity as it was respectful of the significance of the show it was watching—a show, Burke stressed, in comparison to which one's own life would necessarily appear unremarkable. When he wrote that we do not know "whether to blame or to applaud," he was referring both to the overthrow of the French monarchy and to the fact that France was offering his compatriots a gripping spectacle. In this realm of mass spectatorship, political events acquired their significance as much from their status as something to be consumed or ignored as from their consequences for the agents who effected them. In lauding both the audience and the actors, Burke underscored that the performance could be fully appreciated only from a god's-eye view that encompassed those on stage as well as onlookers in England and abroad.

If the French Revolution established the framework for this theater of world history, sustained warfare among the European powers would come to take top billing in the ensuing twenty years. Burke's sense that the emerging mass audience was conscious of its own significance as a witness to world affairs was intensified by the universalizing forces of the French revolutionary wars, which were formalized with the *levée en masse* of August 23, 1793, the proclamation on the basis of which all Frenchmen became part of the army.[4] "Suddenly," as the Prussian soldier and military theorist Carl von Clausewitz wrote, war "became the business of the people."[5] With the advantage of hindsight, Raymond Williams would echo this sentiment, arguing that the modern notion of the "mass" was forged at the turn of the nineteenth century.[6] He might have added that it was first and foremost a mass of spectators consuming war. As Georg Lukács has observed, the French revolutionary and Napoleonic wars made history "for the first time . . . a *mass experience,* and moreover on a European scale" such that "the whole of Europe becomes a war arena."[7]

The new notion of the citizenry as a conglomeration of individuals mobilized to wage war was paralleled by the equally novel idea that the populace was now united in its status as an audience viewing the conflict. For millions in Great Britain and across the Continent, government bulletins and the burgeoning newspaper industry offered an opportunity to monitor the campaigns via published reports, and reading about them became a part of daily life.[8] By 1815 European civilians had all become virtual battlefield spectators, observing from afar. The remote monitoring of war may have been a necessity for British citizens, whose campaigns were not fought on their home soil, but it also became the norm in the rest of Europe since the Napoleonic era did not yet see the mass displacement or annihilation of populations, and relatively few people witnessed the battles firsthand.[9] Henceforth, waging a military campaign required managing the spectacle of battle consumed on the home front as much as defeating one's foe on the field of combat, as clashes of armies came to be assessed not just with reference to the number of dead and wounded but also as objects of observation and analysis: What kinds of reports about them were available?[10] Did these representations of combat enlighten, horrify, or stupefy their audiences?

These questions have proven intractable. Over the past two centuries, both scholars and pundits have engaged in a wide-ranging series of debates about whether human beings abhor or enjoy reading about and viewing the suffering of others, with warfare—the ultimate manmade disaster— serving as the crucial test case. Since the Vietnam War, these conversations have only intensified as advances in telecommunications have offered media consumers a growing wealth of still and moving images of dead bodies and devastated cityscapes. Widespread access to such material has led to no consensus about whether military spectacles fascinate the mass audience, repel it, or simply distract people temporarily from their day-to-day concerns. As the archetype of sublimity, a battle ostensibly promises us a great deal to see, but modern viewers are neither sufficiently appreciative of nor sufficiently traumatized by the show, as if even the most extreme engagement with the combat can never be stimulating enough. Several years after the 2003 U.S. invasion of Iraq, movie and television news producers remained unanimous in their despair about the poor ratings that had been garnered by shows about the war; with little fanfare, the public had moved on to reruns of *Lost* and the new season of *American Idol*.

Our contemporary ambivalence about watching war is the product of several aspects of the Napoleonic inheritance. One is the notion of war as part of the "everyday."[11] As devastating as it may be to think of combat as permanent or routine, the very regularity and ubiquity of violence can make it simply one more thing for media consumers to keep tabs on, like the weather or sports scores. Despite the historically unprecedented degree of death and destruction it effects, war risks being received as commonplace or even monotonous—as if it rendered the distinction between pathos and bathos irrelevant. A second key feature of the Napoleonic legacy is the inherently mediated—today we would say "virtual"—nature of the battlefield. Recent scholarship on war and representational media has tended to underplay the radical changes in war spectatorship that took place at the turn of the nineteenth century, focusing instead on later technological innovations. Beginning with the rise of photography and continuing with the advent of film and digital telecommunications, soldiers have come to wage battles with the same devices that allow audiences around the globe to follow their exploits. Whereas combat was once thought to take the form of engagements of men and arms framed by distinct spatiotemporal parameters, today's military operations are characterized as exchanges between distant parties in which the weapons are electromagnetic waves rather than guns or bombs. These developments are sometimes seen as part of a broader disruption of the very distinction between a medium and what it mediates such that even the event of death, as Jean Baudrillard has observed, fails to serve as the basis for a coherent opposition between the real and the imaginary.[12]

As consequential as technological change has been, it is the argument of this book that the modern perception of warfare was distinguished by a conjunction of physical devastation and elusive simulacra long before the invention of photography or film, much less television or the Internet. If we live in an era of hyperreal wars, we have been doing so for a long time, which is why verbal media that make no claim to facilitate unmediated transmissions of information have been and continue to be as central to war spectatorship as visual media, which appear to offer a more direct encounter with the exigencies of being under fire. In Bonaparte's Europe, information disseminated through print media was an important medium of combat. At the end of the eighteenth century, the emergence of a vast reading public for the burgeoning discourse of newspapers and government bulletins meant that generals could widely disseminate their own interpretations of battles as they fought them. Then, as now, to "win" a battle was as much to secure control of the story in the popular imagination as to rout the opponent's forces or take control of a particular locale. While subsequent refinements in recording and communications media have created new possibilities for experiencing the seemingly impossible speed and destructiveness of twenty-first-century violence, such advances repeat rather than essentially transform a viewing dynamic that had already taken shape at the turn of the nineteenth century, as the modern mass audience assumed its central place on the world stage. Contemporary missiles—be they nuclear or information based—may be faster than Napoleon's artillery or propaganda bulletins, but they only confirm the fact that, for the past two centuries, war has been defined by the interconnection of—even the identity between—the devices used to wage it and the devices used to view it. To speak today of the dissolution of the traditional battlefield as battles are now fought both within electronic networks and on terra firma is to describe something already set in motion at least two hundred years ago, when the scale and complexity of the emerging combat meant that the only observers with any chance of grasping these events were those who were willing to give free rein to their fantasies about what war was like.

Far from transparent in its mechanisms and consequences, Napoleonic combat manifested itself as both an awesome destructive force and a field of signs to be read and interpreted. Whether as a soldier, a bystander, or a civilian reading the newspaper, the individual confronted battles with a range of ideals and prejudices about what warfare was, a set of expectations that made up what I term the *Napoleonic war imaginary*. Under the influence of this military mythology, what one "saw" with one's mind's eye—how the waves of men and arms *should* have appeared—was deemed at least as reliable as what could be seen with one's retina. In turn, the ideal war spectator was characterized not as an eagle-eyed firsthand witness but as an individual with unique creative faculties, such as a novelist thousands of miles away writing about what the battle must have been like. Even the accounts of battles penned by seasoned military veterans of the period betray an apologetic tone for the degree to which their renditions of events could never be empirical enough, as if their retellings were structured by preconceptions about how a war story should sound to its audience. When, more than a century after Waterloo, Ernst Jünger recalled his time in the trenches of the First World War and wondered why it now seemed as if it had been only a fantasy, he was merely pursuing the implications of the Napoleonic war imaginary to their logical conclusion.

Since anyone following from afar could participate vicariously in the imaginative exercise of witnessing the battle "as it must have been," the emergence of these mediated spectatorial dynamics blurred the boundary between the experiences of combatants and the representation of these experiences. The assumption that firsthand witness took priority over secondhand accounts of battles was further challenged by the widespread conviction that soldiers or bystanders could not fully grasp their experience at Austerlitz or Borodino until they had related it to others. A vexed interdependence thus emerged between witnessing a battle "live" and reading and writing about it after the fact, the one remaining incomplete unless it had been supplemented by the other. From the commanding general to the individual soldier under fire, combatants took steps to ensure that what transpired on the battlefield could subsequently be imparted to an audience. In this respect, the European public following the Napoleonic Wars from afar was no less a part of the action than those who were actually there. The resulting array of first-, second- and thirdhand reports helped to perpetuate fantasies about the insights to be won by the immediate experience of a battlefield's horrors at the same time as it unsettled the dichotomy between a direct and an indirect engagement with them.

Contemporary war audiences are frequently said to be under the thumb of an entertainment-military-industrial complex, a fusion of the corporate militarism identified by Eisenhower with the culture industry described by Max Horkheimer and Theodor W. Adorno in *Dialectic of Enlightenment*.[13] In these terms, the spectacle of warfare, whether by intermittently shocking its public or inuring it to the horrors of combat, serves to normalize a permanent war economy and to render peace an anomaly. One of the most commonly discussed features of this system is the profound interdependence between the military and news services. Since the U.S. invasion of Iraq in 2003, there has been intense scrutiny of the relationship between Western governments and the media. In an effort to perfect its own performance, the White House consults with public relations and advertising firms, as well as Hollywood executives, and the Pentagon has demonstrated particular skill at playing to the camera as it tailors its operations for their smooth integration into the twenty-four-hour news cycle. For their part, journalists have been criticized for their reluctance to question official proclamations, often seeming to defer to state authority and to exploit the nationalistic impulses of their audiences in the quest for ratings.[14]

Nevertheless, for all their efforts to entice viewers with the promise of "live" battlefield coverage, the Western media have just as often insisted that their transmissions fail to capture what their reporters are witnessing.[15] Even when the explicit intent of the story is to create a "you were there" effect, the limitations of the medium are openly acknowledged, if not foregrounded, as the "real" story. In a recent online feature, the *New York Times* posted helmet camera video from a soldier in a U.S. military unit's engagement in Afghanistan. Instead of offering the raw film feed, the paper provided an edited version in which the footage of the events was complemented with voiceover narration, intertitles summarizing the "plot" and foreshadowing events to come, and scenes of the soldier who made the video recounting the story at a comfortable remove from the battlefield. Despite the ostensible novelty of the core sequence, the article was explicit that all of this "does not quite capture" the scene and that, in watching the soldiers, what one most directly perceives is the inability to feel what they felt.[16] In fact, the very notion of a flawless conduit of information is profoundly threatening to the experiential authority of war participants and correspondents. To assert that one can impart perfect reproductions of combat experiences is to cede claim to the insight supposedly won by virtue of the fact that one is actually at the battlefield, while one's viewing, listening, or reading public is not. At the very moment when contemporary audiovisual transmissions have threatened to replicate military violence more exactly than ever before, it becomes incumbent on the living, breathing commentator to recast these events in fantastic and even mythological terms. Far from banishing the ghosts of war, technology reinstates their spectral authority in an attempt to preserve the fantasy of a pure immediacy that may never have existed.

Uniquely difficult to observe or share, battles are not merely one object of mass spectatorship among others but have become paradigmatic for the way in which the mass audience processes information in general. In the wake of Austerlitz or Waterloo, to participate in a military campaign as a soldier or an onlooker was to adopt a host of positions on the complex relationship between the perceptual and representational logics that organized the appearance of combat. The result was hardly a triumph of theory over experience. If, as Paul Virilio has claimed, "the history of battle is primarily the history of radically changing fields of perception," it is a history not of the primacy of the abstract over the concrete but of the tangible violence involved when we attempt, as any war watcher must, to control the "immaterial" dimensions of perceptual fields.[17] Since the advent of the Napoleonic war imaginary, this "immateriality," which Virilio also terms war's "magical" or "spiritual" dimension, marks the gap between any given manifestation of war—an array of troops, an explosion-filled sky—and the overarching trajectory of a campaign in which establishing power over the intelligible realm is as important as dominating the corporeal one. It is the persistence of this gap that ensures that war will be uniquely destructive to both mind and body.

To be a member of the war audience is potentially to affirm the natural or inevitable character of the show. Resisting the militarization of society thus means countering the authority of the spectacle—averting one's eyes may not be enough. However, it is far from obvious how the "masses" conceived of as a conglomeration of individuals following war in the press relates to the notion of the "masses" as a collectivity expressing itself at the ballot box or in the shopping mall. In *Society of the Spectacle*, Guy Debord proposed that "the spectacle cannot be understood as a mere visual deception produced by mass-media technologies. It is a world-view that has actually been materialized, a view of a world that has become objective."[18] There is no better example of such an objective materialization of a world-view than a battle, although we must be cognizant of Debord's claim that the spectacle does more than simply unite its audience since the "unification it achieves is nothing but an official language of universal separation."[19] One version of this separation-through-unification may be the semblance of solidarity effected by the communal observation of war. At the end of his essay on art in the age of its technological reproducibility, Walter Benjamin designated war as fascism's strategy for mobilizing the masses without altering the social relations of ownership, implying that the modern military enterprise sustains itself by enjoining populations to watch human beings destroy one another with the same fusion of pleasure and critical appraisal with which they watch Charlie Chaplin films. The spectacle of destruction, Benjamin proposed, had become a common focal point not to mobilize resistance to the status quo but rather to preserve the socioeconomic dynamics that pit people against one another, uniting them by solidifying their divisions.

Benjamin's invocation of film audiences is important because one of the most unrelenting features of Napoleonic war spectatorship is the illusion of choice regarding our status as war watchers, born of the belief that we, like Britons between 1792 and 1815, are securely tucked away in a safe place with the actual combat held at arm's length. In recent years, advances in digital telecommunications have seen the vanity of the sheltered consumer intensify, as Western media consumers wittingly or unwittingly embrace the notion that war is theirs to watch or not: as gripping as live video feeds may be, we can always turn them off. The abiding nature of this sense of spectatorial impunity is difficult to understand given military historians' suggestion that the last two centuries have been distinguished by the advent of total war, the dissolution of any boundary between soldiers and civilians situated safely beyond the reach of violence. This book argues that one of the formative changes in the Napoleonic era was the emergence of an explicit discourse about the fact that it was no longer clear who was left to narrate military events "from the outside."[20] Discussions of the seemingly unlimited nature of combat were accompanied by fantasies of a "total gaze" that could observe and record the proceedings, providing perfect access to the sights and sounds of war. Long before cell-phone cameras became ubiquitous on the field of battle, the military experience was treated as unique because it offered up its gory details to rigorous scrutiny.

Johann Wolfgang von Goethe poignantly posed the question of what the erasure of the distinction between soldiers and their audiences meant for the possibility of telling war stories: "Formerly, somebody could communicate his sufferings to others; he could recount his war experience in old age. These days misery is universal; the individual can no longer lament anymore. Everybody must be on the battlefield—who is there to listen when [warriors] tell their tales?"[21] Once a war story no longer imparts a content experienced by the few but simply repeats what everyone already knows because everyone has collectively experienced it, warfare names less a specific theme or topic than a template for a common discourse, a schema or filter that shapes all stories. In this respect, the total character of modern war heralds the militarization of discursive experience in general. As with Debord's spectacle, this dynamic was unifying precisely because it divided people. What Walter Benjamin wrote about the twentieth-century press was already relevant at the beginning of the nineteenth century: "Newspapers appear in large editions. Few readers can boast of having any information that another reader may need from them."[22] At its birth, the media's hottest topic was stillborn. The gaze of the modern war watcher was defined not by a single pair of curious or horrified eyes—whether myopic or all-seeing—but by the gaze of a mass that surveyed a common property whose interest was by no means self-evident. Far from functioning as a force of discrimination or differentiation, observation served to amalgamate its objects and its viewers indifferently. The shared story of total war both atomized and united the populace since everyone was now independent of everyone else by virtue of not needing any assistance to share in the communal narrative perpetuated by print and word of mouth.

The twenty-first-century citizen's ability to watch war is starkly impacted by corporate and state forces determined to broadcast their versions of events. As we have already mentioned, the communal narrative that emerged in early nineteenth-century Europe was similarly shaped by the powerful information system that developed as warring generals and politicians took advantage of the new mass media, founding a discourse in which waging a war and disseminating their account of operations to the public would be one and the same. Monitoring the press, as well as appointing its editors and in some cases simply acquiring the relevant newspapers,[23] Napoleon's government also issued war bulletins that were distributed well beyond the borders of France.[24] Marveling at the power of this propaganda machine, Prince Klemens von Metternich of Austria opined that "the newspapers are worth an army of three-hundred-thousand men to Napoleon," adding that "the public cannot tell if news is true or false."[25] Naturally, this mass propaganda was accompanied by skepticism about the "official story." The readers who consumed the artful bulletins of the Napoleonic government were far from naïve or uncritical. If the English economist and theologian Richard Whately mockingly commented that "generally speaking, we may say it is on the testimony of the newspapers that men believe in the existence and exploits of Napoleon Bonaparte," he was also aware that much of the European public treated official French reports, in particular their casualty figures, as unreliable, even openly ridiculing them as lies.[26]

Whately was interested less in the credibility of the information itself than in the fact that there was now a common discourse in which war and indeed the very course of history could be followed and evaluated daily on a mass scale. In a sense, Napoleon and his exploits *did* exist by virtue of the mythologies that surrounded them, not to mention the evaluative systems popularized by his war machine, which were designed to help people decide not just who had won or lost a particular engagement but also what that engagement meant for the future of the war and European history in general. This violent interplay of representational systems, physical destruction, and competing interpretive authorities has proven to be one of the most abiding features of the Napoleonic legacy, continuing to shape our cultural experience in the twenty-first century. First and foremost, it is a dynamic that claims to encompass everyone, obliterating any hope that we might critique it "from without." The all-inclusive nature of this system threatens the very identity of war's audience members as observers. If our status as onlookers to the battle is predetermined by the military's own script, then we are playing the role of bystanders from inside the war effort.

As Whatley's comments also suggest, Napoleon Bonaparte was more than one agent among others in this mythohistorical pageant; he was the name for a complex of aesthetic and political doctrines. A collection of emblems and slogans as much as a human being, the first great celebrity in the age of mass media boasted a cult of personality that aimed to make the chaos of modern combat comprehensible and the ubiquitous, predictable story of "another day at the battlefield" fascinating and all-consuming. This attempt to reaffirm order and meaningfulness in the European theater of war took the form of a dual legend of visual authority in which the Little Corporal was at once a superhuman observer, the standard by which all other war watchers would be judged wanting, and a wondrous object who captured the attention of all. His inner eye, "an intellect," wrote Clausewitz, "that, even in the darkest hour, retains some glimmerings of the inner light which leads to truth," was matched only by his outer eye, his purported ability to take in the battlefield and process all of its mysteries in a single glance.[27] Even today, many historical descriptions of Napoleon's defeats turn on key moments at which his line of sight is said to have been blocked. When he was defeated for the last time, his supernatural optic powers were conferred to his vanquisher, Wellington, whose "lynx's eyes seemed to penetrate the smoke, and forestall the movements of the foe."[28]

The French emperor's legendary coup d'œil was complemented by his ability to make a spectacle of himself. The self-styled general as genius and auteur of world history routinely engineered mass events that would be the envy of any twentieth- or twenty-first-century filmmaker, and fictional and nonfictional accounts of his battles invariably include a description of the magical moment when he is espied passing by. Seeing all and being seen by all, the usurper of the Sun King was said to be able to conjure *le soleil* when required. According to legend, the clouds parted at a crucial juncture at Austerlitz, allowing him to review the field of combat and thus to emerge victorious. Gathering light to overcome darkness, this mythical creature devoured the enlightenment emblem of the French Revolution and the Apollonian emblem of the French monarchy in a single gesture.[29] The subject of no one but the object of everyone's gaze, Napoleon was thought to be the individual uniquely able to narrate history as he made it, synchronizing the pen and the sword, since everyone was expected to watch him as both the ultimate exception—a superhuman among men—and the purveyor of the story of war that was everyone's story.

If the French emperor embodied the autoproductive ideal of a historical system that could simultaneously interpret and confirm its own significance as it shaped the course of world history, he was also the embodiment of the inherently incomplete and impermanent authority of this system. Nineteenth-century views of his reign were preoccupied with coming to terms with the spectacular nature of his fall. At the moment at which his tremendous eyesight and his ability to catch everyone else's eye could not save his cause, Napoleon became the greatest star on earth in the act of being deposed. As with the sudden demise of contemporary politicians or celebrities in tabloid feeding frenzies, the real excitement in viewing the Hegelian subject-become-object of world history was watching him go up in flames as his talent for "seeing and being seen" culminated in his spectacular self-destruction.[30]

The intimate relationship between seeing and not seeing that defined Napoleonic war watching makes it difficult to situate its spectatorial logics within the standard accounts of the modern politics of observation. Over the last several decades, Michel Foucault's conception of disciplinary society has inspired numerous studies of the ideological complexities of tele- and microscopic practices and their importance for post-Enlightenment regimes of biopower. The sense that "now more than ever we are under surveillance" has come to inform a variety of descriptions of the Western social order, which is characterized as a field of panoptic systems of limitless observation in which every business transaction, telephone conversation, or walk down the street gives rise to a mnemonic field of electronic traces.[31] Yet despite the manifold ways in which technological reproducibility has come to organize every facet of contemporary life, the legacy of Napoleonic war spectatorship suggests that the most comprehensive or intrusive gaze is not necessarily the most powerful. Discussing the primacy of vision in the military domain, Virilio invokes Napoleon's declaration that "to command is to speak to the eyes" without specifying what sort of authoritative speech is required to permit the eyes to "hear" or "see"—or correspondingly, what sort of political power is at work when vision "speaks."[32] Focusing on the tensions that organize the eminently fallible myth of Napoleonic infallibility, Foucault accords the emperor special ideological significance as "the individual who looms over everything with a single gaze that no detail, however minute, can escape," although he also regards Napoleon as a conflicted formation, a transitional figure with one foot in the old culture of spectacle and the other in the new culture of surveillance:

> At the moment of its full blossoming, the disciplinary society still assumes with the Emperor the old aspect of the power of spectacle. As a monarch who is at one and the same time a usurper of the ancient throne and the organizer of the new state, he combined into a single symbolic, ultimate figure the whole of the long process by which the pomp of sovereignty, the necessarily spectacular manifestations of power, were extinguished one by one in the daily exercise of surveillance, in a panopticism in which the vigilance of intersecting gazes was soon to render useless both the eagle and the sun.[33]

The shift Foucault describes from a society of spectacle to a society of surveillance, from the amphitheater or the stage to the panopticon, was never completed. Both systems persist, coexisting uneasily; at times they are at odds, at others mutually reinforcing.[34] If the "intersecting gazes" have proven insufficiently vigilant, it is because they continue to judge their objects through the earlier paradigm of a singular sovereign power and are therefore at best only half-hearted about what they see. Correspondingly, the individual mechanisms of surveillance are undoubtedly watchful, but they are unable to coordinate with one another to create a comprehensive composite, producing only an incomplete or confused picture, more kaleidoscopic than a perfect panoramic view.

The key question is how these developments have impacted the core of our Napoleonic inheritance, the notion of the battlefield as an unrivaled scene of force and destruction, the ultimate "spectacular manifestation of power." Has its primacy been blunted by the "daily exercise of surveillance," or has this attention only added to its mystique since no degree of scrutiny can compel it to offer up its secrets? In considering the failures of the modern quest for panoptic military vision, existing scholarship has either taken its cue from the classical discourse on the sublime, in which the collision of powerful armies is said to occur at the border of comprehensibility, or it has worked to identify traumatic temporal paradigms, observing not only that witnesses to war may incur long-lasting emotional injuries but also that war is experienced precisely in being missed or forgotten.[35] Broadening our account of the challenges inherent in war spectatorship to include less direct forms of disruption to the viewer-spectacle relationship, this book argues that since the early nineteenth century, war watching has been distinguished by dynamics of obscurity, deferral, and belatedness. Two hundred years after Waterloo, improvements in what can be observed and recorded have not altered the fact that the experience of the battlefield audience is still largely defined by what it does not or cannot see. While the modern theater of war presents itself as a near-universal forum in which everyone is by default an onlooker, it remains a fable about the impotence rather than the triumph of the eye. As with Antonioni's journalist, the fighting may elude the most intrepid viewer. Even in the best of circumstances, what one can see is never sufficient to understand what one wants to know, as if warfare can never make good on its promise to explain the *what, why*, and *how* of its operations through its spectacles. Since war never disavows this offer, its capacity to surprise us is complemented by its equally powerful ability to disappoint. At times beset by shock, the modern war audience has also been marked by distraction, indifference, and boredom.

For many of Napoleon's contemporaries, an inattentive or even indifferent viewing public was a predictable consequence of the empty public discourse created by the nascent mass audience's consumption of wartime news, a discourse that was thought to threaten the very distinction between scholarly letters and sensationalism. One of the first such critiques of the modern news cycle was offered by William Wordsworth, who gave voice to the fear that the shock of war might be difficult to distinguish from the schlock of war when he declared in the 1800 preface to his *Lyrical Ballads* that

> a multitude of causes, unknown to former times, are now acting with a combined force to blunt the discriminating powers of the mind, and, unfitting it

for all voluntary exertion, to reduce it to a state of almost savage torpor. The most effective of these causes are the great national events which are daily taking place, and the increasing accumulation of men in cities, where the uniformity of their occupations produces a craving for extraordinary incident, which the rapid communication of intelligence hourly gratifies. To this tendency of life and manners the literature and theatrical exhibitions of the country have conformed themselves.[36]

This passage is generally treated as part of Wordsworth's views on the expansion of capitalism and the resulting proliferation of reading matter and rapid growth of a reading public.[37] Its specific claim is that the press, in making daily or hourly access to unusual stories a standard feature of modern experience, has ensured that even men and women of letters will be transformed into cheap shock jocks. While Wordsworth does not identify the ongoing European military conflicts by name, they were the primary source of the "great national events" driving the regular consumption of broadsheet sublimity, and the omnipresence of war news was very much on his mind. Two years earlier, he and his friend Samuel Taylor Coleridge had made plans to move to Germany in order to sit out the war, having concluded that their safe vantage point in Britain was no longer safe enough. At that time, Coleridge voiced complaints similar to Wordsworth's: "The insensibility with which we now hear of the most extraordinary Revolutions is a very remarkable symptom of the public temper, and no unambiguous indication of the state of the times. We now read with listless unconcern of events which, but a few years ago, would have filled all Europe with astonishment."[38]

Coleridge's observation that the public had become inured to the significance of the daily news was prompted by criticisms of his 1798 poem "Fears in Solitude," written, as its subtitle explains, "during the alarm of an invasion [by the French]," an invasion that may have been no more than a chimerical fear inspired by government rumors designed to inspire popular resentment of England's neighbors across the Channel.[39] Like Wordsworth in the preface to *Lyrical Ballads*, Coleridge is concerned in this poem with the status of the people of Britain as consumers of spectacle. While their armies have been involved in numerous military clashes abroad, the civilian populace has been content to sit back and take in the trials and tribulations of others: "We, this whole people, have been clamorous / For war and bloodshed; animating sports, / To which we pay for as a thing to talk of, / Spectators and not combatants!"[40] More specifically, Coleridge describes Britain as a nation of newspaper readers eagerly devouring stories about battles occurring elsewhere: "Boys and girls, / And women, that would groan to see a child / Pull off an insect's leg, all read of war, / The best amusement for our morning meal!"[41]

These initial remarks about war as a spectator sport are only the first step in a far-reaching argument that presents the intimate relationship between language and war as crucial to understanding the emerging mass culture. Coleridge himself expressed some skepticism as to whether "Fears in Solitude" was a successful poem, prompting scholars to debate whether politics corrupted the work's aesthetic elegance or whether Coleridge's effort to put a political message in lyric form destroyed the message.[42] The poet's more fundamental concern, however, was whether permanent warfare in Europe was doing irremediable damage to language itself. His addenda to his text suggest that he was well aware that in the course of diagnosing the savage torpor that he and Wordsworth deplored, his lyric opened itself to the charge of exemplifying the very sensationalism it decried. "Fears in Solitude" is not just a poem about the failure of public discourse; it also directly confronts its own status as a symptom of that discourse and acknowledges that its readers may have no choice but to consume it in the same spirit in which they devour their morning newspapers.

In this regard, Coleridge's key insight may be that collective military spectatorship does not facilitate a productive communal conversation in which information and ideas can be shared and debated both rationally and democratically. Instead, wartime is marked by a breakdown in the public sphere that impacts the entire social realm. The forms of speech— prayers, oaths, promises—by virtue of which language ostensibly confirms its power to establish relationships and articulate truths have become mechanical parodies of themselves, performatives that scarcely gesture toward an alignment with constative utterances. In the churches, the words of the Gospel are not preached but muttered in rote fashion by men "too indolent / To deem them falsehoods or to know their truth."[43] The political arena offers a similar scene of discursive bankruptcy, nothing more than a "speech-mouthing, speech-reporting Guild, / [a] One Benefit-Club for mutual flattery."[44] For Coleridge, the threat of war, or rather the threat that Britain's inhabitants will no longer have the luxury of watching war from the sidelines, names not only the danger of invasion or the risk of being oppressed by the reactionary forces that govern

Britain but also the possibility that language itself has been invaded and conquered by a power that no national government can control.

While Coleridge's poem presents the discourse of wartime as a language that consistently undercuts its own promise to deliver meaningful utterances, the result is not a tongue-tied populace but a generalized verbal felicity: "[T]he poor wretch, who has learnt his only prayers / . . . who knows scarcely words enough / To ask a blessing from his Heavenly Father, / Becomes a fluent phraseman, absolute / And technical in victories and defeats, / And all our dainty terms for fratricide."[45] Not only can anyone master this new idiom, but in a kind of universalization of oratorical prowess, war-speak also gives everyone the means to become a skilled speaker, allowing even the uneducated to express themselves with confidence. What is thereby articulated is by no means substantial or even meaningful. Coleridge is explicit that the expostulations war facilitates are "terms which we trundle smoothly o'er our tongues / Like mere abstractions, empty sounds to which / We join no feeling and attach no form!"[46] As I have already suggested, this disjunction between content and expression extends to encompass the very poem that diagnoses it. The presence of the word *phraseman*, coined here for the first time in English according to the *OED*, indicates that "Fears in Solitude" may itself be a product of the military system that guides the smooth empty sounds of others.[47]

Composed at the dawn of the Napoleonic war imaginary, Coleridge's poem considers a theoretical invasion as the impetus for asking whether the real conflict was taking place abroad or at home in the language of self-understanding. One of the principal implications of this exposition of wartime discourse is that any discussion of war may be thoroughly compromised by its object. It is not simply that one inadvertently helps sustain or glorify the war effort by discussing it irrespective of whether one believes that one supports its means or ends. The kinds of self-reflection that emerge in audiences living under the permanent shadow of widespread conflict make it nearly impossible to forge links between the material and the abstract experience of combat. Although there may be no deficit of sympathy or concern in the onlookers, they are fated to talk about warfare "as if the soldier died without a wound; / As if the fibres of this godlike frame / Were gored without a pang; as if the wretch, / Who fell in battle, doing bloody deeds, / Passed off to Heaven, translated and not killed."[48] The central concern of "Fears in Solitude" is that all wartime rhetoric that strives to speak in the name of hope, tranquility, or peace—that is, in the name of something that does not currently exist—may be a language of deception that talks about reality *as if* it were more abstract than is in fact the case. At the same time, any discourse about war that seeks to describe the material immediacy of suffering and despair without any abstraction whatsoever is at risk of being condemned as a series of empty phrases and dainty terms, a flattering mouthing of oaths and promises that has no way of accounting for its own status as true or false.

Allegedly prompted by the threat of an invasion of the British Isles—a conflict that never took place—Coleridge's poem invokes fear as a cathartic force that will help his compatriots understand the reality of the wars that have largely been fought by proxy, but this is only a simulated fear, the projected response to an imaginary attack. The emotional force that is to prompt a return to the "real world" reveals the British populace to be more isolated in its fantasies than ever before. In this respect, the fundamental fear of "Fears in Solitude" is solitude itself. When the poem was reissued in the 1809 edition of *The Friend*, it was titled "Fears *of* Solitude,"[49] which the editors of Coleridge's *Collected Works* indicate "might have been a mistake,"[50] although "[Karl] Kroeber has argued that the reprinted poem conveys Coleridge's intensified fears that his criticisms of his government would isolate him from patriotic Britons."[51] One might instead conclude that this "typographical error" reveals a—in 1809 purely hypothetical—peacetime discourse, a discourse that could not routinely avail itself of figures of fear, to be just as threatening as its wartime counterpart.

"Fears in Solitude" is an experiment in an imaginary violence. Its account of the relationship between the signifying practices and material consequences of modern combat suggests that public discourses about war are constantly at risk of trivializing mass violence in the very act of trying to do the opposite. For the generation that followed Wordsworth and Coleridge, the interplay of physical and linguistic strife and its implications for the theory and practice of war were also of paramount consideration. These problems were perhaps most influentially explored by Clausewitz in his magnum opus *On War*.[52] The text has long been viewed as a compromise formation both in terms of its production—it was famously unfinished at the author's death and appeared posthumously in an edition edited by his wife—and in terms of its conceptual orientation, which lurches between idealist and pragmatic impulses that pit Clausewitz the philosopher against Clausewitz the battlefield engineer, Clausewitz the devotee of Napoleon against Clausewitz the sober scholar of history, and so on. These tensions are compounded by what seem like terminological inconsistencies, especially when it comes to Clausewitz's concepts of "absolute war," "complete war," and "ideal war," as well as his evident uncertainty about whether the Napoleonic campaigns saw these extreme forms of violence realized in practice.

Adding to the confusion is the fact that Clausewitz's work does not seemed to be shaped by an overarching methodology. While eighteenth-century military theorists recognized that both the concept and the phenomenon of war are ridden by precarious and potentially disastrous antitheses, they were nonetheless convinced that war could be analyzed through a scientific (*wissenschaftliche*) exposition that would reveal it to be an ordered system, a set of processes and practices subject to predictable rules.[53] Clausewitz perceived limitations to this approach, and in important respects he sought to develop a discourse whose novelty would rival the uniqueness of his topic. The fact that the idiosyncrasies of his analyses have never adversely impacted his popularity offers one of the strongest indications that the Napoleonic war imaginary and the vicissitudes of wartime rhetoric that preoccupied Coleridge continue to shape our experience of military phenomena. Despite their age, dialectical complexity, and at times fragmentary character, Clausewitz's writings remain standard texts at military colleges and are a favorite reference for academics and journalists, who invoke his pithy formulations at every opportunity.[54]

If a single phrase captures popular unease about warfare in the twenty-first century, it is Clausewitz's "fog of war," a description of the intractable uncertainty that pervades the conception and execution of military campaigns. The metaphor is ubiquitous, whether used negatively to forecast the demise of the best-laid plans or in an exculpatory fashion to excuse the powers that be when their invasions go awry. Examining Clausewitz's texts, it is far from obvious why this expression was fated to become his leitmotif. In *On War* fog first makes its entrance when Clausewitz declares that "war is the realm of uncertainty; three quarters of the factors on which action in war is based lie in a fog of greater or lesser uncertainty."[55] "Fog" functions here to give shape to the vague and unpredictable; it is evidently not as foggy as "uncertainty" itself, which it is supposed to make more tangible.[56] This fog does not obscure so much as it provides a form, albeit a hazy, shifting one, for something more abstract that is not directly accessible to the senses. To reduce this passage to the catchy "fog of war" is to simplify Clausewitz's implicit formula, which might more accurately be expressed as "the fog of the uncertainty of war." The difference between this—admittedly awkward—construction and the familiar version becomes significant when the image of fog returns in a later passage:

> [T]he general unreliability of all information presents a special problem in war: all action takes place, as it were [*gewissermaßen*], in a kind of twilight, which, like fog or moonlight, often tends to make things seem grotesque and larger than they really are. Whatever is hidden from full view in this feeble light has to be guessed at by talent, or simply left to the goodwill of chance [*die Gunst des Zufalls*].[57]

Here, the word *fog* is literal, part of a simile that clarifies the twilight's status as a metaphor for the unreliability of information in war, and, like its earlier metaphorical counterpart, *fog* functions not to obscure but to render something more precise. Fog straddles the literal-figural divide, representing intangibles, clarifying other figurative terms, and sometimes standing in as "itself," a meteorological phenomenon in the atmosphere, as when Clausewitz maintains that one example of the role that chance plays in war is the weather, then goes on to specify fog as one such happenstance. Yet even in this final capacity, fog is always more than fog. Shortly after his discussion of military action in the twilight, Clausewitz writes: "It is rarer still for weather to be a decisive factor [in war]. As a rule only fog makes any difference."[58] Initially invoked as an example of how the weather can profoundly influence a battle, fog is subsequently declared to be the only form of weather that can be truly decisive, which is particularly surprising given that in other sections of *On War*, Clausewitz emphasizes the importance of a variety of meteorological phenomena, including the famous example of Waterloo, where rain softened the ground and made it difficult to move the artillery. Functioning as an uncertain standard of uncertainty and unreliability, fog, both a metaphor of metaphor and an example of exemplarity, perpetually under- and overperforms where its promise to obscure is concerned, which is to say that fog is simultaneously the most literal and the most figurative term in Clausewitz's discourse.

While Clausewitz is sometimes accused of being "too theoretical" in rendering the physical immediacies of war abstract, his exposition of fog suggests that his study of war systematically confronts tensions between the ideal, the actual, and the virtual. These same difficulties arise when he wrestles with the word *friction*, which he describes as "the only concept that pretty generally [*ziemlich allgemein*] corresponds to the factors that distinguish real war from war on paper."[59] A physics term that refers to the resistance between two bodies or surfaces, friction functions here metaphorically as a concept to describe the resistance between theory and practice, between expectations and their realization, between planning and execution, or at least Clausewitz maintains that friction comes closer to characterizing these resistances than any other concept. Given that it is not the perfect word for this tension, what is it that actually takes place—in theory, in practice—when *friction* is employed to perform a descriptive labor that it can only "pretty generally" execute? In a memorable passage Clausewitz writes: "This tremendous friction [in war], which cannot, *as in mechanics*, be reduced to a few points, is everywhere in contact with chance, and brings about effects that cannot be measured, just because they are largely due to chance. One, for example, is the weather. Fog can prevent the enemy from being seen in time, a gun from firing when it should, a report from reaching the commanding officer."[60] In war, a metaphorical friction encounters the eminently volatile concept of chance, and these two enigmatic words "rub together" to produce incalculable effects, one of which is termed "fog." War is thus as much a conflict between literal and metaphorical registers as it is a collision of bodies and weapons, and friction names the unstable parallel, verging on identity, between the fog of language and the fog of military experience. Clausewitz's claim that "friction, as we choose to call it, is the force that makes the apparently easy difficult" applies equally to the challenge of moving a piece of artillery through the mud, penning a treatise in which one predicts what will happen to an artillery unit under specific weather conditions and speculating on why chance is likely to disrupt such a unit's plans no matter how carefully they are made.[61] The distinction between the theory and practice of war or between war as a conceptual discourse and war as a physical exercise is fated to remain clouded "in a kind of twilight."

Nowhere is this intractable tension more in evidence than when we turn to another of Clausewitz's famous pronouncements, his canonical

declaration that war is "a mere continuation of politics by other means."[62]
The enthusiasm with which generals, politicians, and political theorists
embrace this definition as the kernel of his thought bespeaks their hope
that its ostensible clarity and straightforwardness will provide a way out
of the foggy discourses about the fog of war, revealing Clausewitz to be at
heart an eminently pragmatic thinker who did in fact succeed in boiling
his object of study down to its nonparadoxical essence. It is important to
realize, however, that he arrived at this formulation only by considering a
series of propositions that he regarded as more fundamental statements
about his object of study. In the first chapter of *On War* Clausewitz follows
Machiavelli by avoiding any simple identification of war with destruction. War, he writes, is not an act of God such as an earthquake or a tsu-
nami but "an act of force to compel our enemy to do our will."[63] In these
terms war is to be measured by its utility—it is a means to an end—and
it is always subordinate to the thinking being who employs it.[64] Even this
statement, however, is derived from a more basic claim that war is "nothing but a duel on a larger scale" or, as Clausewitz also writes, the sum of
"countless duels."[65] As a duel, war follows specific rules and has a precise
beginning and end. A ritual or performance, it is a staged spectacle that
obeys its own rhetorical logic irrespective of the uses to which it is put by
its performers or audience members.

In the course of *On War* Clausewitz considers a number of ways in
which the "duel nature" of warfare may compromise rather than facilitate
its usefulness. In one memorable passage he argues that "the fact that
slaughter is a horrifying spectacle" may prompt us to "blunt our swords
in the name of humanity."[66] Although such an abdication of violence will,
he allows, feel morally responsible, it is not prudent in the long term since
"sooner or later someone will come along with a sharp sword and hack
off our arms."[67] By making the costs of war appear too dreadful, the perlocutionary force of war's spectacular performances can compromise our
ability to assess the concrete threats posed by potential enemies. The duel
also demonstrates a procedural independence, a formal autonomy that
can supersede even its own capacity to horrify. Fashioning a rudimentary
game theory, Clausewitz proposes that because combat is by nature reciprocal, the sustained collision of competitive energies should rise without limit. One increases one's efforts to best the enemy, the enemy does
likewise, and "competition will intensify again and, in pure theory [*in der
bloßen Vorstellung*], it must again force you both to strive for extremes."[68]

Once invoked, this specter of a notional striving for extremes is not easily dispelled, and, as Clausewitz subsequently explains, "more than any other type of action, battle exists for its own sake alone."[69] As an autotelic enterprise, a kind of deathly *l'art pour l'art*, organized combat cannot be judged in terms of its usefulness for furthering any given political program because it is an autonomous praxis governed by the ruthless principle of reciprocal intensification.

Clausewitz repeatedly revisits this tension between war as a spectacle that influences its audiences and war as an autonomous dynamic that realizes its true character in an abstract striving for notional extremes. In the process it becomes difficult to distinguish between his accounts of the intellectual labor peculiar to conducting military operations and his reflections on the challenges involved in thinking and writing about war. Is he referring to the work of the theoretician, the general, or the politician when he announces that "in the abstract field of the pure concept, the inquiring mind can never rest until it reaches the extreme, for here it is dealing with an extreme: a clash of forces freely operating and obedient to no law but their own"?[70] The concept of war threatens to short-circuit any effort to show that it is not "just" a concept because the extremity war sets in motion is a force of transgression that inexorably assumes a semblance of spontaneity and autonomy. Many scholars have tried to minimize this threat, arguing that, in revising his book, Clausewitz gradually shifted his allegiance from theoretical to practical models of warfare, as if with intellectual maturity he felt compelled to rein in his philosophical bent.[71] Yet throughout *On War* his most prosaic advice about getting troops across rivers or moving artillery through the mud is interrupted by images of war as free play, a game of chance, or a theatrical spectacle for aesthetic contemplation. Each time Clausewitz entertains a schema that might facilitate a stable dualism between the theory and practice of war or between a war of concepts and a war of flesh-and-blood soldiers, a dynamic of extremity imposes itself, blurring the proposed distinctions. Clausewitz thus finds himself having to remind his readers that war—arguably the most concretely consequential of human endeavors—"is no pastime; it is no mere joy in daring and winning, no place of irresponsible enthusiasts" and "all its colorful resemblance to a game of chance, all the vicissitudes of passion, courage, imagination, and enthusiasm it includes are merely its 'special characteristics' [*Eigentümlichkeiten*]."[72] In the face of these numerous disclaimers, one senses that the gentleman doth protest too much. It may well be that these *Eigentümlichkeiten* are not merely war's peculiarities but also what is most proper (*eigen*) to it. At the very least Clausewitz reveals that war is good at masquerading as everything he says it is not.

Clausewitz claims that the autonomy characteristic of human reason is identical to or best expressed in and by the independence of military praxis even as this praxis invariably misrepresents its own true nature. In considering the relationship between warfare as an idea and warfare as a material act, he comes to write explicitly about war as a language. "The main lines along which military events progress, and to which they are restricted," he explains,

> are political lines that continue throughout the war into the subsequent peace. How could it be thinkable otherwise? [*Und wie wäre es anders denkbar?*] Do political relations between peoples and between their governments stop when diplomatic notes are no longer exchanged? Is not war simply another mode of the writing and speech of their thinking? [*Ist nicht der Krieg bloß eine andere Art vom Schrift und Sprache ihres Denkens?*] Its grammar, indeed, may be its own, but not its logic.[73]

As decisive as the final statement about war's grammar and logic is, the preceding lines cannot be discounted as "merely rhetorical" questions. If war is politics by "other" means, if war is the "other" of politics that is not entirely other to it, then it is only "thinkable otherwise." The striving toward extremes that distinguishes war's autonomy ensures that any act of warfare will elude the form imposed upon it by a particular conceptual determination or pragmatic mobilization. The inversion of "war is politics" should thus be complete since politics now appears to be an excuse for the excesses of military grammar, produced after the fact and then cast as the cause of the system of which it is an effect.

Clausewitz claims that when war speaks or writes, it does so doubly, expressing both a logic that is not entirely its own and the absolute authority of its grammar. He also makes it clear that the relationship between war's grammar and logic is less stable than this observation allows, offering two distinct accounts of what it means to say that war, considered independently of its status as an act of policy, has a grammar of its own. First, he describes its pure, unregulated praxis as "an absolute expression of violence" that "would of its own independent will usurp the place of policy the moment policy had brought it into being; it would then drive policy out of office and rule by the laws of its own nature, very much like a mine that can explode only in the manner or direction predetermined by the setting."[74] Different from the earlier image of military autonomy as notional striving, this new figure of mechanized inflexibility presents the free play of war's performance as a trick of physics rather than an intelligible activity, indicating that the absoluteness of war's expressivity depends on its constancy and rigidity and on the fact that it can explode in only one fashion. This is warfare as not only a destructive detonation but also a predictable, localizable phenomenon, something that can be anticipated and survived. Clausewitz's second explanation of the grammar of war describes the ideal execution of a military operation as a realm of inevitability in which "everything results from necessary causes and one action rapidly affects another, [such that] there is, if we may use the phrase, no intervening neutral void."[75] This is war as the metaphysical fantasy of a perfect system of cause and effect, devoid of literal or metaphorical friction. With no limits to its purview or power, no distinction between the ideal and the actual, this dynamic is potentially far more threatening than an entire field of exploding mines.

The grammar of war is defined by an autonomy that no general or political leader can fully tame, yet for Clausewitz, war's status as a means to an end is inconceivable without reference to this radical independence, whether it is conceived of as physical or metaphysical. Still, neither of these characterizations of war's grammar—the exploding mine or the realm of perfect cause and effect—can be termed a "literal" model. Both are symptoms of the degree to which the third part of the classical trivium, the rhetoric of war, haunts Clausewitz's understanding of military praxis and confounds both the absoluteness of its grammar and the utility of its logic with the paraforces of "friction" and "fog." Never reducible to a pure reflex of one-upmanship or the pure utility of a means to an end, war inexorably takes the form of phenomena that assert their independence of both the theoretical and the empirical modes of military praxis. To the extent that military programs are only partly governed by the abstract laws of competition and the concrete dictates of policymakers, they are forever fated to surprise those who fight them, as well as those who follow them from a distance.

Clausewitz convincingly demonstrates that as an expressive medium, a mode of speech and writing, war invariably gives rise to representational dynamics that go beyond any given set of formal processes or tactical goals. With the emergence of warfare as mass spectacle in the Napoleonic era, it became possible to identify this extra "something" that battles put on display as an essential dynamic of the military experience. *Watching War* explores the dimensions of battlefield spectacle that cannot be explained either by the absolute mechanics of war's grammar or by the practical ambitions of its logic. The first section of the book focuses on the ideological systems that organized the execution and the reception of the Napoleonic campaigns. Chapter 1, "How to Tell a War Story," asks why the burgeoning violence at the turn of the nineteenth century proved so difficult to assimilate to existing narrative paradigms. Earlier thinkers such as Thomas Hobbes and Jean-Jacques Rousseau sought to distinguish between war and individual battles and were skeptical that watching a clash of troops could help one understand why it was occurring or what it meant. In contrast, Napoleonic military doctrine was based on the idealized vision of a decisive one-day clash whose significance was held to be self-evidently manifest. Juxtaposing Victor Hugo's description of Waterloo in *Les Misérables* with Chateaubriand's tale about accidentally hearing the same battle one morning while out on a stroll in the Belgian countryside, the chapter describes attempts to articulate aesthetic, political, or historical models that could account for the modern military spectacle.

With the advent of a mass audience that followed war remotely, the opportunity to witness a battle firsthand acquired an almost mythological status, as if being under fire offered revelatory insights into the human condition. Chapter 2 considers the paradoxical implications of this ambition to experience combat "live." So large and fast paced as to be unintelligible even to the men who fought in them, the titanic conflicts of the Napoleonic era became required viewing at the very moment that they became incomprehensible. For the nineteenth-century authors who reflected on this seeming contradiction, the ability to imagine what a clash of armies must have looked like was more powerful than witnessing one firsthand. They argued that the enormity of the physical devastation was best grasped by avoiding any direct sensory engagement with it and regarded actually being present at a battle as anything but a gripping experience. In Goethe's memoirs about the Austro-Prussian invasion of France, Stendhal's *Charterhouse of Parma*, and Tolstoy's *War and Peace*, the witness to the battles of Valmy, Waterloo, or Borodino was plagued by distraction and confusion and found little to confirm the import of what he saw.

Chapter 2 concludes with an examination of the short-lived phenomenon of the panorama as a unique attempt to recraft the public's mediated engagement with the battlefield by allowing it to be viewed indoors, like a museum exhibit or laboratory experiment.

The second half of *Watching War* explores the legacy of the Napoleonic era in the later nineteenth, twentieth, and twenty-first centuries. Chapter 3 considers how the emergence of battlefield photography further complicated the relationship between the direct experience of combat and its mediated records. Focusing on the question of what one can learn about war by looking at photographs of dead soldiers, I propose that the pictures of corpses taken during the American Civil War created a new spectatorial dynamic in which viewers were invited to participate in an intimate encounter with the plight of a fellow human while constantly being reminded that they were being confronted with something outside their own realm of experience. The dimensions of human existence the pictures exhibited proved difficult to incorporate into the prevailing conceptions of war's social and cultural significance, and the modern mass audience to war was forced to ask whether battlefield spectacles were best grasped with the eyes or in the imagination. This concern continued to haunt twentieth-century representations of the battlefield, which seemed to demonstrate that the modern individual perceives the world as a fragmented field of disjointed trauma. Ultimately, war photography, far from enhancing the human gaze, has challenged the notion that any gaze—human or mechanical—can help us understand war.

Chapter 4 examines the legacy of Napoleonic military ideology in early twentieth-century debates about total war, asking what it meant to be a war spectator in the First World War, when the border between soldier and civilian had been all but completely erased. While historians have long debated the relationship between the concept of total war and its empirical manifestations, I argue that the fantasy of a total view of warfare, the conviction that an all-encompassing gaze can control even the unbounded battlefield, has played a crucial and largely unexamined role in the development of modern militarism. The question of how to watch a war that is by nature invisible became pressing during the First World War since the commanding generals rarely visited the front, and the soldiers in the trenches were acutely aware that in the course of the daily fighting they rarely caught a glimpse of their foes. Combatants' memoirs from this period, as well as from the Second World War, describe not only the tangible misery of battlefield horrors but also the prominent role that irony and abstraction played in organizing the highly mediated experience of danger and death. Both major wars of the twentieth century thus came to be compared with the Cold War, as authors from Faulkner to Pynchon struggled to understand a theater of world history in which the disappointing quality of the war spectacle had become the norm and questioned whether it was still possible to formulate a historical account of military operations when a battle was no longer something that one could see.

In the Conclusion, I demonstrate that uncertainties about imaginary visions of combat and tensions between the ideals of war and its empirical instantiations continue to shape war spectatorship in the age of the Internet, when technology has made live video feeds from conflicts around the globe instantly available to hundreds of millions of prospective viewers. The most striking thing about contemporary accounts of war's scope and significance is how sharply they contradict one another. While some argue that the globe is engulfed in perpetual strife, others propose that war as a conflict between nation-states has become obsolete, having been replaced by large-scale police actions. The basic question that plagued Hobbes and Rousseau about how to understand the relationship between a war and the individual engagements fought in its name remains unresolved, and the battlefield, idealized in the Napoleonic era as a clearly circumscribed field on which history could be made, persists as the ultimate example of mass destruction that is nonetheless ephemeral, at once all-encompassing and intangible.

Since the Napoleonic era, notions of what battles must be like have proven as important as political and economic changes for how war has been fought and how it has impacted the cultures that have waged it. Far from simply constituting an observational forum, watching war has become a field of combat in its own right, a battleground on which our most basic ideas about violence and human sociality are explored in an ongoing debate about what it means to be part of an audience to mass destruction. The fact that modern viewers of war's spectacles have not been entirely consumed by them, at times seeming more detached than enthralled, suggests the possibility of a resistance to the military logics that conflate war spectatorship with human perception as such. In these terms, the battlefield's inability to effect an unbridled sublimity betrays its limits, in particular its inability to become a general paradigm for historical or political agency. At the same time, our capacity to imagine ourselves as observers rather than participants in the ongoing programs of armed state violence may suspend us in an uncertain powerlessness: Either we are not part of the larger military enterprise and hence lack the power to influence, much less end it, or we are the unwitting pawns of a military system that casts us in the role of a benign audience. We can therefore not take it for granted that the self-reflective observer enjoys a methodological advantage over the bystanders who fail to take stock of the perspective from which they survey the cultural terrain. The more self-aware the audience to war is about the significance of its own status as a viewing force, the more unsure it becomes about the meaning of what it is watching and its relationship to it. War, consistently designated as a feature of every society that has ever existed, remains a perennial surprise; it besets us in a fashion that we can never fully anticipate, striking close to home at the very instant that it seems most foreign. The experience of watching war is always an experience of the frontiers of experience, the experience of an inevitability that cannot assume a predictable form. Judgments of war's omnipresence or obsolescence will never suffice to disarm its complex logics of simulation and dissimulation. To do something different with war, to challenge war in terms that are not entirely its own, we must conceive of ourselves as both less and more than onlookers to the greatest horror show on earth.

§ 1 How to Tell a War Story

Men are reduced to walk-on parts in a monster documentary film which has no spectators, since the least of them has his bit to do on the screen.

—Theodor W. Adorno, *Minima Moralia*

The central tenet of the Napoleonic ideology of warfare is that the course of world history is shaped by titanic one-day clashes of men under arms. The decisions made by generals at key moments in these engagements are thought to impact the fates of nations for generations to come. To fully appreciate the implications and the abiding influence of this doctrine, it is important to understand that it emerged as a reaction against seventeenth- and eighteenth-century theories of the battlefield that had in turn sought to reject earlier military thinking. More than a century before Waterloo, Thomas Hobbes opened the *Leviathan* with the assertion of a sharp distinction between combat and the semblance of a commitment to pursue it, declaring that war consisted "not of Battle only, or the act of fighting, but in a tract of time, wherein the Will to contend by Battle is sufficiently known. . . . [T]he nature of War consists not in actual fighting, but in the known disposition thereto. . . . All other time is Peace."[1] For Hobbes, war was both a series of violent conflicts and a condition of hostility in which no shots need be fired. What we today refer to as the spectacle of war is therefore not principally a matter of landscapes covered in clashing armies or the fireworks of aerial bombardments. To wage war, we must demonstrate a capacity for self-expression; we must be able to make our readiness to fight apparent to the enemy. Hobbes's warring posture aims to manifest something metaphysical—a will—as something physical that is accessible to the senses.

Since our relationship to any alleged intention to fight—even when it is our own—is highly mediated, Hobbes's distinction between war and battle creates a realm ripe for duplicity. If war is the ultimate example of a sequence of events with consequences, it is equally a field of simulation since any war is permanently under suspicion of being a phony war, emerging only in virtue of an opposition between an act and the announcement of an alleged plan to act. War is as much a matter of signifying performances—declarations and threats, feints and bluffs—as of hand-to-hand combat. Pretense and facades are as central to its arsenal as cannonballs and bullets.

The lasting influence of Hobbes's doctrine is manifest in the work of Paul Virilio, a contemporary theorist who has extensively explored the logic of battlefield spectatorship. Best known for his lapidary formulation "war is cinema, and cinema is war," Virilio characterizes combat as a struggle to see, which means not just seeing the enemy before the enemy sees and targets us but also being seen in such a way as to demoralize and intimidate our opponent, perhaps eliminating the very need to come to blows.[2] In these Hobbesian terms, to wage war is to direct a show; it means managing appearances, in particular one's own, as much as slaying foes—hence, it is an aesthetic, as well as a physical, moral, or economic struggle.

Virilio sometimes gives the impression that the forces of self-expression peculiar to warfare are more easily governed than is actually the case. Designed to regulate semantic missives, as well as material projectiles, military ventures unfold as projects in which the ability to dissimulate the difference between a real intention to attack and an imitation thereof is as important as the deployment of troops and munitions. Still, we should not assume that warring parties are ever in complete control of their presentations, whether they regard them as sincere articulations of their inner feelings or as pure fakery. On the one hand, the deception at work in military posturing may be a form of self-deception—nowhere is self-awareness a more precarious state of mind than when commanding officers, governments, or people consider trading death blows with a foe. On the other hand, even the most heartfelt performances of intent may not succeed in realizing their illocutionary or perlocutionary goals. If the physical violence of warfare tends to outstrip the aims of its purveyors, this is equally the case in the signifying realm. Fighting a war means engaging in a struggle to make one's threats meaningful and convincing to oneself, as well as to one's enemy, and it is a struggle that no warring force can ever bring to a close. Much of the instability and inherent unpredictability of military campaigns, which never seem to follow the script, stems from the fact that no party ever masters this particular facet of combat.

The argument for the inherently self-expressive nature of the military program comes close to conceiving of war as a self-validating, almost completely self-contained process. In his 1985 *Simulation and Simulacra* Jean Baudrillard proposed that contemporary warfare had lost its antagonistic core. Although it still boasted bloody engagements in which tens of thousands of people were injured and killed, it no longer took place in the name of anything external to the destructive process, whether a noble ideal or a crass grab for power. In short, war had become war for war's sake.[3] Ten years later in his infamous *The Gulf War Did Not Take Place*, Baudrillard described the solipsism of war as a system preening for its grand entrance: "The war . . . watches itself in a mirror: Am I pretty enough, am I operational enough, am I spectacular enough, am I sophisticated enough to make an entry onto the historical stage?"[4] The "will to spectacle," as Baudrillard termed it, threatened to become the dominant impulse governing military operations such that we would no longer be able to evaluate a war as just or unjust, righteous or evil, but would have to assess it entirely by its ability to create a scene.[5] This has been one of the great challenges in understanding the spectacle of war in the post-Napoleonic era. War imposes itself upon a mass audience, presenting itself as a show that no one can afford to miss, but this wartime performance unfolds according to solipsistic standards that can be appreciated only by a warring compatriot or an armed foe.[6] Small wonder that the modern viewer so often feels cheated, as if for all the millions of lives and trillions of dollars that have been poured into the production of the theater of war, there has been precious little return for its public.

In conceiving of war as the sum of social and cultural practices that confirm a commitment to fighting one's opponents, Hobbes opened the door to what in the twentieth century would be termed "total war." Once we suspend the distinction between threatened and actual combat, between battle imagined and battle realized, all wars become at once cold and hot and yet neither cold nor hot, neither completely dormant nor fully actualized.[7] It is thus no longer clear on what basis we can distinguish between military and civilian operations. While the suffering and destruction that have occurred as a result of armed conflict over the past two centuries have been unparalleled in their scale and consequence, war's significance has never simply been a factor of the immediacy of its physical consequences for the material well-being of peoples and property. Equally consequential has been the way in which any given campaign has necessitated a reconceptualization of the boundaries between the material and ideal realities of violence. Each warring party has had to reinvent its audience, setting forth an account of what people should see when they confront its expressions of willingness to fight. Beyond what we commonly recognize as propaganda—boasts of imminent or realized success in clashes with the enemy—war unfolds as a presentation of standards against which onlookers are to evaluate the significance of what they observe. Every war asks its audience to learn to read the sociocultural landscape all over again.

This point has important implications for what it means to represent a war. Following Hobbes, any depiction of a battle must illustrate the disjunction between war as an act of demolition and war as a set of signifying practices that aim to perform an intent. From painting and lyric poetry to novels, photography, and film, the challenge has been how to capture both war's immediate consequentiality in the physical world and the fact that it is organized by semantic systems designed to regulate its legibility. Any story about a military operation—whether imparted verbally or visually—runs the risk of coming into conflict with the interpretive paradigms that the warring forces have set forth on their own behalf. To represent a war is to participate in a struggle for control of how it is to be understood, a contest waged not with colleagues or competitors in the pressroom but with combat's autorepresentational forces themselves.

In a study of French battle paintings in the ancien régime, Norman Bryson elucidates one of the key aspects of this dynamic and suggests that the intermingling of allegorical and historical figures within a single canvas reveals that "event is Scripture even as it happens: the battle is already narrative at the moment it takes place."[8] A battle is marked by the formal logics of signification and expression as it occurs and not simply in being reconstructed by an artist after the fact. As a result, Bryson maintains that when "Tolstoy or Stendhal describe their battles, narrative is not super-added to a scene which lacks discursive intelligibility, but is instead the repetition of a discourse which is pre-existent. War is perhaps the most ancient, and certainly one of the most powerful, of rhetorical *topoi*."[9] Far from simply a topic selected by an author who writes about it, war has a narrative impulse of its own that is integral to its elaboration. "In war," Bryson writes, "events acquire a dimension that has already all the intelligibility, visibility, and recountability of the narrative act."[10] The novelist's depiction of a battle reproduces a dynamic internal to that battle. However ghastly or incomprehensible the events of war may seem, they unfold such that this horror performs a demonstrative function. The scene is a means to an end, part of a larger presentational system.

Once the acts of war are no longer self-evidently consequential—that is, once we accept that war is as much the performance and interpretation of specific signifying intentions as it is a program of harming people and property—the concrete physical parameters of military engagement cease to have the same organizational primacy, and war, no matter how bloody or destructive, threatens to become a conflict of meanings and ideas. Bryson's conclusion is that the ultimate achievement of warfare is to make a drive or rationale perceptible. A battlefield, he proposes, is a distillation of the relations between intention and cause and effect that organize a narrative so that "in the battle, human action consolidates into a united purposiveness that is patent and visible at all points."[11] There is no room for compromise; the battle must culminate in a "public violence" that is "fully displayed and intelligible."[12] Can the display ever be absolute enough, however, to ensure that the battle is "*fully* displayed"? By allowing for a distinction between a battle as something processed with the senses (its "visibility") and a battle as something grasped through logical or narratological abstractions (its "recountability"), Bryson raises the possibility that these two different manifestations of combat may not be mutually reinforcing or even compatible. What if the historical and allegorical figures constitute such different representational modalities that "full display" and "intelligibility" prove contrary aims? Bryson appears to acknowledge—albeit indirectly—that the intended effect of a battle's show may not be realized: "[W]hat is *sought* is absolute publicity, for the battle is a form of aggression that takes place without guile, deceit, or any aspect of the clandestine. In the swordplay of the duel, there is room for the artistry of fencing, which is full of feints and misdirections: but in the swordplay of battle, intentions and action are far more co-extensive."[13] The recourse to the figure of the duel, itself a form of argumentative "misdirection," bespeaks a recognition that a battle must at every stage defend itself against the charge of having succumbed to the trickery of fencing. This need to simulate a lack of simulation introduces an element of mediation that compromises any claim to a direct display of intention. Proceeding from the attempt to sidestep or ignore the difficulties of distinguishing between purposiveness rendered visible and the semblance of purposiveness—the distinction that for Hobbes is constitutive of warfare as such—Bryson nonetheless arrives at a rather Hobbesian conclusion when he acknowledges that military combat is defined by a signifying excess and that "battles possess a spectacularity that is heraldic: each side blazons its identity with a clarity that is not at all exhausted by strategic need."[14]

It is not by chance, then, that war stories—whether verbal narratives, photographs, or films—are perpetually attacked for not seeming real enough. The standards of "reality" that reality fails to meet are themselves the very real products of such war stories. The point is not that war is "unrepresentable" but rather that war itself is partly a contest between different paradigms of representation that are not easily coordinated with one another. If, as Bryson would have it, war is a rhetorical topos, it is far from clear what form of knowledge this topos makes available. Following Hobbes, telling a story or painting a picture of a battle is as much an effort to illustrate a signifying dynamic as an attempt to depict the physical horror of men and machines in a sea of blood. Of course, if the difference between a willingness to aggress and actualized conflict is what distinguishes war from mere violence, then war constitutes a rather shaky reference point for a narrative of historical events since it comprises possibilities and virtual phenomena as much as instantiated acts. Classically regarded as the ultimate forum of historical praxis, the grandest stage on which the designs of an individual warmonger or an entire population could be displayed for all to see, war is equally the one sphere in which the intent to act may be just as consequential as (or more so than) the action itself.

One consequence of Bryson's position is that he is reluctant to dismiss military historiography's tendency—widely regarded today as hopelessly old-fashioned—to focus on a given era's battles as the key to understanding it. "Childlike" in its simplicity, such an approach nonetheless rehearses something complex fashioned "from history itself" since the battle has already performed its own interpretation and told its own story. As a result, "far from shaping the event into meaning, all the historian there has to do is to repeat the writing that emanates spontaneously from history itself."[15] Like painters or novelists, historians who confront war find that a key aspect of their work is done before they start since war takes place by articulating criteria for what will count as meaningful incidents, e.g., battles, as well as what will qualify as mere happenstance.[16]

Part of the reason, then, that war is so extraordinarily destructive on a social, cultural, and corporeal level is that it is a profoundly presumptuous activity, a series of events that seeks to dictate how it is to be represented, interpreted, and understood as it occurs. To study war, we must analyze the ways in which military operations aim to recast aesthetic and historiographical paradigms, and we must consider whether these ambitions can be resisted. To date, even the sustained efforts of social and cultural historians to challenge the dominant narratives of great generals on horseback have failed to unsettle the fundamental model according to which battles are the ultimate example of self-evidently meaningful phenomena.[17]

To understand more precisely what it would mean to write about a war without ceding authority to its participants' interpretive systems, we must recognize a key difference between Hobbes and his inheritors, such as Bryson. Despite acknowledging that a battle may not always succeed in realizing a full display of its purveyors' ambition for absolute publicity, Bryson privileges both the battle and the battlefield as the essence of war since the clash of opposing armies is what provides "the consolidation of open intelligibility."[18] In contrast, Hobbes's conception of warlike postures and war spectacles rests on a clear distinction between a war and the battles waged in its name, which may never be as significant as the aggressive posing that precedes and follows them. Indeed, in his terms it may not be necessary for the battles to be part of the discussion at all since what is constitutive of wartime is the expression of a willingness to fight rather than actual combat per se.

A century after Hobbes, Jean-Jacques Rousseau takes up this distinction between war and battles, casting a skeptical eye on the study of military events as he attempts to unsettle the awesome authority that the battlefield spectacle has enjoyed in Western historiography. Rousseau maintains that the pedagogical benefit of history is that it allows the student to see "men from afar"; history will "show [people] in other times or other places and in such a way that [the pupil] can see the stage without ever being able to act on it."[19] At the outset, the pupil should observe people as "a simple spectator, disinterested and without passion, as their judge and not as their accomplice or as their accuser."[20] On this score, Rousseau considers Thucydides to be the preeminent historian because "he reports the facts without judging them, but he omits none of the circumstances proper to make us judge them ourselves. He puts all he recounts before the reader's eyes. . . . The reader no longer believes he reads; he believes he sees."[21]

If the value of history as a pedagogical tool is that it moves us from reading to seeing, the question is whether the historian can assume an observational stance that provides access to all of the relevant data. The decisive test of history's value as the theatrical stage that displays "men from afar" turns out to be a battle: "How many times did a tree more or less, a stone to the right or to the left, a cloud of dust raised by the wind determine the result of a combat without anyone's having noticed it? Does this prevent the historian from telling you the cause of the defeat or the victory with as much assurance as if he had been everywhere?"[22]

Any claim to insight through observation founders because any given line of sight will be only one of hundreds or thousands of possible views, and historians can never see the difference between what they see and what they have missed. Exposed as just one position among others, a particular standpoint loses any claim to being a reliable ground of knowledge; that is, no individual network of causal relations can demonstrate its own completeness. As a result, the anticipated transition between watching war and telling a story to explain it never takes place. What one sees is not what one wants to be able to narrate.

Rousseau's reference to the "*cause* of the defeat or victory" suggests that whatever it is that the pupil ought to experience is not for the eye to see. Although history's strength as a heuristic device is supposed to be its ability to create an illusion of visual immediacy—"the reader no longer believes he reads; he believes he sees"—it turns out that what really needs to be revealed are invisible forces since the facts are useless if one does not know "the reason for them."[23] The supposed immediacy of seeing notwithstanding, reading, as flawed as it may be, turns out to be the better part of valor. As long as we confine ourselves to the theater of history, the "slow and progressive causes of these facts . . . remain unknown."[24]

Reflecting on these tensions, Rousseau revisits the military stage, but now his critique is damning. Thucydides, his hero among historians, "unhappily . . . always speaks of war; and one sees in his narratives almost nothing but the least instructive thing in the world—that is, battles."[25] Battles are not worthy objects of inquiry in their own right because they are only the symptoms of a more fundamental dynamic: "One often finds in a battle won or lost the reason for a revolution which even before this battle had already become inevitable. War hardly does anything more than make manifest outcomes already determined by moral causes which historians rarely know how to see."[26] This changes the argument subtly but decisively. Whereas the analysis of a battle was initially fated to fail because anything could be the decisive factor and no observer could hope to master all of the variables, a battle can now be treated as a product of moral forces, the set of which is implied to be finite rather than open-ended. The result is that battles are no longer to be regarded as objects of study in their own right.

War renders visible the results of processes to which historians such as Thucydides otherwise remain blind, but by letting historians *see* things, it encourages them to forget the distinction between cause and effect. For Hobbes, posturing *is* war. Although Rousseau is in agreement, he draws somewhat different conclusions, fearing that in attending the theater of Thucydidean history, his pupil will learn about imposters and their impostures rather than the hearts of men; the student will study poses instead of the reasons for them. For Rousseau, war is an inherently misleading display because it presents as its own power an inevitability that preexists it. War misrepresents itself as an autonomous dynamic, as origin rather than product. As a result, even the most sophisticated historian is likely to end up treating war as complete in its own terms rather than as the symptom of something logically or ontologically prior to it. What had previously been the argument for history—it reveals the actions of men, piercing the veils of people's disguises—has now become its fatal flaw. History is condemned because it "shows actions far more than men"; it treats what happened in isolation from the agents who caused it.[27]

If Bryson sees war as a narrative system that aims at ensuring its own visibility and recountability, Rousseau maintains that any war will necessarily be misrepresented since war itself is a system of misrepresentation. This argument raises doubts about the efficacy of *any* gaze that takes a battle as its object. Viewing military actions, whether as a participant or as a bystander, does not allow one to draw inferences about the agents who execute them or about the putative status of such actions as consequential events. The sense that any account of war is misleading is not a product of the efforts of self-interested governments or media interests to lead audiences astray; it arises because war can only distinguish itself from routine violence—that is, it can only articulate Hobbes's distinction between a willingness to aggress and actualized conflict—on the basis of a representational analysis that inexorably bifurcates actants and events.

We find ourselves faced with a series of contradictory injunctions: War demands to be explained but wreaks havoc with any teleological model of history; war demands to be viewed but is distinguished from random violence by the difference between what it is and what it offers to be seen. War spectacles thus acquire enormous authority even as they present themselves as inherently flawed productions. Situated precariously at the limits of the visible and the intelligible, war's show imposes itself as the standard for what can be known about the past, but it does so by unsettling the very logics of origin and priority in virtue of which it would be possible for something to "make an appearance" on the world-historical stage. Taking the instability of Hobbes's model to the extreme, Rousseau demonstrates that the inherently misleading nature of warfare condemns it to present the past as something with which it has lost contact.

Rousseau's attempt to unsettle the battle's status as the ultimate historical forum is a serious challenge to efforts in the Napoleonic era to glorify the field of combat as the essential scene of world history. First and foremost, it was Napoleon himself who put the battle at the center of the theory and practice of warfare, conceiving of it as a kind of algorithm designed to produce a definitive result—a "victory" or "defeat"—that would manifest itself in the course of a day's fighting and be shared across Europe posthaste.[28] This logic of abstraction, which reduces the collision of tens or hundreds of thousands of men under arms to an unambiguous verdict about winners and losers, was to be one of the most influential aspects of the Napoleonic heritage and would remain the preeminent standard for assessing military engagements in future wars, even in situations where there were no clearly opposed adversaries or it was not obvious that anyone was left standing to have won or lost.

The ramifications of Napoleon's combat algorithm were anything but abstract. His famous disregard for the well-being of the men he casually fed to slaughter was a product of his view that all that mattered was the "answer"—victory or defeat—and that showing one's "work"—the dead and injured—was not integral to the demonstration. His schematic formalization of military operations specified the elements that would compose the decisive day. In one of his most programmatic prescriptions he wrote: "A battle is a dramatic action which has its beginning, its middle,

and its end. The battle order of the opposing armies and their prelimi-
nary maneuvers until they come to grips form the exposition. The coun-
termaneuvers of the army which has been attacked constitute the dramatic complication. They lead in turn to new measures and bring about
the crisis, and from this results the outcome or denouement."[29] It is difficult to overstate the degree to which this rhetoric dominates subsequent
discussions of the Napoleonic campaigns. One could be excused for concluding that the French commander had genuinely realized his abstract
conceptions in the physical world, with virtually no mediation. Even
scholars with little inclination to poetic flights of fancy have a tendency
to characterize Napoleon's battles in dramatic terms, with turning points,
supporting characters, and unexpected plot twists. The appeal of impos-
ing such a strict narrative template onto the phenomenon of clashing
armies is that it creates a sense of order, a schema of visible causes followed by equally visible effects and countereffects, as if formal game theory
could be instantiated in a set of transparent figures whose interactions are
the product of the interventions of generals whose intentions manifest
themselves as events with definite consequences. Rousseau himself could
not have penned a more cogent response to the theoretical concerns of
Emile.

Does the violence inherent in the abstract logic of Napoleon's schemas
rival the violence of his battlefields? The endpoint of Napoleonic military
doctrine was the reduction of the vast and bloody combat to a unique act
of the mind occurring at a unique point in time: "The issue of a battle,"
Napoleon wrote, "is the result of a single instant, a single thought. The
adversaries come into each other's presence with various combinations;
they mingle; they fight for a length of time, the decisive moment appears;
a psychological spark makes the decision; and a few reserve troops are
enough to carry it out."[30] In accounts of the development of modern military tactics, the influence of this ideology of the instant is evident in the
credit Napoleon is accorded for developing a new form of rapid attack,
often seen as a precursor to the German blitzkrieg of the Second World
War.[31] It is not simply the ideology of speed that is crucial but also the
asserted coincidence of the single moment and the single thought, the
reduction of an entire sequence of events and an entire field of strategy
and tactics to a singular form without extension such that a decision can
be expressed as something that takes place in an autonomous instant
standing outside any chain of causes and effects. On the one hand, this

implies the condensation of reflection and contemplation into a split second; thinking no longer occurs over or even in time. On the other hand, the interplay of causal forces is seen as entirely hierarchical since an infinite number of actual and possible moments are subordinated to a privileged one that governs them precisely insofar as it has no regard for them at all. This vision of the decisive thought-instant constitutes both the ultimate control fantasy and the most precarious ontological system since the "spark" that creates the decision cannot be predicted or known after the fact yet remains a point of irrationality or madness around which the entire world revolves.

Even Carl von Clausewitz, the preeminent student of Napoleonic warfare, shied away from this aspect of Napoleon's philosophy. Acknowledging the horror of the single thought/single moment/single result conflation, he writes that as terrible as the slaughter and blood of battle may be, "the human spirit recoils even more from the idea of a decision brought about by a single blow."[32] Indeed, Clausewitz was so disturbed by this argument that he suggested that Napoleon must be being metaphorical when he maintained that at the decisive moment "all action is compressed into a *single point* in time and space" since what is actually of concern to the commanding general is the less stressful notion of staking the fate of an entire campaign on one battle.[33] It is as if Napoleon's abstraction of spatiotemporal singularity were so radical that it not only eclipsed the sight of tens of thousands of dead and injured but could not be integrated into a theory of warfare at all. According to Clausewitz, war takes place in a place over time, whereas Napoleon's ideal of the decisive essence of the battle seems to leave any kind of narrative or dramatic schema behind, eschewing both the power of sequence and the authority of an arena of combat, a site on which military praxis may unfold. For Clausewitz, it is thus ultimately irrelevant whether Napoleon's decisive decision is understood as the manifestation of an instant of pure freedom or of the indomitable slavery of destiny because it is impossible to anticipate or prepare for either.

Seeking to heal the rift between war and battle opened up by Hobbes and widened by Rousseau, Napoleon's philosophy of warfare demands that a battle be considered entirely in its own terms, with reference to the events of the single day or moment, and that winning or losing a particular engagement should have nothing to do with what precedes or follows that exact period of time. Napoleon's own experiences seem to belie his theoretical proclamations; for example, his army "won" the giant engagement of troops at Borodino, but his Russian campaign failed because of overextended supply lines, bad weather, and disease. This tension is reflected in Clausewitz's writings, which stress that a general's preparations prior to the period of armed engagement are vital to ensuring victory, yet follow Napoleon's lead in according the battle absolute explanatory privilege and consequentiality. In a memorable passage, Clausewitz attempts to negotiate this tension: "The major battle is therefore to be regarded as concentrated war, as the center of gravity of the entire conflict or campaign. Just as the focal point of a concave mirror causes the sun's rays to converge into a perfect image and heats them to maximum intensity, so all forces and circumstances of war are united and compressed to maximum effectiveness in the major battle."[34] Aiming to acknowledge the dimensions of war that lie beyond the battle while at the same time confirming that the battle is the distilled essence of war, Clausewitz invokes two different models from physics—the notion of a center of gravity and the convergence of light rays through a concave mirror—suggesting that the ideology of the battle's absolute primacy rests on an unstable conceptual field. Considered alone, the light image is dynamic, shifting quickly from the visual to the thermal; as the motif starts to run away with the show, we get a picture of the onset of a raging fire that is anything but governable and predictable—hardly an insignificant figural event in the work of a military theorist who declares that war is the realm of human experience in which chance is given the greatest expression. The question here is the same problem that haunts Clausewitz with regard to Napoleon's notion of the decisive instant, namely, whether war, "heated to maximum intensity"—boiled down to its purest essence—is still war or whether the kernel of the event (the battle) is a negation of the spatial and temporal forces that shape war. Ironically, Clausewitz's efforts to rework Napoleon's arguments suggest that Napoleon's own attempts to negate Rousseau's stark distinction between war and battle may achieve the exact opposite, furthering the opposition between the two rather than making the battle into the culmination of war.

Nineteenth-century historians such as Ranke or Michelet follow Napoleon rather than Rousseau in allowing battles to occupy a privileged place in the war narrative. In contrast, many nineteenth-century works of fiction take Rousseau's concerns to heart, according battles a privileged thematic status in order to call into question the self-evidence of their significance. Telling a war story becomes a test case for assessing both the possibility of recounting historical events meaningfully and the limits of literary representation. When Georg Lukács dates the emergence of the historical novel in Europe "at about the time of Napoleon's collapse," he underscores the fact that the Napoleonic war imaginary failed to vanish with the death of its flesh-and-blood avatar, becoming more powerful in his absence as a new space of speculation opened up in which the radical changes of the Napoleonic era and their implications for the understanding of war, history, and literary praxis were rethought.[35] Across several national literary traditions, the theoretical questions of *Emile* reemerge: Can a military engagement, even one of the epic proportions found in Europe in the first decades of the nineteenth century, ever be consequential in its own right? Can a single day's events alone constitute a "turning point" or "watershed"—or are they an effect of broader forces, epiphenomena whose outcome is perhaps a foregone conclusion long before they occur? Finally, is a war story invariably constructed after the fact, or do battles by their nature unfold according to narrative principles?

In the nineteenth-century novel, these issues are repeatedly explored with reference to an engagement that was revisited countless times but never entirely mastered: the clash of armies on June 18, 1815, which came to be known as the Battle of Waterloo. Bringing to a close the decades of war that had gripped Europe, Waterloo inaugurated an era of comparative peace on the Continent and over time would be seen as the start of a host of sociopolitical trends or transformations. From Thackeray's *Vanity Fair*, which describes people going to or returning from combat, to Hugo's *Les Misérables*, in which an omniscient narrator purports to relate the "hard facts" about what transpired on the field, Waterloo was the object of a variety of different representational strategies. The central question was whether it was the quintessential historical event or the perfect example of why such events prove more spectral than substantive, concatenations of chance and contingency rather than determined connections of causes and effects. For this reason, Waterloo became the ultimate exercise in entertaining counterfactuals: What if it had not rained? What if the Prussian forces had arrived a little later? What if the French cavalry had attacked at a different point? At issue was not simply whether the course of world history would have been different but whether one day, one battalion's efforts, or one individual's decision could have world-historical significance. In short, Waterloo became the test case for nineteenth-century thinking about historical agency and the enigma to be unraveled if Napoleon's ideology of the decisive battle was to be preserved.

Almost before the battle was fought, the basic historiographical paradox latent in Rousseau's argument was at the forefront of the discourse about it. On the one hand, if Waterloo was to be properly termed "an event," the actions that composed it must not have been inevitable, in which case they would have been merely the side effects of a broader dynamic. In other words, if the outcome of the battle turned out to have been preordained from the start, it would be necessary to examine pre-battle preparations to understand why and how what transpired took place. To be truly consequential in its own right and not the product of some external logic or mechanism, Waterloo had to be shown to have occurred in such a way that it was clear that its outcome was the product of that day on those fields. As a result, any explanation of it—whether fictional or nonfictional—had to dwell on specific details (e.g., Rousseau's "tree" or "cloud of dust") that could be shown to have had a crucial influence on the outcome. A survey of the last two centuries of the historical and literary treatments of the "battle of battles" thus reveals a series of attempts to isolate one or two unique features and present them as the keys to the fateful day's proceedings.

On the other hand, if Waterloo were to lay claim to being the cornerstone or emblem of an entire epoch of European history, it had to prove its significance for processes and dynamics far beyond June 18, 1815. The battle, "the hinge of the Nineteenth Century," as Victor Hugo termed it, gained its broader significance by coming to stand as the symptom or impetus—literal or metaphoric—for far-reaching change at every level of European society, much of which began long before Napoleon and Wellington exchanged cannon fire. To confirm Waterloo's autonomy as a day standing above and beyond the influence of the days that preceded and followed it, much less to demonstrate that its outcome was a result of a haphazard quirk of fate that occurred on a specific morning or afternoon, was potentially to deny its systemic significance, leaving it isolated outside the broader developments that shaped pre- and post-Napoleonic Europe.

In *Les Misérables* Hugo addresses precisely this tension between Waterloo as a decisive instant and Waterloo as an integral part of long-term patterns of change. Three hundred pages into the novel, the narrator offers a lengthy account of the battle, a discussion that at first glance is notable for how little it claims to be doing:

> It goes without saying that we do not claim to be writing a history of Waterloo. . . . For our part, we leave to the experts their task, being ourselves no more than a remote observer, a traveler across the plain, scrutinizing that earth sodden with human blood and perhaps mistaking the appearance for the reality. . . . It appears to us that a series of hazards dictated the course of events at Waterloo; and as for Destiny, that mysterious culprit, we judge it like those simple-minded judges, the common people.[36]

It would be easy to take this self-deprecating tone for false modesty, but one might also see it as Hugo's acknowledgement that a demonstration that purports to show step by step why such an event has transpired in a certain fashion may turn out to be as misleadingly persuasive as Rousseau feared. If one can string together accounts of the interrelationships between various factors, charting the play of "a series of hazards," the results will inevitably be convincing, even if along the way one has to make disclaimers about the limitations of one's perspective and grant that appearance and reality may be confused. In short, the impulse to connect the dots may beguile even the steeliest skeptic. This in mind, Hugo, having disavowed any authority, embarks on a blow-by-blow account of the proceedings with a command of detail that would make any military historian proud. Seemingly liberated by his declaration that he will not even attempt to offer "a history," the narrator presents a host of precise observations that go well beyond what any individual pair of eyes or group of observers could hope to have discerned.

This richly detailed story is punctuated with reflections on the mode of representation proper to a battle:

> There is no logic in the flow of blood; the army fronts are like waves on the seashore, advancing and retreating regiments forming bays and headlands, impermanent as a shifting sand. Where there was infantry, artillery appears; artillery is replaced by cavalry; battalions are like puffs of smoke. At a given place there was a given object: look for it again and it is gone. The light shifts, the dark patches advance and retreat, a graveyard wind blows, driving and scattering the tragic multitude of men. All is movement and oscillation. The immobility of a mathematical plan or diagram may present a moment but never a day. To depict a battle we need a painter with chaos in his brush.

Rembrandt is better than Van der Meulen; he who was accurate at noon is a liar by three o'clock.[37]

The chaos in the painter's brush marks the way in which this passage strains at the limits of the visual order. The landscape imagery and the play of light and darkness gradually give way to tactile elements ("wind blows"), culminating in the abstractions of movement and oscillation. In the midst of these shifts between sensory registers and between the sensory and the supersensible, a simile presents battalions as "puffs of smoke," an oddly chosen figure since the artillery of the first part of the sentence indicates that "real" clouds of smoke were hovering above the battlefield. If anything, the army is self-cloaking, obscuring visibility and making it impossible to see the men and their weapons. A similar unease haunts the phrase "graveyard wind," which is both literal and metaphorical since after June 18, 1815, there were few places that could lay as much claim to the status of graveyard as these fields in Belgium. Given that this is a passage about the challenges faced in representing a battle, one could say that the proliferation of tropes and figures in these sentences rivals the driving and scattering of the soldiers, to the point that it is no longer clear which terms hold priority in the various comparisons. The dynamic recalls Nietzsche's famous line about truth as a "mobile army of metaphors, metonyms, and anthropomorphisms"—in Hugo's narrative, the violence of language that attends the effort to characterize the ways of war manifests itself as a profound uncertainty about where to locate the literal level of the text, which constantly verges on going up in smoke (*s'en aller en fumée*).

The chaos of the painter's brush is also the chaos of the poet's pen, so the implicit privileging of the painter over the writer may be in bad faith. The passage is not, however, simply an allegory of writing as painting or vice versa because the writer-painter is also competing with the artistry and the violence of the battle's generals. Paul Virilio has encouraged us to regard the battlefield as one representational medium among others: "Since the battlefield has always been a field of perception, the war machine appears to the military commander as an instrument of representation, comparable to the painter's palette and brush."[38] For Hugo's narrator, the resulting artwork is unstable. On the one hand, the battle appears as "an ugly cloud," the details of which can only be summarized, grasped in "broad outline," but never presented in their "exact shape."[39] On the other hand, peering into this obscurity, one finds a limitless supply of disjointed details: "[T]here is an element of tempestuous convulsion in every battle—*quid obscurum, quid divinum*—and every historian, peering into the mêlée, can find what he looks for."[40] This is the flip side of Rousseau's concern that the historian can never be sure that he has identified all the relevant contingencies: The creative observer "with chaos in his brush" could find whatever he wanted in the tumult, and the artist-historians in question were not simply painters, authors, or scholars studying and illustrating the events from the vantage point of the past but the men fighting the battle. As Hugo concludes: "The battle of Waterloo is an enigma as incomprehensible to the winners as to the loser. To Napoleon, it was a panic: Blücher saw it simply as a matter of fire-power, and Wellington did not understand it at all. . . . All other historians are in some degree bewildered by it and grope in their bewilderment."[41]

Given this insight, how can the story of a battle be told, that is, how can Hugo's narrator defend himself against the charge that he is merely seeing what he wants to see in the events of June 18? The claim is that any reconstruction of the battle will inevitably manifest itself as the precarious conjunction of a vague approximation of the whole with a seemingly random privileging of one or two details. Nonetheless, the narrator immediately turns to an account of the fateful day as if to underscore the fact that—however rigorously self-reflexive one's investigation may be—one has no choice but to tell the story by crudely conjoining the particular and the general, magically summoning a conclusive result out of a handful of minor facts:

> Had it not rained in the night of 17–18 June 1815, the future of Europe would have been different. A few drops of water, more or less, were what decided Napoleon's fate. Providence needed only a downpour of rain to make Waterloo the retort to Austerlitz. An unseasonably clouded sky sufficed to bring about the collapse of a world. The Battle of Waterloo could not start until eleven-thirty because the ground was too wet. It had to dry out a little before the artillery could maneuver. And it was this that enabled Blücher to arrive in time. . . . Had the ground been dry, so that the artillery could move, the battle would have begun at six in the morning; it would have been over and done with by two, three hours before the Prussians could turn the scales.[42]

Even the most scrupulous historian of the battle cannot avoid falling into the very traps in which he locates others, finding "whatever he looks for"

in a few drops of water. Hugo's novel reflects directly on this methodological predicament by immediately complementing this vital detail
about the rain with another—equally "crucial"—one as the narrator relates that a peasant guide either incorrectly informed Napoleon about the
existence of a ditch at a key spot on the field or simply lied to him: "It can
almost be said that the shaking of a peasant's head [to indicate the absence of any obstacle in the terrain that might hinder the cavalry charge]
was the cause of Napoleon's downfall."[43] This juicy piece of gossip is
presented in such a way as to invite the reader to interrogate each substage
of the process: Was the peasant ignorant or lying? Was the "shake" of his
head an unambiguous gesture, was it somehow misinterpreted, or was he
simply avoiding a mosquito? Finally, how does this "essential" detail of
the battle relate to the earlier one about the downpour? Like the plurality
of similes describing the troops, which only a painter with chaos in his
brush can depict, it would appear that where Waterloo is concerned only
a plurality of critical explanations will suffice, as if a battle were distinguished by an overdetermined multiplicity of singularly crucial turning
points.

Hugo seems to imply that it does not matter which minor detail was
"true" as long as we recognize that the outcome of a battle with such enormous consequences rested on fleeting, fragile factors that could very well
have been different. It is also possible that the narrator is parodying the
notion that such miniscule facts could be the key to such a grand historical
change, demonstrating by example that the "tempestuous convulsion of
the battle" overwhelms the efforts of even the best painter to give it a
cloudless form. As if to make it impossible to decide which of these views is
accurate, Hugo's tale explodes into an array of contrasting interpretations
of Waterloo. Prefiguring Tolstoy's historiographic reflections in *War and
Peace*, the narrator of *Les Misérables* attempts to review and acknowledge
the legitimacy of every conceivable explanation for the course of events.
Equal attention is given to "those principles and elements" that order the
universe, luck, and an equilibrium theory of power according to which
Napoleon had to fall because he had become too mighty. Of concern is not
just the fact that war is governed by some peculiar concatenation of forces
but also the recognition that reflecting on its controlling dynamics inexorably generates all manner of causal models without making it possible to
privilege a single one.[44]

Although there are clearly tensions between these different explanatory paradigms, they are of no obvious consequence for the execution of this highly self-conscious narrative. Having demonstrated that a smooth transition between particular and general is impossible when it comes to "painting" the battlefield, Hugo shifts back and forth between dissections of precise "facts" about local causes and effects and broad reflections on human destiny. Brief celebrations of the power of chance are interspersed throughout, as if the entire discussion of Waterloo and the challenges of telling a war story were merely one subtopic in a larger argument about determination and happenstance. It is thus no great surprise when the "hinge of the nineteenth century" is abruptly subordinated to the life of the mind: "Overshadowing Blücher, in that epoch when Waterloo was no more than a clashing of sabers, was the Germany of Goethe, and overshadowing Wellington was the England of Byron. A huge upsurge of ideas is the keynote of our century."[45] Having devoted dozens of pages to this event of events, the critical day around which modern military history and theory would come to be organized, Hugo's narrator ultimately remains faithful to Rousseau in declaring that war does not dominate its age, even between 1792 and 1815.

Hugo closes his lengthy reflections on the implications of Waterloo for the nineteenth century by declaring that "our story requires us to return to the battlefield."[46] Suddenly, however, the site of combat is not the impetus for a philosophical disquisition on the nature of human history but the setting for a scene involving figures in the novel. We are no longer dealing with the fable or "true fiction" of Waterloo but with a "fictitious fiction" about characters in a book. Looting corpses shortly after the close of the fighting, M. Thénardier chances upon the wounded Baron Pontmercy, who thanks him for saving his life. In an effort to disguise his criminal activities from the man upon whom he has stumbled, Thénardier pretends to be a French sergeant, and with each retelling, the tale gradually acquires a life of its own as his supposed escapades during Waterloo are embellished and exaggerated.[47] In other words, in picking over the detritus of the battlefield, Thénardier becomes part of the day's proceedings by accidentally helping someone who was injured there, and the consequence is that he has to start writing himself into his own battle narrative, miming the efforts of the novel's narrator in the preceding section to find an appropriate explanatory paradigm for the day.

This suggests that the extended—if inconclusive—discussion of Waterloo offered by *Les Misérables* may have been prompted by a similar accident, an effort on the part of the book to excuse itself from the charge of being a "looter" of the past. What does this say about Waterloo as an event if its principal function in the novel is to serve as a figure of determined happenstance, a plot device that functions to facilitate a chance meeting of two figures? This would amount to a complete inversion of the particular and the general, a reduction of the battle of battles to a trick for generating a haphazard encounter between two characters that will be crucial for later aspects of the story. Does this imply that in the earlier section the narrator was only paying lip service to the power of chance to decide a contest between armies since it was really this more important chance meeting of fictional personages that was at issue? Or is the scene with Thénardier and Pontmercy an implicit acknowledgment that, in bringing a battle into the picture even as a mere plot device, one introduces an element of randomness that no amount of emplotment can dispel? If this final inference is correct, then everything that happens in *Les Misérables* after the encounter between Thénardier and Pontmercy may be a "consequence" of their "chance" meeting.

The ensuing chain of events may also constitute an attempt to protect the book from the conundrums that arise when a battle becomes, even contingently, an object of narrative representation. What takes place here is therefore either an inversion of part and whole or a polarization of the two such that the part is no longer a part of the whole. This uncertainty is a version of the theoretical tension that is repeatedly encountered in efforts from Hobbes to Clausewitz to characterize the relationship between war and battle. The introduction of the Battle of Waterloo into Hugo's novel may be the "convergence" of the book's representational forces into an "image" of "maximum intensity," or it may be the novel's "Waterloo," the moment at which it stumbles, never to right itself again. Exposing its narrative dynamics to the volatility of military forces without simply assuming that its own representational powers will win the day, *Les Misérables* distinguishes itself as a true war story—a story about the way in which war compels its own tale to be told while making it impossible to conclude that narrative with a logical end or a tidy moral rather than a paradox about the uncertain status of warfare as theme, narrative form, or arbitrary motif.

With the conclusion of hostilities on the Continent, the nineteenth-century public, which had been transformed into the modern war audience between 1792 and 1815, was reluctant to give up its viewing privileges. If Waterloo constituted Napoleon's strongest rejoinder to Rousseau's claim that studying a battle cannot teach one anything about warfare, Hugo's account of looters picking over the dead is a fitting allegory for popular attempts to understand the meaning of this colossal clash in the war's aftermath, as if one could make sense of the conflict only now that it was over. This was an investigation pursued not by a handful of scholars but also by hosts of people from all social classes who rushed to visit the Belgian fields where Waterloo had been fought, some arriving on the heels of the looters as early as the nineteenth of June.[48] These mass excursions to the scene of the recently concluded conflict contrasted with the efforts of eighteenth-century men of means to seek out the sites of ancient battlefields while on the Grand Tour. Armed only with textual descriptions of the events, these gentlemen had typically encountered local populations who had no sense that the place where they lived figured prominently in venerable narratives about great generals and their armies. Waterloo offered a populist alternative by requiring no knowledge of the classics and offering, at least ostensibly, a more tangible scene of historical combat complemented by a souvenir-hawking local population, which was more than eager to profit from the newfound notoriety of its locale.

Since this plot of land in Belgium had recently been the arena of such an immense conflict, one might imagine that relatively little was left to the visitor's imagination. In fact, the opposite was the case. Almost from the outset, the pastoral setting was regarded as a kind of contemplative retreat in which one could let one's fantasies run wild. Despite their temporal proximity to the event, the new war tourists were no less reliant on printed resources than their eighteenth-century forerunners who took their cues from classical literature when trying to identify ancient battle sites. Visitors to Waterloo carried accounts of the fateful day as guidebooks, and in walking across the fields they hoped to revisit the past through their imaginations or, better, to confirm the truth of their preexisting notions of what it must have been like. John Scott, the editor of the *London Magazine*, succinctly described the situation of the noncombatant confronted with a battlefield for the first time: "[T]he great cause of excitement lies in his being on the point of converting into a visible reality what had previously existed in his mind as a shadowy, uncertain but awful fancy."[49] When Scott goes on to designate this experience as second in significance only to the comparison between one's ideas of the afterworld and what one will encounter there in death, he underscores that coordinating the stories of Waterloo with their traces in "reality" was a serious task. Still, the visits to Belgium differed starkly from the disaster tourism of our own time surrounding the World Trade Center ruins or the city of New Orleans after Hurricane Katrina. Waterloo was distinctive as a historical ruin precisely because it was an empty field rather than a ruined city—in the end, its very innocuousness, the fact that the battle had been on this particular ordinary plot of ground rather than a different, equally ordinary plot of ground, added to the spectral quality of the scene. For those who visited the site, it remained an open question whether the excursion allowed one to engage with the past at all or whether some trees and fields were simply experienced in their utter ordinariness. Even onlookers who arrived as the fighting was still taking place mentioned the carnage and heaps of bodies they had witnessed in the same breath as they offered details of what they had eaten and where they had slept, as if the curious surreality that surrounded the setting of the conflict underwrote a continuity between the banal details of the trip and its singular horrors.[50]

If the trips to Belgium were predicated on a commitment to the substance of physical immediacy—tourists were determined to see the very hill on which a particular charge took place—the fact that the landscape had to be decoded with a map or guidebook introduced an element of mediation. As time passed, the fixity of the terrain itself seemed to lose its supposed authenticity, and even the best guides became suspect. By the 1830s the area around the town of Waterloo resembled a modern-day theme park, complete with map sellers, relic vendors, and refreshment stands.[51] People flocked there, purchased relics from the event such as buttons from soldiers' coats (most of them fake), and lamented that the topography had changed in the intervening decades or at least no longer corresponded to the stories they had heard, as if the very materiality of nature should reflect not simply the world-historical significance of what had transpired there but all of the reports, rumors, and fantasies it had engendered as well. Somehow, the site of "Waterloo" could not possibly measure up to the imaginary sight of Waterloo. As Hugo described it more than forty years after the storied day:

> Everyone is aware that the variously inclined undulations of the plains, where
> the engagement between Napoleon and Wellington took place, are no longer

what they were on June 18, 1815. By taking from this mournful field the where-withal to make a monument to it, its real relief has been taken away, and history, disconcerted, no longer finds her bearings there. It has been disfig-ured for the sake of glorifying it. Wellington, when he beheld Waterloo once more, two years later, exclaimed, "They have altered my field of battle!"[52]

In the wake of the events of July 15, 1815, one of the major questions that arose for both writers and artists was whether Waterloo could be accu-rately described or recorded for posterity, verbally or visually. Focusing on the British experience of the immediate aftermath of the Napoleonic Wars, Philip Shaw has argued that "whether the battle was represented through the medium of the sonnet, the extempore effusion, or the lyric 'song,' the idea that Waterloo was as yet too big for the imagination to comprehend its sublimity was a notable feature of these early attempts at representation."[53] While the sheer scale of the battle and the seeming enormity of its historical implications pushed against the borders of the comprehensible, its elusive qualities had as much to do with what it lacked as with its tangible power. Despite or perhaps because of the fact that Wellington's field of battle was just "a place," it proved to be impossible to preserve the site to the satisfaction of those who had fought there, as well as those who came to see where they had fought. What the nineteenth century lamented was not the loss of the exact topographic contours that had existed on June 18, 1815, but the fact that "Waterloo" was always a kind of empty placeholder as much as it was the true center of gravity of the age, a blank canvas available for whatever picture one wanted to paint.

It is often observed that the clash of French and Anglo-Allied armies that ended Napoleon's career could very well have happened elsewhere, meaning that the notoriety that fell upon this specific setting was contin-gent upon inessential factors, a point only reinforced by the accidental quality of the very label "Waterloo." The battlefield was situated about five kilometers south of the Belgian municipality that would become known the world over. While Wellington's decision to head his victory dispatch with the name of that district ultimately carried the day, for al-most a century the victor did not have absolute authority over this partic-ular section of the historical record. Some French battle dispatches referred to the "Bataille de Waterloo," and some to the "Bataille de Soignies," and for several years after the fact it was referenced in Parisian publications as "la journée de Mont-Saint-Jean," a nearby village. Until the First World

War, German historians spoke of the *Schlacht bei Belle-Alliance*, which was Blücher's term for the event.[54] If "Waterloo" became not simply a term to designate a particularly consequential engagement but the generic label for a world-historical event or catastrophe, this was precisely because it was not the name of a crucial city or strategic site. Hardly "Rome" or "Constantinople," "Waterloo" was a fantasy of the untouched, nameless field not yet "disfigured," as Hugo wrote, by humans moving earth to make a monument. On the evening after the battle, as the fictional Thénardier was looting corpses, "Waterloo" was already lost in the mists of the past because it had never precisely existed in the first place. What the tourists who arrived the next day or in the ensuing decades came to see, then, was less a physical locale than a stage set or even the site of a séance.

The most popular activity at the proto-amusement park that sprang up at the site was to stand on the observation tower where Napoleon himself had stood to survey the action, as if one could participate vicariously in his legendary scopic prowess by pretending to view a scene of hundreds of thousands of colliding soldiers.[55] The visitors do not seem to have been motivated by a desire to see what had happened, since by and large there was nothing left to see; instead, they sought to participate in the ghostly aftermath of a place where, as Hugo put it, "spectral armies whirl in mutual extermination."[56] This exercise in fantasy role-playing offered an opportunity to enjoy the thrill of pretending to conquer the world, but it also meant engaging with the inevitable "game over" since "Waterloo" was the place where Napoleon's reign came to a close. Simon Bainbridge has argued that, for Romantic writers such as William Wordsworth, "Napoleon's real power lies in his tyrannical hold over the 'imaginations of men,' not in his domination of Europe."[57] As an ideological construct, however, Napoleon was more a site of contestation than a representative of the imagination understood as a force of intelligible creativity shaping material reality. Bainbridge stresses that for Wordsworth the imagination "fights against Napoleon. . . . [It] is a militant, active and political force that both evolves out of and is directly engaged in Wordsworth's contest with Napoleon."[58] In these terms, "Napoleon" named not a magical individual whose word was ontological law, someone around whom idea and actuality coincided, but a symptom of the impossibility of controlling the imagination, which was liable to assume the form of a military or political program gone awry. Waterloo was sublime not because it offered a spectacle of might but because it revealed a fundamental representational contradiction: Almost before the battle was complete, it was widely asserted that no single glance, picture, or narrative could hope to capture it, yet for all its resistance to framing or demarcation, it was embraced as the ultimate figure of closure because it had brought to an end one crucial era in European history and inaugurated another. Waterloo was a manifestation of both the ungovernable and the controlled, the unanticipated and the thoroughly predictable. It was the site at which the Romantic imagination pit its productive powers against its own propensity for chaos or unlawfulness.

Over time, the self-evident meaningfulness of June 18, 1815, became something of a joke. Everyone could acknowledge the battle's significance, but no one could say what it revealed about the course of human affairs or the destiny of civilization. Waterloo was the ideal of a battle as a broken ideal; it marked the end of an age of idealized conflict, proving to be a monument not just to the collapse of empire but also to the collapse of monumentality itself. If Waterloo became the ultimate impetus for a war story, inspiring countless fictional and nonfictional meditations on its myriad dimensions, it is no easy task to distinguish between stories about the battle and stories about the battle's status as the ultimate stumbling block for the ambition to impart such a story. While "Waterloo" remains to this day a name for a colossal clash of armies and a colossal defeat, it is thus equally the name for Rousseau's struggle against the conviction that battlefields should be the focus of historical inquiry. It is in this sense that Hugo's *Les Misérables* narrates the Battle of Waterloo only by exposing the limitations of traditional third-person battle narratives, confirming Rousseau's fears about the futility of studying individual clashes of troops.

Firsthand accounts of the closing event of the Napoleonic era indicate that the citizenry of Europe had an uneasy relationship to their new status as spectators to mass destruction. By the time of Waterloo, the public had for decades been actively conceiving of itself as an audience to a world history of which it was and was not a part, but regardless of whether one looked on from the sidelines or followed the news reports in the paper, the experience of being a witness to modern war was often tinged with a Rousseauist skepticism about what one could hope to learn from the show. François-René de Chateaubriand, for example, relates an unusual morning in his *Memoirs*:

On June 18, 1815, I left Ghent about noon by the Brussels gate; I was going to finish my walk alone along the highroad. I had taken Caesar's *Commentaries* with me and I strolled along, immersed in my reading. I was over two miles from the town when I thought I heard a dull rumbling: I stopped and looked up at the sky, which was fairly cloudy, wondering whether I should walk on or turn back towards Ghent for fear of a storm. I listened; I heard nothing more but the cry of a moor-hen in the rushes and the sound of a village clock. I continued on my way: I had not taken thirty steps before the rumbling began again, now short, now drawn out at irregular intervals; sometimes it was perceptible only through trembling of the air, which was so far away that it communicated itself to the ground as it passed over those vast plains. The detonations, less prolonged, less undulating, less interrelated than those of thunder, gave rise in my mind to the idea of a battle. I found myself opposite a poplar planted at the corner of a hop-field. I crossed the road and leant against the trunk of the tree, with my face turned in the direction of Brussels. A southerly wind sprang up and brought me more distinctly the sound of artillery. That great battle, nameless as yet, whose echoes I was listening to at the foot of a poplar, and for whose unknown obsequies a village clock had just struck, was the Battle of Waterloo![59]

This passage weaves together many of the complex and often contradictory motifs that structured accounts of the Napoleonic battlefield. Chateaubriand presents his experience as a philosophical exercise in which he attempts to coordinate his sensory perceptions and his cognitive faculties to answer the seemingly straightforward question, what am I hearing? Insofar as his first thoughts are of the weather, his description invokes the well-established convention of comparing battles with natural phenomena such as earthquakes or tidal waves, although his inferential progression moves in the opposite direction, from the natural to the manmade since he detects in the sounds of detonations connections "less interrelated than those of thunder." His key insight is the jump from auditory data to "the idea of a battle," although this development does not entirely remove him from the pastoral setting, complete with a moorhen in the rushes. When a wind springs up and brings him "more distinctly the sound of artillery," the natural world, in addition to its possible significance as the cause of the sensory phenomena with which he is engaged, acquires a secondary role as the medium that imparts data that may resolve the uncertainty about what he is hearing, helping to answer the question of whether what his ears discern is a product of nature or of human hands.

Chateaubriand's status as a battle spectator is rather tenuous since he hears only echoes and sees nothing. He does not race toward the sounds in an effort to supplement his auditory experience with a visual one, but he does not flee in the opposite direction, either. There but not "there," the war almost falls in his lap; it infringes upon his daily routine, yet remains an object of contemplation that prompts speculation precisely to the extent it does not infringe upon his routine too egregiously and can almost be renormalized back to a part of the natural scenery. This might be regarded as a struggle between the authority of what Chateaubriand can process with his senses and what he can "see" with his mind's eye, but what is most striking is the way in which he confers authority upon neither type of vision. He does not make an effort to look at the field of combat "in the flesh," and he does not try to imagine how it must appear.

The final sentence of the passage interrupts these calm musings as Chateaubriand triumphantly declares that what he was hearing was the as-yet-nameless Waterloo. This formulation calls attention to the retrospective quality of the narrative, which, having ostensibly moved from detail to detail "in real time," now takes an enormous leap, a step thoroughly conditioned by the vantage of hindsight and an awareness of just how consequential the events unfolding on that day would prove to be. Interestingly, Chateaubriand declares that the clock rings *for* the battle. As his emphasis on the "unknown" ("for whose unknown obsequies a village clock had just struck") suggests, juxtaposing the noise of the clock with the first set of noises is, even after the fact, an arbitrary alignment and doubly so when considered from the perspective of his immediate perception of the events of June 18, 1815, as they unfolded. In this way, his narrative of a liminal encounter with something monumental seems to test the strength of its own conjunctions, as if the narrative were forced to concede that its various pieces might not hold together. Chateaubriand thus insists that, although he cannot see what is going on, he is situated in exactly the right spot to be moved by the event:

> A silent and solitary hearer of the solemn judgment of the fates, I would have been less moved if I had found myself in the fray: the danger, the firing, the press of death would have left me no time for meditation; but, alone under a tree, in the countryside near Ghent, like the shepherd of the flocks grazing around me, I was overwhelmed by the weight of my reflections. What was this battle? Was it going to be decisive? Was Napoleon there in person? Were lots being cast for the world, as for Christ's garments?[60]

The initial puzzle over curious noises now turns into an abstract reflection on the theoretical and allegorical aspects of the scene that Chateaubriand has decided he is almost encountering, and in fact he stresses that dealing with the battle from afar, at the edge of where it is possible to know what one is confronting, allows him to experience it "better." The idea of being situated at just the right distance from the spectacle in order to appreciate its colossal character is a refashioning of Immanuel Kant's discussion of the mathematical sublime in the *Critique of Judgment*, in which Kant cites a French general's claim that "in order to get the full emotional effect from the magnitude of the [Egyptian] pyramids, one must neither get too close to them nor stay too far away."[61] Seemingly aware of this reference, Chateaubriand likens his relationship to the unfolding battle to an experience he had had in Egypt: "A few miles from an immense catastrophe, I did not see it; I could not touch the huge funeral monument growing minute by minute at Waterloo, just as from the shores of Bulak, on the banks of the Nile, I had stretched out my hands in vain towards the Pyramids."[62] Having arrived in Egypt in flood season, he could not get close to the famed monuments and had to commission a friend to carve his name on them in his stead.

The invocation of this prior travel reveals a tension in Chateaubriand's account of his brush with Waterloo: On the one hand he claims to be in just the right position to experience it; on the other hand, as at the banks of the Nile, he may not be able to leave his own mark on the day, suggesting that the reality of Waterloo, even as it unfolded, was already part of an untouchable past. As in Egypt, there is definitely something to "see" that day in Belgium—albeit a monument of bodies rather than of stones— but the contingent quality of Chateaubriand's encounter with history threatens to turn his reminiscences into a series of hypothetical musings on experiences that could have been. If his walk had taken a slightly different turn, he might have found himself in the midst of Kant's dynamic sublime, terrorized by a storm of artillery instead of lurking on the margin, reflecting on a prior engagement with the mathematical sublime. Indeed, one of the striking things about his story is that although it flirts with an intimation of natural sublimity, the rumblings never become a raging tempest of lighting and thunder, and the armies of Napoleon and Wellington never manifest themselves directly enough to warrant comparison with the fearful power that Kant attributes to hurricanes or volcanoes. Instead, Chateaubriand presents an antishock experience set in motion not by the view of clashing soldiers but by a vague concern about what turns out to be a nonexistent weather system. The result is a curious mixture of understatement and overstatement: "There was a catastrophe (or so I would learn later), but I did not see it, and for this reason, I could be gripped by deep thoughts about what was taking place."

War has a well-established pedigree as the archetypal instance of the sublime. Canonized by Longinus, the motif stretches from Homer's *Iliad*, in which the scale of the fighting demands a host of different perspectival and ocular innovations such that ultimately only the gods can grasp everything that is taking place, to contemporary invasions waged under the banner of "shock and awe." Understood as a fearsome figure of might, the battlefield is a show perpetually on the verge of undermining any stable observational framework that might delimit it, threatening to break the boundary between viewer and viewed and spill into its audience with potentially disastrous consequences. Far more likely than that this battle will swell to encompass Chateaubriand, however, is the possibility that he will miss it entirely. His story thus exaggerates—to the point of ironizing—a core feature of Kant's aesthetic doctrine, the notion that the enjoyment of fear that defines the experience of the sublime is predicated on an underlying security. Confronted with nature's violence in the form of rushing water or flowing lava, Kant proposes that we not run and hide but instead grasp that "property, health, and life" are small matters in comparison to the supreme authority of reason, hence "the sight of [such terrors] becomes all the more attractive the more fearful it is, *provided we are in a safe place* [*in Sicherheit*] when we watch them."[63] Given that "it is impossible to like terror that we take seriously," sublime spectacles of astonishing power must be regarded as products of pseudothreats rather than brushes with real danger.[64] We can watch these remarkable events with pleasure only insofar as we can avoid taking them to heart.

Chateaubriand's memoirs take Kant at his word and push his model of safety to the limit, to the point that Chateaubriand is only indirectly confronted by a figure of force. The result is not, however, an aesthetic judgment of Waterloo's sublimity or its beauty. Although Chateaubriand presents the scene as a classical philosophical consideration of the relationship between sensation, affect, and cognition, he never actually sees the source of the sounds that give him pause, meaning that the experience culminates, somewhat disappointingly, in an assertion of the supremacy of the mind over the world it encounters as his own ruminations quickly become more important than the world-historical event upon which he has stumbled. This is initially legible in the shift from impersonal questions about the fate of the world to a simile—"as for Christ's garments"— that feels rather hubristic given that Chateaubriand has earlier cast himself as a shepherd tending his flock. As he goes on to consider his experiences in the twenty-four hours after Waterloo before he has learned who won the battle, his reflections become almost childish as he ponders which result would suit him best, weighing the trade-offs of glory versus liberty, his own inconvenience versus the honor of the French state, and so on.

In the bulletins and other public announcements that Napoleon penned describing his own triumphs, texts that were widely distributed throughout Europe, he imitated Caesar in his *Commentaries* and wrote about himself in the third person. As a faithful reader of both the Roman Caesar and the Little Caesar of France, Chateaubriand is concerned with how a first-person witness can hope to relate to the great historical personages it may chance to encounter, that is, how his "I" can claim to talk with, to, and about a monolithic "he" on the nearby field of combat. Like Rousseau in his *Reveries*, Chateaubriand can contemplate the monumentality of what is taking place precisely because he is not quite present either at the event or to himself. The effect of this doubly liminal state is to invert the relative significance of observer and observed, as if the real struggle were not between the French and the English but between the walker and his reflections. Even in this most tangential of encounters with a battle, it is incumbent upon the war watcher to become part of the war mythology. Our strolling "I" has to locate himself within the titanic struggle in virtue of being weighed down by the enormity of the reflections his chance brush with world history prompts. In other words, Chateaubriand himself must have pretensions to being an immortal; otherwise, Napoleon, and by extension the storied Caesar, may be exposed as ordinary men. The sublimity of world-historical grandeur and battlefield genius thus threatens to lapse into the commonplace or the bathetic, as if the ordinariness of a passerby on his daily walk could infect the epic field of combat and lay it low more efficiently than any enemy army.

As an object of observation, Chateaubriand's battlefield oscillates between an occurrence of monumental significance that should be all-consuming for any bystander and an event that is gripping not in its own terms but on the basis of the abstract musings it prompts. In turn, Chateaubriand himself is a figure of both spectatorship and fantasy, poised at the uncertain juncture between the informational authority won by "being there"—although he is not quite there—and the conceptual authority won by the ability of his mind to imagine precisely what must be happening "over there" and what it means, although at this point he is not quite sure of the consequences. Nineteenth-century reflections on the Napoleonic era were riddled with similarly ambiguous battlefield scenes and liminal onlookers situated neither precisely inside nor outside the war effort. These individuals became spectacles in their own right, and following their escapades as they did or did not take in the sights and sounds around them became as interesting or disturbing as the mass killing they were watching—or failing to watch, as they became consumed by self-observation to the point that they forgot to look at the battle itself. Notwithstanding its unparalleled dimensions and destructiveness, the Napoleonic battlefield was thus routinely characterized by viewers and combatants alike as elusive or ephemeral, as if it were never quite large or violent enough to ensure that it was impossible to miss. At the very least, there was always a risk of confusing a skirmish or preparatory engagement with the "real" thing. Given the material limitations on viewers of the period, who did not enjoy the advantage of air transportation, much less the advanced visual transmission and recording devices we take for granted today, it is perhaps to be expected that any single observer's perspective proved to be both limited and fallible. At the same time, Chateaubriand's experience was typical in illustrating the challenge of winning a disinterested view of military proceedings. The Napoleonic engagements were mythologized so quickly that it seemed that reliable insights into the events were to be won only by those who lacked a proper role to play in them and who did not (yet) realize what they had stumbled upon and could therefore by happenstance make an aesthetic rather than a teleological judgment of the scene.

Chateaubriand's presentation of his own near encounter with Waterloo implicitly grounds the legitimacy of his experience in the accidental quality of this brush with the battlefield, but it is hard to take this dimension of the narrative at face value. As his readers, we are asked to believe that if the wind had been blowing in a slightly different direction or if Chateaubriand had taken a slightly different route on his stroll, his brief pseudoencounter with the battle of battles would never have come to pass. However casual his opening description of the mysterious thunderlike sounds may appear, his story seems completely overdetermined in retrospect. Surely he did not just happen to be wandering by that exact spot on that exact day such that he could almost, but not quite, espy what was going on at Waterloo. His claim that the battle noises roused him from an ambulatory study of Caesar's *Commentaries* about the Gallic Wars, as if his subject matter had suddenly come to life in a modern form, is similarly implausible. We are invited to accept a tale in which a man reading about famous generals and their exploits sees them—or almost sees them—materialize right before his eyes. Chateaubriand clearly perceives that the credibility of his story rests on his ability to produce a semblance of chance that in retrospect will seem entirely contrived, as if he can lay claim to being a true wartime observer only if his position vis-à-vis the scene is more or less than merely artificial. The price to be paid for the integrity of his account is the reduction of the clash of armies—an engineering marvel in which tens of thousands of men and a brutal array of firepower were brought together in an extremely restricted space—to a quasi-spectral phenomenon, potentially no more than a fantasy of the author out for a stroll, something he concocted upon hearing some stray thunder.

It is also not by chance that the semblance of coincidence in this narrative is produced by a detail about reading Caesar's *Commentaries*. In the very process of asserting the primacy of happenstance in war spectatorship, Chateaubriand confirms that the endeavor to know the battlefield is fundamentally a contest between looking and reading, a struggle to coordinate accounts of the visual event—one's own or others'—with the narratives one peruses in a newspaper, a government bulletin, or a personal account composed long after the fact. In Chateaubriand's memoirs there is a strong suggestion that it is only because he was reading about the ancient Caesar that he realized that he had just stumbled upon the work of the modern one; although it is equally implied that if he had kept his nose in his book, he might have learned a lot more about war than he did from trying to decipher the sounds he heard. The real achievement of the passage is thus that it pits a firsthand sensory encounter with a battle—albeit an auditory rather than a visual one—against a firsthand encounter with a classical text about a battle, yet leaves open the question of which one "wins." In this regard Caesar's book is not the only text caught up in the fray. When Chateaubriand reflects on the sounds he hears that morning in Belgium—"What was this battle? Was it going to be decisive?"—he is wittingly or unwittingly speaking in a Napoleonic vocabulary that resonates just as loudly in the *Memoirs* as the works of overt forerunners such as Kant or Rousseau.

We may conclude that Chateaubriand on the road in Belgium is an emblem for the masses of Europe reading newspapers about the Napoleonic wars as they take place. Who or what, then, sets the standards for legibility in the historical realm? In other words, what makes it possible for the public to learn how to read a war—assuming that they (or Chateaubriand) ever do? In "watching" a battle from an extra-safe place, Chateaubriand confirms that the ability to remember or impart information about such a conflict is only tangentially a factor of how much of an opportunity one has had to experience it directly. Leaning against a tree as he ponders the profundity of a struggle he cannot quite see or know, he situates himself and the modern battlefield at a curious juncture of the aesthetic, the political, and the historical. This is a site at which all three discourses meet but do not quite mutually inform one another. In the end it is unclear whether any of them offers a paradigm with which to understand what is taking place on the nearby meadows.

§ 2 The Witness Under Fire

> Child with its mother in the panorama. The panorama is presenting the Battle of Sedan. The child finds it all very lovely: "Only it's too bad the sky is so dreary."—"That's what the weather is like in war," answers the mother.
>
> —Walter Benjamin, *The Arcades Project*

Throughout the Napoleonic Wars, bystanders and combatants alike were constantly struck by the impenetrability and implausibility of the battles being fought. Horrific scenes of injury and death that they were, the giant clashes of armies were nonetheless delimited by precise spatio-temporal parameters, as if the Aristotelian unities were being observed. This formal organization of unparalleled suffering and slaughter often appeared pointedly artificial, even surreal. The chessboard of military strife in which would-be Caesars directed their human pawns on exposed fields thus reached its grandest scale on what seemed to be open-air stages.[1] The quintessential example was Waterloo, which Victor Hugo called "more a massacre than a battlefield."[2] Historian Alessandro Barbero concurs, observing that on that morning in Belgium "nearly 200,000 men confronted one another on a scrap of land barely four kilometers (2.5 miles) square; never, either before or after, have such a great number of soldiers been massed on so circumscribed a battlefield."[3] As it assumed its most gruesome guise, this horrific theater of war was starting to betray its status as unsustainable. The enormous casualties were the result of improvements in the mobility and accuracy of artillery that were bringing the direct collision of massed troops on open fields to the brink of tactical obsolescence. In subsequent generations the widespread use of better rifles and machine guns would complete the antiquation of this style of combat.

If there is no question that Napoleonic battles offered would-be onlookers massive collisions of men under arms that acquired the scale and force of natural disasters, the scope and pace of the events and the weapons the combatants employed ensured that this theater of warfare had few, if any, clear lines of sight. The well-known paintings of brightly clad troops firing upon one another are misleading, for the function of the colorful uniforms was to help the soldiers distinguish friend from foe in the midst of the clouds of smoke that covered the field. Although historians disagree about precisely how poor visibility was, firsthand accounts of these engagements suggest that discharge from muskets and artillery obscured most participants' view of the proceedings. Reports of Waterloo in particular describe a thick smoke that reduced visibility to ten yards or less.[4] Even to the eye of the professional soldier, these engagements were mystifying phenomena. At best, one could take in a piece of the action, with no glimpse of the whole; at worst, one was surrounded by chaos, with no discernible narrative thread to organize what was transpiring. War thus became required viewing at the very moment at which its immense engagements became too large and complex to be followed by the best-trained observers.

Accounts of battles from this period are distinguished by their elaborate strategies for addressing these difficulties, particularly when it came to the question of how the—often sketchy—details of what had taken place on the field of combat could be best presented in support of one's claim to have won the day. In 1807 at the Battle of Eylau, the French fought a bloody and largely inconclusive engagement with the Russians in which both sides suffered enormous casualties and neither could boast of having destroyed the opponent's forces. This was the first time that the *Grande Armée* was seriously tested, if not fought to a draw, and the subsequent effort to tell the story of its "victory" became a crucial challenge for the French propaganda machine. At stake was not simply the supposed invincibility of Napoleon's forces but also the viability of the one-day battle and its ability to guarantee a clear result in the form of a definite winner and loser. To set the record straight, Napoleon himself penned several supplementary bulletins for the official press releases, focusing on his own experiences on the field after the fighting was over rather than during it. Writing about himself in the third person, the emperor thus narrates his victory not as a blow-by-blow account of the battle but as an interpretation of its remains:

> After the Battle of Eylau, the Emperor spent several hours daily on the battlefield. . . . To visualize the scene one must imagine, within the space of one square league, nine or ten thousand corpses; four or five thousand dead horses; rows upon rows of Russian field packs; the remnants of guns and swords; the ground covered with cannon balls, shells, and other ammunition; and

twenty-four artillery pieces, near which could be seen the corpses of the drivers who were killed while trying to move them—all this sharply outlined on a background of snow.[5]

Here, the power of the wartime spectacle lies not in the immediacy of unfolding action—men dismembered by swords or cavalry trampling bloodied bodies—but in the remnants of such events, "sharply outlined on a background of snow." Combining the perspectival logic of landscape painting with an engineer's geometric ordering of a square field divided by rows, Napoleon's description of the scene presents these remains as both traces of material transformations (death and destruction) and as formal units or numbered objects, precisely arrayed.

Napoleon's implicit claim in this bulletin is that victory goes to the one who is left to peruse the carnage, suggesting that, to win a battle, it is not enough to rout the enemy with weapons; one must also prevail in the exegesis of the aftermath. By inviting us to visualize the scene and thereby shifting the medium from what he sees to our mind's eye, Napoleon does not necessarily unsettle his own authority and may even augment it since now we are asked to imagine things as he imagined them, as well as to see them as he saw them, meaning that he has become the model for processing data in both the sensible and intelligible realms. At the same time, once the identity between seeing and understanding is broken, it is unclear that Napoleon or anyone else can reign sovereign over the ensuing dynamics of simulation, irrespective of how well one claims to be able to see or fantasize, because the very fact that the emperor has to interpret what he witnessed firsthand means that he can be second-guessed by people who were not there. The injunction—"one must imagine"—allows the addressee more independence than may have been intended. In this vein Michael Marrinan has argued that "despite Napoleon's very real control of most historical information across the Empire, his obsession with absolute authority—to control every aspect of a text's 'lexie' as both narrator and observer—inadvertently configured a space where the reader's unconscious could run free."[6] In the case of the Battle of Eylau, the French government, apparently perceiving that its press releases were not sufficient to ensure the authority of its interpretation of the event, held a competition for the best painting of Napoleon visiting the battle after the victory. His verbal recounting of his inspection of the scene needed to be supplemented by a visual one, almost as if the original command to the reader—

"Visualize!"—had to be recast as an ostensibly more direct order: "Look!" Unsurprisingly, the resulting images only extended rather than obviated the original problem. Scholars have shown that the paintings made for the contest were highly ambiguous, confirming once again that the interpretation of Napoleonic spectacle was not entirely in Napoleon's control.[7]

It is instructive to compare Napoleon's text about Eylau with Walter Scott's comments on visiting the site of the Battle of Waterloo only a few weeks after the epic day:

> To recollect, that within a short month, the man whose name had been the terror of Europe, stood on the very ground which I now occupied . . . —that the landscape, now solitary and peaceful around me, presented so lately a scene of such horrid magnificence—that the very individual who was now at my side, had then stood by that of Napoleon, and witnessed every change in his countenance, from hope to anxiety, from anxiety to fear and to despair—to recollect all this, oppressed me with sensations which I find it impossible to describe. The scene seemed to have shifted so rapidly, that even while I stood on the very stage where it was exhibited, I felt an inclination to doubt the reality of what had passed.[8]

Scott's encounter is entirely at odds with what Napoleon enjoins us to experience at Eylau. Standing on the main stage, at the center of world history, on the very spot where the emperor had been, Scott finds that the "indescribable" disjunction between the setting and what had allegedly taken place there makes him skeptical about the "story" with which he has been presented since what he sees offers him no information about what supposedly happened. Moreover, far from following Napoleon's instructions and trying to imagine what the landscape must have looked like only hours after the battle, Scott is not prompted to any flights of fancy whatsoever. What he "experiences" is a stark challenge to the understanding of the past through a study of what persists in the present, for the very fact that Waterloo the physical locale endures whereas Waterloo the battle came and went in less than twenty-four hours becomes a reason to doubt the significance of what transpired there on June 18. Precisely because one can imagine, as Napoleon would have it, the details of the battle, one can also imagine that the battle did not take place or at least that it did not take place in the manner one has been told.[9] While such a suggestion in no way questions the extent of the suffering and death that occurred, in both Scott's musings and Napoleon's bulletin, the power of the theater of war is as much a factor of what the mind can see as of what the eye can see. If anything, it would appear that the force of a war story is compromised rather than intensified the moment it is tied to a specific representation or locale. As a narrative, war asserts its independence from the firsthand empirical observations of it.

Another example will reinforce the point. In April of 1793, with the French revolutionary wars still in their infancy and the years of the mammoth Napoleonic conflicts in the future, William Godwin paused in the middle of a treatise on ethics and politics to consider the evil of war:

> We can have no adequate idea of this evil unless we visit, at least in imagination, a field of battle. Here men deliberately destroy each other by thousands, without resentment against, or even knowledge of, each other. The plain is strewed with death in all its forms. Anguish and wounds display the diversified modes in which they can torment the human frame. Towns are burned; ships are blown up in the air, while the mangled limbs descend on every side; the fields are laid desolate; the wives of the inhabitants exposed to brutal insult; and their children driven forth to hunger and nakedness.[10]

To illustrate the horrors of war, Godwin demands that we visit a concrete incarnation of its tragedies, the field of battle. His recommendation is not based on his own experiences of a specific military struggle; it occurs as a thought experiment rather than a review of empirical data. Whether he had wanted to cast his gaze on the Wars of Reformation or to turn to the classical accounts of Thucydides or Caesar, Godwin faced no shortage of past battles to exemplify his point. Instead of using history as a guide, however, he proposes that we consider war abstractly, "as" it happens and not as it has happened or as it will happen. If the following two decades in Europe were to witness forms of concentrated slaughter unprecedented in 1793, for Godwin the mere idea of war was already powerful enough that it could be unfolded in exact and terrible detail. Yet precisely because he treated war first and foremost as an idea, its exposition could not be restricted to a visual review of combat. As a war "in" and "of" the mind, his demonstration quickly starts to run away—temporally and spatially—from the parameters with which it begins, moving from a field of battle to towns, to ships at sea, and finally to the long-term consequences of soldiers' deaths as their children are left to perish without protection. Godwin does not propose that by describing a war he will bring its terrors home to us. We are to do this on our own, as if, curiously, the singular horror that

is war were universally accessible to the imaginative capacities of his readership. In the process we are to survey the world not as a war correspondent would observe the manifold complexities of a battle firsthand but as
an omniscient narrator relating the fates of countless individuals across
an entire society. In other words, we are asked to review extended se-
quences of causes and effects for which there may be no visible evidence,
as if we could "see" months or years into the future. The power of Godwin's illustration of the evils of war lies in his invitation to his reader to
become the author of a novel about war.

In all three of these texts the observational authority of the solitary
watcher—the witness whose testimony ostensibly wins credibility due to
the singularity of his privileged vantage point—is undermined by the
need to generalize the substance of the experience via the mind's power
to envision something that is not or cannot be directly viewed. At best,
firsthand witness is incomplete and must be supplemented by some sort
of inventive reconstruction or projection. At worst, seeing something in
person—in Scott's case, the field where a battle was supposedly fought—
becomes a challenge to the claim that anything happened at all. Crucially,
"observation" is not modeled here in micro-, macro-, or telescopic terms.
If anything, war spectatorship is defined in contradistinction to rather
than on the basis of the faculties of human perception. The result is that
the spatiotemporal integrity of the military event is shattered. With Napoleon's Eylau, the conflict can be grasped only by reading the traces of its
aftermath; with Godwin, the full horrors of the battle become apparent
only as one moves far beyond it. Responding to Rousseau's claim in *Emile*
that in watching a battle one can never hope to distinguish between the
forces shaping the course of the event and irrelevant incidents, these
authors propose that only a hypothetical or an imaginary viewer can comprehend the complexity and totality of the war experience. Henceforth,
the story about what and how one *should* see when witnessing a military
venture will be just as important as what one does see. Watching a war and
imagining what it must have been like to have done so thus prove to be
inextricably intertwined. The story of a combatant or bystander viewing
a battle unfold "live" becomes a testimony to the mediated, even ephemeral quality of an event that ostensibly gains its significance from the
immediacy of its physical horrors.

This uncertain identity between the imperative to see and the imperative to envision was often experienced as a form of theatricality. In a study

of the performative nature of military behavior and its significance for British society of the Napoleonic era, Gillian Russell has argued that war and theater became "mutually sustaining not only in material terms but also culturally, ideologically, and politically."[11] Russell emphasizes the way in which patriotic efforts to organize volunteer forces relied on the "theatricality of the military" and ultimately "broke down the boundaries between the military and the general population, making it feasible for all men to 'play' at being soldiers," to the point that "the identities of the actor and the soldier" became "interchangeable in late Georgian society."[12] In *The Great War and Modern Memory* Paul Fussell similarly argues that the intimate link between playacting and being soldier was forged in the Napoleonic Wars because the demand for troops far exceeded the supply of professional combatants: "The most obvious reason why 'theater' and modern war seem so compatible is that modern wars are fought by conscripted armies, whose members know they are only temporarily playing their ill-learned parts."[13] At issue was not simply a matter of recruits being conditioned to military discipline through marching and other training rituals but also the very way in which these men experienced battle itself.

Reflecting on the theatricality of these dynamics, Carl von Clausewitz, the preeminent military theorist of the Napoleonic era and a veteran of numerous combat engagements, offers an intriguing hypothetical account of a first visit to the field of combat:

Let us accompany a novice to the battlefield. As we approach the rumble of guns grows louder and alternates with the whir of cannonballs, which begin to attract his attention. Shots begin to strike close around us. We hurry up the slope where the commanding general is stationed with his large staff. Here cannonballs and bursting shells are frequent, and the seriousness of life pierces the youthful fantasy. Suddenly an acquaintance is wounded; then a shell falls among the staff and produces an involuntary movement. One begins to feel that one is no longer completely calm and collected; even the bravest becomes somewhat muddle-headed [*zerstreut*]. Now we enter the battle raging before us, still almost like a play [*Schauspiel*], and join the nearest divisional commander. Shot is falling like hail, and the thunder of our own guns adds to the din. Forward to the brigadier, a soldier of acknowledged bravery, but he is careful to take cover behind a rise, a house or a clump of trees. A noise is heard that is a certain indication of increasing danger—the rattling of grapeshot on roofs and on the ground. Cannonballs tear past, whizzing in all directions, and musketballs begin to whistle around us. A little further we reach the firing line, where the infantry endures the hammering for hours with incredible steadfastness. The air is filled with hissing bullets that sound like a sharp crack if they pass close to one's head. For a final shock, the sight of men being killed and mutilated moves our pounding hearts to awe and pity.[14]

As in numerous fictional and nonfictional battle narratives, Clausewitz sets the scene by describing the distinctive sounds of the engagement, which invariably precede one's precise cognizance of artillery or gunfire. The notion that the novice's attention needs to be piqued may seem somewhat counterintuitive, as if one could ever be distracted in the course of this unique experience, but it is precisely the incompleteness of the auditory data that propels the party forward to get a better view, at which point everything is "still almost like a play." From both a sensory and an emotional perspective, the initial encounter is not overwhelming. Instead, the dangers the neophyte confronts intensify gradually, as if someone were slowly turning up the dial on the battlefield meter, and this progression toward the sight of death and mutilation is carefully paralleled at each increment with a corresponding step down in the military chain of command as we move from the vantage point of the general to the side of a divisional leader to a brave soldier to the common infantrymen dying in droves. Indeed, with the introduction of each subsequent personage, it feels more like one is meeting characters in a costume drama than processing an account of what the firsthand witness to a clash of armies would be like.

Clausewitz's tale succinctly captures the basic tensions of the Napoleonic battle. On the one hand, the field of combat stages order. The ultimate "public" event, it places social logics on display in grand terms, graphically exhibiting the communal construction of identity, the division of labor, and the centrality of hierarchy.[15] This accounts for the highly self-reflexive experience of being in battle: the soldiers are aware of themselves as actors in a drama for which they are the primary audience. On the other hand, the battlefield stages the incomprehensible and inconceivable. As the limit case of human agency, it exposes a potential for aggression and cruelty that normally remains hidden or at least muted. The question for Clausewitz as for the generations of nineteenth-century historians and philosophers who reflected on the Napoleonic Wars is how these two tendencies can be understood together, as facets of a single event and in particular a single spectacle. In this regard, it is notable that Clausewitz offers a markedly impersonal rendering of the novice's first encounter with the "real thing," which is narrated not from an individual's eye view but from the perspective of a bird flying overhead across the field. Clausewitz's point is not so much that no subjective perspective can be illuminating but rather that we must reject the layperson's romantic fantasy that one experiences the battlefield in a fit of impulsive rampage: "You charge the enemy, ignoring the bullets and casualties, in a surge of excitement. Blindly you hurl yourself toward icy death, not knowing whether you or anyone else will escape him."[16] Clausewitz disputes that such a moment of headstrong blunder, even if it were to come to pass, would be perceived as instantaneous, "like a heartbeat," and proposes that this impulse would be felt "rather like a medicine, in recurring doses, the state diluted by time."[17] If encountering a real battle demystifies one's preconceptions about it, it is not in a rending tear but through the revelation that the horror of the scene comes upon one in a methodical, even leisurely fashion. For Clausewitz, the experience of warfare is never a matter of getting carried away by the moment but always a process of reflection and repeated reorganization that in essence is neither spontaneous nor intuitive.

Clausewitz's narration of the novice's first excursion into combat underscores the inherent abstractness of the event, as if the effort to emphasize the sensory dimensions of the experience were constantly at risk of being obscured by the overtly imprecise plot details (the brigadier takes refuge behind a rise, a house, *or* a clump of trees). The disorientation introduced by the uncertain role of the hypothetical in the passage is augmented by the shifting focus of the involved parties, who are said to oscillate between attentiveness and disorientation, a detail that sits oddly with the profoundly controlled way in which Clausewitz sets out the story. When he concludes by telling us that at the close of the scene we are moved to awe and pity, it is as if he is describing the audience at a classical drama experiencing the catharsis prescribed by Aristotle's *Poetics*. In the final analysis the account of the raw recruit's first encounter with the realities of warfare serves only to illustrate that a battle is experienced as a play by those who fight it.

Guided by a similar concern with the degree to which traditional poetic conventions inform the experience of war, Paul Fussell comes to the same conclusion: "If killing and avoiding being killed are the ultimate melodramatic actions, then military training is very largely training in melodrama."[18] For these authors, the recourse to generic categories such as tragedy or melodrama is not designed to deny the reality of the physical and psychological suffering that soldiers endure but works instead to expose the fallacy of relying on any notion of a "natural" or "normal" response to witnessing extreme scenes of death and destruction. In fact, the profound trauma visited by a battlefield upon those who find themselves in it has everything to do with its inherent theatricality, that is, with the irreducible gap that obtains in warfare between identity and performance, between an immediate intuition of sensory data and the reflection and reorganization that for Clausewitz imposes itself as or even before one first cognizes the surrounding misery. To be under fire is to experience the loss of control of one's own signifying practices. As much as a battle overwhelms soldiers with physical threats, it also crushes them with an onslaught of performative logics that leaves them with the sense that only overplaying or underplaying their hand will give them any hope of reasserting control over the apparent meaningfulness of their actions.[19]

It is therefore not by chance that many of the most insightful reflections on the dynamics of Napoleonic war spectacle center on the question of what happens when someone blunders onto the battlefield stage before he has learned his lines. One of the most memorable such figures makes his entrance in the first part of Stendhal's *Charterhouse of Parma* (1839) as the seventeen-year-old Fabrice leaves his home in Italy and rushes north, desperate to serve his idealized hero, the emperor of France, recently returned from exile on Elba.[20] Fabrice's quest to become an actor in the world-historical theater of the Hundred Days quickly turns comical as the naïve young man is robbed and then arrested as a suspected spy. Finally managing to find his way to the French army, he arrives, the narrator explains, on the eve of the Battle of Waterloo.[21] Fabrice devotes the fateful day of June 18 to attempting, with limited success, to become a cog in the Napoleonic war machine. Having purchased the uniform of a hussar who recently died in jail, he attaches himself to a squad of men and tries to sightsee, as well as to take part in the engagement. While his newfound comrades support his efforts to catch glimpses of the famous generals who pass by, they are not fooled by his impersonation of a soldier, and many cast inquisitive glances his way—as if the major thing of note that occurred that day were the disruption of an adult play by an upstart child actor. Evidently unaware of the show he is putting on, Fabrice is relieved when they are attacked: " 'Aha! Now we're under fire at last. [*Ah! m'y voilà donc enfin au feu!*] I've seen action!' he kept telling himself, with a

certain satisfaction. 'Now I'm a true soldier [*Me voici un vrai militaire*].'"[22]
In his youthful enthusiasm Fabrice is committed to the notion that to see
the cannonade, to be under fire, is to be "a true soldier" regardless of the
fact that he is there as an imposter with no training, rank, or assignment,
much less any past experience in combat. This jejune conception of military identity is immediately called into question: "At this moment, the
escort began galloping at breakneck speed, and our hero realized that
these were cannonballs tearing up the earth. Though he tried to see where
they were coming from, there was nothing but white smoke from the
battery a great way off, and amid the continuous roaring of cannon-fire,
he seemed to hear explosions much closer to him [*beaucoup plus voisines*];
he could make nothing of it."[23] If "being there" is the essence of "being a
soldier," it is no guarantee of access to reliable information about what is
taking place in one's immediate surroundings. Fabrice successfully infers
that gunshot is making the earth fly up, but when he looks for its source,
he cannot reconcile what he sees with what he hears, passing from pre-
liminary comprehension ("our hero realized that these were cannonballs")
to the utter lack thereof ("he could make nothing of it"). His repeated
emphasis on the link between location and self-identity ("here *I* am because I am *here*") is asserted in a toposcopic lexicon of imperatives (voici—
vois ici / voilà—*vois là*). The coordination of place and sight is interrupted,
however, by the confusing appearance of something "much closer," "beaucoup plus *voisines*," a contiguity in which identity becomes literally too
close for comfort. At the level of the letter, *voisines* extends the chain of
terms beginning with v-o-i, but it does so with a word whose root is the
Latin *vicinus* (neighbor) rather than *videre* (from which *voir* is derived).
Putting together the sights and sounds of the novel's verbal description of
Fabrice's confusion is no easier than the coordination of perceptions that
Fabrice undertakes. His *baptême du feu* (baptism by fire) introduces an
uncertainty that divides his efforts at self-expression since, despite what
he asserts, it is now possible that being *au feu* (under fire) is not the same
thing as seeing *le feu* (the action)—indeed, it may be that being *au feu* is
the name for a situation in which one cannot see what is going on. In this
combat experience the *coup de feu* (shot) becomes a disruptive *coup d'œil*
(glance); it is not a glimpse but a blow to the eye that shatters the authority of vision and exposes the immediacy of combat as irremediably *après
coup* (after the fact).

From this point on, Fabrice's most notable "firsthand" perceptions will be oversights and errors. He cannot make out the figure of Napoleon passing by, and he infers that he has shot a Prussian, only to learn that someone else actually felled him. As his attempts to define himself as a soldier founder, Fabrice redirects his attention to the identity of the proceedings around him and asks one of his new comrades whether they are actually in the midst of a battle: "'Monsieur, this is the first time I've seen a battle,' he finally said to the sergeant, 'but is this a real battle?'"[24] Fabrice's obsession with this question blinds him to the sarcasm of the answer he receives—"Somewhat"/"Un peu"—and he never considers whether his query might be laughable.[25] Well after the action was over, "what distressed him most," explains the narrator, "was that he had not asked Corporal Aubry the question: 'Have I really taken part in a battle?'"[26] It would be inaccurate to say that Fabrice's escapades are the product of a disjunction between his actions and his consciousness of them, for he cannot even begin the reflection on his own behavior that would allow such a disjunction to emerge. The desire to shift the focus away from issues of identity ("Am I a real soldier?" "Is this a real battle?") and toward some consideration of what he *has* done ("Have I really taken part in a battle?") is an effort to stabilize his experience by putting a past he could claim as his own in the place of a past that has gone missing. Unfortunately, this decisive question about what he has already done is never posed in such a way as to produce a response he can accept.

In a blithe and thoroughly entertaining fashion, the experiences of Stendhal's pseudohero offer a viewpoint that is neither epic nor panoramic but fragmentary, limited, and, above all, confused. There is no grand scene of battle and no overarching narrative. Fabrice's Waterloo is a series of disparate encounters, none of which are self-evidently significant in their own right and none of which appear to be essentially connected to what preceded or followed them. As in Clausewitz's story about the novice's first taste of combat, we have frequent glimpses of authority figures, but there is no corresponding sense of how authority is disseminated through the ranks; instead, the novel gives the impression that one is following a military force constantly on the verge of dissolution, which was of course the fate of more than half the French regiments at the conclusion of the battle.

One might object that even to take Fabrice's mishaps and his ensuing self-interrogation seriously is to miss the point, which is that inexperience and incompetence more than suffice to explain his uncertainty about what he is seeing and doing on June 18, 1815. The fact that Fabrice will be plagued by a studied naïveté throughout Stendhal's novel suggests that his confusion about his situation on this storied day in Belgium is simply an introduction to a lifetime of bumbling behavior to come and not evidence that a battlefield is by nature incomprehensible to the point that someone participating in it might not know that it was taking place around him. At the same time there are clear indications that the perplexing vicissitudes of battlefield spectatorship are central to the understanding of history in *The Charterhouse of Parma* and not simply a product of Fabrice's youthful folly. The first lines of the novel's opening chapter characterize the grand entrance of Napoleon into Italy:

> On May 15, 1796, General Bonaparte entered Milan at the head of that young army which had lately crossed the Lodi Bridge and taught the world that after so many centuries Caesar and Alexander had a successor. The miracles of valor and genius Italy had witnessed in a few months awakened a slumbering nation: just eight days before the French arrived, the Milanese still regarded them as no more than a band of brigands who habitually fled before the troops of His Imperial and Royal Majesty: at least so they were told three times a week by a little news-sheet the size of a man's hand, printed on dirty paper.[27]

This inaugural scene establishes a clear standard for world-historical events, which are to unfold as poignant revelations of the truth. Mired in the falsities of news reports, the Italian populace is roused from its confusion as it bears direct witness to miracles of bravery and genius. This is the ideal of Thucydidean history, in which war appears as self-evidently meaningful. In these terms Fabrice at Waterloo is completely excluded from the Napoleonic pageant, unable to participate either as a member of a formative military force or as a spectator who can see the battle for what it really is. Is this simply to state the obvious, namely, that on that particular day Fabrice was on the losing side? In fact, once it is set in motion, Fabrice's comical spectacle of faux soldiering, like the inexorable march of Napoleon's army into Italy, gains considerable momentum, albeit as a para- or an antihistorical story rather than an onslaught of truth. As the novel continues, members of Fabrice's family attempt to protect him by insisting that he was not in Belgium on that day in June, but secondhand accounts of his past ultimately come to describe him as having once been "one of the bravest colonels in Napoleon's army."[28] In the end, Fabrice is "a true soldier" precisely in virtue of his failure to coordinate his expectations for himself with his expectations for the event that unfolds around him. In his dual role as a would-be combatant (he kills no one) and a would-be spectator (he cannot even be sure that he was present at the spectacle), he exemplifies the experience of the battlefield as a disorganized melodrama, a confrontation with a performative system to which one desperately wants to submit oneself but with which one can never be entirely in synch.

If Scott and Godwin help clarify the role of the imagination in grasping the significance of a battle, Stendhal's hero—at once imaginative and unimaginative in the extreme—suggests that any encounter with a battle may lead both to a demand for a better "perspective" on the scene and to an indictment of that very demand as a fantasy. In the course of Fabrice's exploits the assertion of a difference between a wartime engagement and its model or ideal—"a real battle"—underscores the fact that every empirical military operation has to be interpreted with reference to standards that are anything but physically tangible. Fabrice's repeated queries to his would-be comrades indicate that his experiences, far from self-evident in their meaning, require constant interpretation. What guarantees, then, that a meaningful overview of an event such as Waterloo can ever be won, whether by a bystander on site or by a historian or novelist decades after the fact?

The question is whether this dynamic of military posturing that perverts the sanctity and authority of the "true" march of history is inherent to warfare or to the dynamics of this novel. One could argue that Stendhal's entire book works to undermine the logic expressed in its opening lines and that our hapless imposter at Waterloo is just the first in a series of characters who play at being what they are not. It has often been observed that for large sections of *The Charterhouse of Parma* Fabrice does not seem to be the principal figure in his own bildungsroman; at times, for example, the spotlight is stolen by Gina, the duchess who assumes the role of his aunt. Maurice Samuels has emphasized the paradigmatic status of another character, the prince of Parma. Modeling himself on Louis XIV, the prince turns his state "into a giant Romantic historical drama" such that the town essentially becomes a stage set and the inhabitants have to pretend that recently constructed buildings date from the Middle Ages.[29] "Through the example of Fabrice and the court of Parma," argues

Samuels, "the novel reveals the absurdity, as well as the danger, of looking to the past as a model," exposing "the historical obsession of the nineteenth century as a Romantic delusion, as incapable of providing a basis for the formation of either individual or national identity."[30]

In the quarter century from Napoleon's final defeat to the appearance of *The Charterhouse of Parma* the Battle of Waterloo had acquired considerable mythic status and had become ripe for debunking. The problem with subsuming Fabrice's experience of June 18 into Samuel's broader claims for the ironic logic of the novel is that Fabrice's "delusions" in Belgium stem not from the instability of the past as a model of self-identity but from the inability of an experience of the present to serve as a ground of truth, as if the scene at the start of the book, in which the Italian people bear witness to the genius of the invading French, were a onetime fluke. The key to understanding Fabrice's convoluted relationship to world-historical events lies in the connection that the novel establishes between war and reading. In the opening lines of the first chapter, reading appears as a diversion from veracity in the reference to the "little news-sheet" that misleads the Italian people about the real nature of the French forces. Later Fabrice's "Aunt" Gina explains: "You know that I had, in my private apartments in the Palazzo Dugnani, the engravings of the battles won by Napoleon: it was by studying the captions of these engravings that my nephew learned to read."[31] The idea that children's acquisition of their *ABCs* would be facilitated by observing the alignment between illustrations of the exploits of the French emperor and a verbal account of them wryly gestures toward the infantile essence of "great men," but it also suggests that in Fabrice's representational universe the experience of war as something to be read was prior to the experience of war as something to be seen or fought. It is not surprising that the latter forum would have a hard time measuring up to the mythological authority of the former.

If the modern experience of war as spectacle rests on the possibility that "watching" war primarily comes to mean reading about war—and reading about other people watching war—Fabrice's travails do not bode well for the clarity of the public discourse that emerges. The claim that this sometime protagonist learned his *ABCs* by inspecting the captions of illustrations of Napoleon invites us to look more closely at Fabrice's activities in the weeks immediately following Waterloo, when he tries to put words and pictures together as he searches for some corroboration that the sights he remembers were what he hopes they were:

During the fifteen days Fabrice spent in the Amiens inn . . . the Allies were invading France, and Fabrice became an entirely different man, so many and so deep were his reflections upon the things which had just happened to him. He remained a child only on this one point: had what he had seen been a battle and, furthermore, had this battle been Waterloo? For the first time in his life, he took pleasure in reading; he still hoped to find in the newspapers or in the accounts of battle some description that might allow him to recognize the places he had passed through with Marshal Ney's escort, and later with the other general.[32]

Like the opening paragraph of the novel, this passage suggests a clear relationship between world history and an individual's experience of it: The allies take France, and Fabrice's profound reflections on these events make him "an entirely different man." Yet, whereas earlier the Italian people were witnesses to the immediacy of the Napoleonic force and were thereby made aware that what they had been reading about the invaders was false, here the press is enlisted to confirm that what Fabrice experienced was what he wanted it to have been. Unfortunately, nothing in the newspapers corroborates the accuracy of his memories, his "mental engravings," of June 18. Watching war and constructing a story about how one watches it seem to be discordant, if not antithetically opposed, activities.

In the model of literacy offered by his "aunt," Fabrice's inability to match words with pictures means that effectively he cannot read at all. Because these investigations generate no insights into "his" experiences, he reflects much later in the novel that he would like to visit the site where Waterloo was fought—by then a standard tourist attraction—in order to see whether the landscape there in fact included the meadow where he remembered losing his horse. It remains uncertain whether Fabrice's experience of the Belgian countryside would have echoed Scott's disbelief that such an innocuous terrain could have been the scene of terrible destruction, for the return to the Waterloo-that-was-not-quite-Waterloo never takes place. In this respect the fact that the narrator of the novel states matter-of-factly that our hero *was* at Waterloo helps us little. The sometime protagonist's failed experience of a battle near the start of *The Charterhouse of Parma* is uniquely disruptive because we cannot be sure whether it should be treated as an account of a historical event or as a parody of a historical event. In other words, there is no way to decide whether Fabrice's Waterloo prefigures the elaborately staged forms of artificial history that will constitute the Court of Parma later in the novel or whether his day in Belgium is an indication that there is no clear distinction between the "delusion," as Samuels terms it, of looking to the past as a model for identity and the delusion of looking to the present or the future for the same. In the final analysis *The Charterhouse of Parma* offers a conception of war reading that makes it impossible for us—or the narrator—to articulate a clear standard with which to establish whether Fabrice was ever truly "under fire."

Fabrice tries to legitimate his own experience through the newspaper, but his failure to do so reveals that precisely what the emerging mass media will not help him manufacture is an intimate story of an individual's engagement with world history.[33] Insofar as his conception of a war narrative founders in its search for a schema of personal battlefield agency, his travails suggest that the wartime public sphere paradoxically celebrates Waterloo as the paragon of historical experience that no individual can experience. Enjoining the citizens of Europe to envision what battlefields must have been like, the media's dissemination of wartime news established a standard for what constitutes a social or political event that is still in force today. A phenomenon can make an "appearance" only by being implicated in a simulacral dynamic in which it is what one learns through mediated transmissions that makes firsthand experience possible at all. "Virtuality"—what might otherwise be called iterability or reproducibility—thus became a sine qua non of actuality.[34]

The reader of Stendhal's novel does not escape these difficulties simply by virtue of identifying them. Fabrice's failure to confirm the factual status of his experiences offers an ironic reflection on our own efforts to read him more effectively than he reads Waterloo. Does our interpretation of the novel stand or fall on our ability to confirm that what we saw/read *was* what we saw/read? What sort of correspondences or self-identities between words and images must we posit if we are not to "remain a child," as Fabrice fears he does? There is certainly no guarantee that we will pose the questions he forgets to ask, and it is far from obvious what medium of transmission legitimates our "firsthand" experience of the book.

Perhaps the most threatening aspect of Fabrice's day at Waterloo is the simple fact that his experience of this monumentally consequential clash of men and arms could be so empty. This question of how a bystander could miss the significance of such a spectacle preoccupied Leo Tolstoy, and his *War and Peace* betrays many debts to Stendhal. Unlike *The Charterhouse of Parma*, however, Tolstoy's novel is peppered with lengthy historiographical musings, which have struck many readers as unnecessary digressions from an otherwise gripping story. Tolstoy is particularly derisive when it comes to the notion that battles are won or lost because of the decisions made by "great" generals. Like his contemporary Victor Hugo, he expresses considerable skepticism about the myth of Napoleon, averring that no individual, from the lowliest soldier to the grandest marshal, had more control over the events at Austerlitz or Waterloo than anyone else. When it comes to the course of a battle, to attribute authority to a specific person is to impose a false causal schema on events: "[O]nly later did historians furnish the already accomplished facts with ingenious arguments for the foresight and genius of the commanders, who, of all the involuntary instruments of world events, were the most enslaved and involuntary agents."[35] His harshest words are reserved for Bonaparte himself. Tolstoy's narrator deems his influence on military proceedings "only external and fictitious," adding that "Napoleon . . . was like a child who, holding the straps tied inside a carriage, fancies that he is driving it."[36] Against the view that the leaders of armies shape the fate of their troops, *War and Peace* entertains a host of alternative dynamics, including broader sociohistorical forces that transcend individuals, as well as more nebulous powers such as "fate" or "chance."

If these features of *War and Peace* are relatively well known, it has not been recognized that the novel has a great deal to say about modern war spectatorship. Scholars have often observed that Tolstoy drew heavily on the escapades of Fabrice in crafting a lengthy scene in which the nobleman Pierre Bezukhov observes the grisly Battle of Borodino firsthand. However, in contrast to Fabrice, who is driven by his youthful idealization of the French emperor, Pierre is unable to explain his motives. On the eve of the battle an officer asks him what a civilian nobleman is doing at the front, to which he replies: "'I just wanted to have a look.'"[37] Confronted with the question again later, his response is no clearer: "'I've come . . . just . . . you know . . . I've come . . . it's interesting,' said Pierre, who had repeated the senseless word 'interesting' so many times that day, 'I wanted to see the battle.'"[38] Pierre's reaction to what may have been the bloodiest single day of the Napoleonic Wars verges on boredom. Cannonballs mow men down right beside him, and he ultimately ends up grappling with a French soldier, but, like Fabrice, he betrays no anxiety about his own mortality, remaining curiously comfortable in his seeming oblivion:

[B]ut, despite the incessant shooting that was going on there, it never occurred to him that this was precisely the field of battle. He did not hear the
sounds of the bullets whining on all sides, and of the shells that flew over his
head, did not see the enemy on the other side of the river, and for a long time
did not see the dead and wounded, though many fell not far from him. With
a smile that never left his face, he looked about him.[39]

Pierre is a spectator without any expectations for the spectacle he observes. He has no inclination to romanticize the event, no scientific or
philosophical urge to explain the causal dynamics at work, and no desire
to treat the proceedings sentimentally. Most important, he does not regard the life-and-death struggle around him as a medium through which
to reflect on his own identity. The tone of the passage is antitragic, anti-
epic, and antimelodramatic. That Pierre realizes little—and only long after
he should—is not evidence of the sublimity of his experience, as if the
scale or force of the proceedings were impossible to comprehend. He
watches with no claim to being able to judge what he sees. More than
seventy-five thousand people died at Borodino, but intensifying the irony
with which Stendhal flirts, Tolstoy suggests that to understand a battle
one must conceive of it as an event that will not move its onlookers if they
fail to mobilize their own imaginative powers. *War and Peace* thus faith-
fully extends the insights of Rousseau's *Emile*, which emphasizes that war
spectacles acquire an appearance of autonomy from the historical dynamics to which they belong. By the standard of spectacle established by
Napoleon's triumphant march into Italy in the opening paragraph of *The
Charterhouse of Parma*, what Tolstoy's Pierre views from the front row of
the theater of world history is entirely unhistorical. He experiences the
impotence of his experience, its inability to lay claim to any larger significance, and, like Fabrice, he will subsequently ponder the cataclysmic clash
he witnessed as one might consider the glimpse of an apparition that may
never have been there. As hapless an observer as Fabrice is, he is better situated than Pierre because he can still speak as though he cares about what
he is saying even if he sounds childish in the process.

One might see the devolution of Pierre's narrative into a nontragic,
nonsublime mode that borders on the comic as a symptom of his inability to process the horrors he witnesses, whether because of the workings
of a psychological defense mechanism or a filtering process organized
by his cultural or class background. Yet the role of distraction or quasi
oblivion in the battle narratives of this period is so widespread that one

must ask whether it is of a more systemic nature. To take another example, in the summer of 1792, at the start of the French revolutionary wars, Johann Wolfgang von Goethe accompanied the Prussian army and its Austrian allies on their invasion of France as an "embedded reporter." The renowned German author was the invited guest of his sovereign, Duke Carl August of Saxe-Weimar, who evidently hoped that the prominent poet's pen would do justice to the glories about to be won. Goethe did not record his experiences until almost thirty years later, by which time he had few personal records on which to rely. When one compares letters Goethe sent in 1792 with the narrative he wrote decades after the fact, the story does seem to have been reworked with all the benefits of hindsight and some poetic license to boot.[40] As a result, while some historians regard these reflections as valuable source material, others treat the account as an allegory of European politics of the 1820s rather than a report about revolutionary France.[41]

Whether one reads what came to be called *Campaign in France* as a faithful record of the past or as a thinly veiled allegory of the present, its strategies and goals are far from self-evident. One senses from the outset that the author is unsure how he will be able to organize his reminiscences within a single narrative or aesthetic model. Goethe frames his description of the trip as an attempt to experience the proverbial "theater of war," a term that appears on the first and final pages of his text, and as things get under way, he seems to regard himself as an audience member in front of a grand stage upon which ranks of troops collide in an elegant tableau: "The lines upon lines of horsemen made a handsome picture against the pleasant landscape. . . . To be sure several villages were on fire ahead of us, but smoke can hardly detract from a war scene."[42] Yet Goethe's account of the proceedings is striking for how little there is to see—if, like him, what one expects to see are men in combat. Under his gaze, formations of soldiers turn out to be far less interesting than the natural settings in which he finds himself. Ostensibly present to survey the fighting, the longer Goethe remains with the army, the more time he spends musing on the hues of various rock formations or on the behavior of sunbeams striking the water in a nearby well. As he is further consumed by his lifelong passion for the study of light and the philosophy of color, any hope of serving as a spectator at a confrontation between world-historical forces is displaced by a series of contented reflections on the nature of perception.

This notion that a battlefield might serve as a sort of perceptual laboratory was common in nineteenth-century efforts to make sense of the challenges that Napoleonic combat presented to the coherence of historical
experience. Superficially, what is at stake in Goethe's text is the uncertain
relationship between the perceptual autonomy of the individual observer
and the unique sensory stimuli that characterized the modern exchange
of fire.[43] This becomes clearest in the most famous passage from *Campaign
in France*, which describes a fierce artillery barrage at Valmy followed by
a brief clash of infantrymen that halted the Austro-Prussian army's
advance. While in 1792 the Valmy engagement appeared to be of minor
tactical or symbolic significance, it was subsequently identified as the
first demonstration by French revolutionary troops that the "people's
forces" could best the established armies of aristocratic Europe, and by
the time Goethe was writing his account of the day decades later, Valmy
was regarded as an event of considerable historical significance.[44] Even
reworked from the vantage of hindsight, however, Goethe's description
of the clash lacks grandeur or any pretension to sublimity. When he finally
ventures forth into the line of fire, the experience of a hail of cannon balls
prompts only a peaceful transformation of his sensory faculties:

> It seemed as though I were in a very hot place, and thoroughly permeated by
> that same heat, so that I felt completely at one with the element in which I
> found myself. My eyes lost nothing of their strength or clarity of vision, yet
> it was as though the world had a certain reddish brown tone, which made
> my own condition, as well as the objects around me, still more ominous. . . .
> When I had ridden back and was out of danger, I found it remarkable that
> all that burning had been instantly extinguished and not the slightest trace
> of feverish agitation remained.[45]

Unlike Pierre at Borodino, Goethe has no broad view of the proceedings; his field of vision is more local and intimate. Like Pierre, however,
he stands directly in harm's way, perceiving the barrage of projectiles
around him not as an immediate threat to his own person or as an opportunity to experience the violent power of the sublime but as the impetus
for achieving a curious equilibrium. "At one with the element" in which
he finds himself, his perceptual capacities, far from being interrupted or
distorted by the battle going on around him, are heightened. He emerges
unscathed, the event marking him with no trace of adversity once it has

passed. Indeed, the shift in his senses seems to have little to do with the specific objects of sensation he encountered. His account of the world turning reddish brown is solipsistic, the self- assertion of an autonomous subjectivity scrupulously maintaining an indifferent posture to the horrors of modern warfare surrounding it. Goethe does declare that everything becomes "more ominous," but it is hardly obvious that this is a direct consequence of the battle he witnesses. If anything, his experience of the field of combat becomes a kind of paraexperience, an exercise in what it would mean to have an experience of being under duress. In these terms war is far from an all-consuming event that overwhelms one's sensory capacities. Goethe recounts the tale as if he were only half there, as in a dream. The effect is similar to Stendhal's description of Fabrice on the field of Waterloo, drowsy from drink and only half certain that he is processing the key details around him.

A century after Valmy, Ernst Jünger also dwelt on the odd quality of the battlefield experiences he and his comrades endured, emphasizing that although the ghastly conflict of the First World War "was so palpable, and rested heavily, like lead, on our senses," we still wondered whether it was "perhaps only a phantasm of our brains."[46] Friedrich Kittler has argued that this reduction of inner experience to neurophysiology heralded the end of Goethe's conception of literature, quoting Jünger: "When red life clashes against the black cliffs of death, what we get are sharp pictures composed of bright colors. . . . There is no time to read one's *Werther* with teary eyes."[47] Yet Goethe's own ruminations in *Campaign in France* already suggest the same dissociation of self-affection and sensory data that Kittler locates in accounts of the First World War, and they may even bespeak a more radical opposition between the first-person war narrative and its narrator. Like Tolstoy's Pierre, Goethe exhibits strikingly little concern for his own security even when he is under fire and has cannonballs falling all around him. Although he repeatedly stresses that he is witnessing far more terror than anyone should have to endure, these pronouncements sound like the invocation of a pathos he does not feel, and the references lack detail. Goethe certainly seems self-involved in the sense that he ignores what is going on around him—one has to look hard to find, for example, any mention of the fact that the Prussian army began to fall apart due to dysentery and poor supply lines long before their main clash with the French. Nonetheless, the overt solipsism does not confirm the inherent worth of the observer or the authority of his observational position.

At times the indirect quality of Goethe's reminiscences is almost farcical, for after light and color he is preoccupied primarily with food. Large sections of his narrative read like a piece of tourist literature recounting its protagonist's efforts to enjoy the culinary delicacies of various regions. "After such a quick conquest of Verdun," Goethe relates in an upbeat tone, "no one any longer doubted that we would soon move on and recover splendidly from our previous hardships with the help of the good wines of Châlons and Epernay."[48] Even when we begin to suspect that the entire army is on the brink of starvation, an almost celebratory irony informs Goethe's account of their plight. At one point, he describes joining a group of famished soldiers in an attempt to pilfer a locked kitchen cabinet for foodstuffs. All they find inside is a cookbook, so the men pass the time "exciting the imagination" by reading the "most delicious recipes" aloud and "intensifying [their] hunger."[49] As the decline of the Prussian forces continues, Goethe's periodic references to the discomforts of the illness now widespread among the ranks are largely obscured by his energetic day excursions, including a trip to taste "the incomparable Verdun pastries," an enterprise that proves a failure when it turns out that the famous baker has no butter.[50] Throughout these episodes, many of which border on picaresque comedy, Goethe intersperses lamentations about the tragedies he is experiencing, but these expressions of sorrow tend to assume an allegorical abstraction at odds with the direct sympathy for his fellow man to which he claims to give voice. More often than not, it is weary animals or the ruins of old buildings that move him rather than the ubiquitous sight of dead and wounded soldiers.

One might argue that *Campaign in France* testifies to the all-pervasive nature of total war, revealing it to be a force that co-opts those who attempt to document it, turning their efforts to illustrate its harsh realities into mystified digressions that make light of piles of corpses in the very act of supposedly enshrining human loss for posterity. Alternatively, one might see the genius of a war spectator such as Goethe or Tolstoy's Pierre as consisting precisely in his ability to avoid treating armed combat as either a tool of statecraft or an aesthetic phenomenon that follows its own rules. In these terms, the distracted, sometimes comical follies of these war chroniclers are proof of their ability to resist being transformed into puppets in the theater of war, like the tourists who flocked to Belgium to stand where Napoleon had stood at Waterloo.

Another memorable passage from *War and Peace* offers insight into the potential autonomy a battlefield observer may achieve vis-à-vis a battle. At Austerlitz, where the sudden appearance of the sun at a fortuitous moment ensures a French victory and solidifies the myth of their emperor's command of the visual order, Prince Andrei Bolkonsky has been struck down. In the aftermath of the struggle, the living sift through the carnage, and, by chance, Napoleon Bonaparte, the preeminent reader of battlefield traces himself,

> stopped over Prince Andrei, who lay on his back, the staff of the standard fallen beside him (the standard had already been taken as a trophy by the French).
>
> "*Voilà une belle mort*," said Napoleon, looking at Bolkonsky.
>
> Prince Andrei understood that it had been said about him, and that it was Napoleon speaking. He heard the man who said these words being addressed as *sire*. But he heard these words as if he was hearing the buzzing of a fly. He not only was not interested, he did not even notice, and at once forgot them. He had a burning in his head; he felt that he was losing blood, and he saw above him that distant, lofty, and eternal sky. He knew that it was Napoleon—his hero—but at that moment, Napoleon seemed to him such a small, insignificant man compared with what was now happening between his soul and this lofty, infinite sky with clouds racing across it. To him it was all completely the same at that moment who was standing over him or what he said about him; he was only glad that people had stopped over him and only wished that those people would help him and bring him back to life, which seemed so beautiful to him, because he now understood it so differently. He gathered all his strength in order to stir and produce some sound. He stirred his leg weakly and produced a weak, painful moan that moved even him to pity.
>
> "Ah! He's alive," said Napoleon. "Lift up this young man, *ce jeune homme*, and take him to the first-aid station!"[51]

As at Eylau, Napoleon tours the field of battle studying its nuances, searching for meaning and beauty as one might poke through an antique store or a museum gallery. At first glance the eagle-eyed French leader appears to be far less visually gifted than he would have us imagine, mistaking the living for the dead, and not just for the dead but also for a classical tableau: a beautiful death. The sovereign's error does give Prince Andrei the privilege of hearing the impossible—the pronouncement of his own demise—but it is far from a revelation. Although Bolkonsky is aware that it is his hero uttering the magical words, his nonengagement with the event is so extreme that it can be expressed only as kettle logic: He does not notice, he is not interested, and he immediately forgets what has happened. As for Goethe at Valmy, the battlefield facilitates an experience for the prince that is entirely personal to the point of excluding any external stimulus even when it stems from Napoleon, the most idealized figure in his psyche. At the same time, what Bolkonsky endures follows the formal script of classical aesthetics rather than any private reflection, for he sees the sky as sublime and eternal, as one might contemplate a landscape painting, in effect countering Napoleon's *belle mort* with a different tableau. Once again the inherently formal nature of the battlefield imposes itself within even the most intimate and consequential of individual experiences. If for Goethe the battlefield became a laboratory in which to study the nature of perception, here the clash of soldiers becomes a competition between stylized representations, each vying for mastery of the traces of the battle.

The real irony of the scene, however, comes to the fore when Prince Andrei, who in his capacity as a piece of the battlefield landscape is entirely indifferent to who his audience is or to what they are saying about him, asks only that his viewing public "bring him back to life," which is precisely what the magician Napoleon accomplishes in recognizing the error of his original judgment about the fallen figure: "Ah! He's alive." The ultimate war spectator after all, the French emperor proves his mastery of the battlefield by resurrecting its victims, a trick he is able to pull off only because he is such a poor observer of the surroundings that he mistakes a wounded man for a dead one. If Austerlitz was the site of Napoleon's greatest triumph because the sun came out at the key moment, allowing him to see the colliding armies and adjust his tactics to seize victory, in the aftermath of the conflict he is unable to make out the most basic detail. Tolstoy's novel upends the authority of Napoleonic vision, although not entirely at Napoleon's expense, for in his failure to process the nuances of the battle's denouement, Napoleon wins nothing less than the power to resurrect the dead.

Still, the emperor's newfound authority is far from absolute. Prince Andrei survives the day but not the Napoleonic Age; disillusioned with war, he leaves the army for almost half a decade, only to return to fight at Pierre's Borodino and subsequently to die from the wounds he suffers there. The question, then, is whether the prince ever quite recovers from his brush with the powers of life and death or whether his near-death experience—his momentary role as a corpse scattered on the field among the rest of the dead and dying—reveals that the only true vantage point from which to watch the Napoleonic spectacle lies neither inside nor outside the struggle but from beyond the grave. This would mean that paradoxically it is only by giving up one's very status as a sentient being that one can experience one's own war story but avoid the evacuation of the interior self that besets Goethe or Pierre.

The encounters with Napoleonic combat that we have been considering focused on individuals in the midst of masses of soldiers and storms of projectiles. As early as the first part of the nineteenth century, however, it was clear that one of the unique features of war watching in the Napoleonic era was its status as a group activity. With the close of combat on the Continent in 1815, the inherently communal medium of the panorama thus came to play an increasingly important role in efforts to revisit the bloody events as part of an imaginary viewing public. An artistic phenomenon that aimed to reengineer the traditional relationship between the artwork and its viewers, the panorama's "primary object," as John Ruskin famously described it, was "to place the spectator, so far as art can do, in the scene represented, and to give him the perfect sensation of reality, wholly unmodified by the artists' execution."[52] This emphasis on a reality principle was already canonized in Robert Baker's 1787 patent for the panorama, which declared that it was "to make the observers, on whatever situations [the artist] may wish they should imagine themselves, feel as if really on the spot."[53] By allowing the audience to situate itself at once inside and outside a battle, this new forum ostensibly simulated the all-consuming war experience that Goethe, Fabrice, and Pierre could never achieve.

As representations of battles, panoramas would appear to be a logical outgrowth of earlier pictorial representations, as if the size of the paintings had to expand exponentially to keep pace with the burgeoning armies.[54] At the same time, Baker's sense of putting the viewer on the spot is suggestive: The social force of this art form had more to do with control than with convincing viewers that they really were looking at the cityscape of London or standing in the middle of the Battle of Waterloo. In fact,

panoramic viewing should be thought of not in terms of verisimilitude—
there was nothing realistic about entering a chamber through an under-
ground tunnel or being positioned in the center of a darkened room—
but as an attempt to construct and guide a collective gaze. A kind of
organized group observation, the panorama is the cousin of the panopticon and functions by demanding that something be seen in a precisely
prescribed fashion. It is an experiment in disciplinary vision that tells
its audience that they will have a unique spectatorial experience if they
do as they are told. In this respect, the panorama anticipates the movie
camera, which will acquire an even greater power to direct the gaze of its
audience wherever it sees fit.[55]

In addition to controlling its viewers, the panorama also aims to win
command of the view. Bernard Comment has argued that it should be
understood as a response to the growth of cities: "The city exploded, becoming opaque, no longer visible. In conditions like these, the panorama
had a decisive role to play. Not only did it express the perceptual and representational strategies that befitted such troubled times; it was also a way
of regaining control of sprawling collective space."[56] Like the eighteenth-
century salon, the panorama facilitated a collective act of visualization
by offering a show to be watched in a group, but it did so by bringing the
outside inside, safely placing the external scene within the confines of a
museum exhibition or under the laboratory microscope. With the cityscape, the result was an inversion of part for whole whereby the entire
metropolis came to serve a backdrop for the theater in which audience
members were playacting, pretending to be looking at exterior surroundings that they could just as well have taken in by going outside and standing on the rooftop. With the battlefield, itself already a theatrical scene,
the shift was both more and less violent. The panorama highlighted the
inherently staged quality of combat, but only in the guise of the belief
that the strife could be somehow controlled if it were cast in a geometry
of the round—what the spectators were viewing could decidedly not be
replicated by going outdoors and scanning the horizon. In either case,
the viewing experience was defined by the lack of freedom it afforded the
eye since everything transpired in a windowless room, which is to say that
the panorama provided a magical view by failing to facilitate a view onto
anything.[57] Far from constituting a vantage point—a hillside, a tower, or
a lighthouse—it situated its audience in an imaginary center that was

surrounded by somewhere but was itself nowhere. Like Prince Andrei, who found himself precariously situated between the living and the dead, the panorama's viewers found themselves in a faux crypt or tomb. This was the key link between viewing a cityscape and viewing a battle, the two most popular subjects of the panorama. The Napoleonic battlefield was an alternative public space; by bringing it into an artificial interior, the panorama revealed that the sheer numbers of men involved in the engagement transformed it into a temporary city, although it was an antisocial social space, a metropolis rapidly becoming a necropolis.

Like the Napoleonic battlefield, which collapsed under the contradictions of its tactics and was not to be restaged in later nineteenth-century wars, the panorama was a relatively short-lived phenomenon. Its brief tenure has been explored by Canadian artist Jeff Wall, who has reflected on the legacy of this distinctive art form and its implications for the representation of war. In his 1993 photograph *Restoration*, Wall constructed a fictitious scene in which actual conservators were posed as if they were in the process of restoring a panoramic painting, Edouard Castres's *Bourbaki Panorama* (1881), which was not in fact undergoing restoration at the time. Castres's circular work shows the plight of the French troops of General Bourbaki in 1871, during the Franco-Prussian War. Recently routed by the enemy, they are seen receiving aid from Swiss troops and peasants as they seek refuge in neutral Switzerland while awaiting a formal cease-fire. Although the event has considerable historical symbolism inasmuch as it marks both the end of the reign of the third Napoleon and the advent of a unified Germany, Wall notes that this is not an ordinary battle scene: "Usually, huge war pictures deal with victory, spectacle or defeat and not with assistance, sanctuary and healing, as Castres' does."[58]

FIGURE 2.1 Jeff Wall, *Restoration*, 1993. Transparency in lightbox, 119 cm × 489.5 cm. Courtesy of the artist.

Wall's image of part of a battle image is thus both a war photo and an antiwar photo.

Wall photographed the panorama with a panoramic camera, but he recorded only 180 degrees of the 360-degree view.[59] According to him, this balance between inclusion and exclusion is the essence of his picture. Wall proposes that the distinctive feature of the panorama as an art form was that its viewer had to turn in a circle to see it in its entirety and was never looking at more than a segment of it at any one time. In other words, as much as this art form supposedly depicts an entire landscape, cityscape, or battlescape, it constantly hides a large part of itself in plain sight. Wall thus highlights the importance of the female curator on the scaffolding "looking into the space, . . . into part of the picture you can't see, to make a little accent to that notion that there's a space outside."[60] For the viewer of *Restoration* the result is a sense of competing visual cues, as if one's eye were being drawn in different directions, moving between the scenes on the wall, the individual curators, and the darkened viewing platform, with no sense of the parts coalescing into a whole.

For Wall, the constitutive blindness at the heart of the panoramic experience, the fact that at any given moment an individual viewer cannot see a large part of the painting, is complemented by the impossibility of representing a panorama in any other medium. The panorama, he argues, is "unrepresentable"; it cannot be accurately illustrated—there cannot even be a panorama of a panorama.[61] Even in the case of a photograph that aims to capture only part of the setup, something always escapes regardless of how successfully the illusion of volume and a curving wall is created in flat space. Still, it is not enough to say that the inability of a photo to represent a panorama reproduces the panorama's own failure to reproduce the battlefield.[62] Even in declaring the panorama unrepresentable, Wall implies that his photo is designed to represent that unrepresentability by reproducing the fragmentary experience of being inside one. In this regard it is significant that Wall took his picture from a perspective that no visitor to the panorama would ever have had. Shot from in front of a section of the circular outer wall, the photo hints at a kind of antipanopticon in which the center viewing point would be empty and the figures in the painting would eye each other across the room. In this way *Restoration* exposes the core ideology of the panorama as a regime of controlled seeing, an effort to direct or structure the gaze common to both the artist, who tries to represent the battlefield, and to each of the individuals in the battle, who seek to win military supremacy through visual supremacy.

Wall's photograph also attempts to liberate us from the conventional platitudes about the panorama's perfect replication of reality. He argues:

> The fact that panoramas emerged so strikingly, and then died out so quickly, suggests that they were an experimental response to a deeply-felt need, a need for a medium that could surround the spectators and plunge them into a spectacular illusion. The panorama turned out to be entirely inadequate to the challenge. The cinema and the amusement park more or less accomplished what the panorama only indicated.[63]

We might ask whether this "failure" was equally the panorama's triumph, that is, whether by plunging its spectators into a spectacular illusion that was never quite spectacular enough, the panorama exposed the constitutive gap between anticipation and satisfaction that marked the mass audience's fantastic relationship to the terrain of the Napoleonic battlescape each time a painting, fictional narrative, or memoir prompted the public to try to imagine "what it had been like." In this manner, *Restoration* illustrates the landscape of the nineteenth-century visual order by presenting us not with a scene of a battle or of the carnage on a field after a battle but with a scene of survivors who have managed to flee elsewhere. The modern-day curators who pose as though they were restoring this artwork extend this logic of defeat and displacement, as if their fake efforts to attend to the painting were somehow in parallel with the vanquished army in the painting seeking refuge. It is as if art itself had to seek shelter from the aftermath of the panorama's downfall and the breakdown of its fantasy of an all-encompassing vision of warfare.

Wall's suggestion that the cinema or the amusement park ultimately served the public better than the panorama implies that the mass war audience failed to embrace the task of historical excavation that the panorama's visual investigation invited. Nonetheless, one must be careful not to mistake the panorama's representational ambitions, its claim to show everything, for a progressive impulse. Wall observes: "*Restoration* has a post-revolutionary, even counter-revolutionary implication. I was interested in the double entendre in the title, the idea that the panorama and the 'regime' of representation in which it is involved could be identified

with an *ancien régime*, which ironically we are preserving, and even re-
suscitating, bringing back to life."[64]

Wall's picture stages the representational paradox of the panorama as a
clash between eighteenth-century aristocratic demonstrations of sovereign power and the nineteenth-century surveillance culture of the panopticon without implying that either visual order wins the day, whether
in the 1870s or in the twenty-first century. To the extent that his photograph at least temporarily resuscitates either of these ideological systems
of observation and representation, it does so by invoking them in their
collapse. We are shown not the detritus of the forces of a glorious ancien
régime but the scattered remains of one of its weak repetitions. Moreover,
since half of *Restoration* is occupied by the viewing platform, the historical scene on the wall functions primarily as a backdrop to the centerpiece
of the illustration, the mechanics of panoramic viewing themselves. What
we see is not a replication of what it would have been like to have stood
in the darkened center and looked outward at the painting illuminated
on the wall but something more akin to a view of the room of a haunted
house the day after Halloween, when the cover of darkness has been pulled
back to expose the banality of mechanical tricks that are no longer startling by the light of day.

FIGURE 2.2 *Restoration* (detail).

In demystifying the nineteenth-century techniques of scopic fantasy and underscoring their considerable authority for a host of different political ideologies, Wall's photograph retains a whimsical quality that affirms its position in the line of battlefield meditations we have explored in Stendhal, Tolstoy, and Goethe. Most of the curators that we see in his image are not hard at work on the walls, as in the famous picture of Diego Riviera industriously producing his murals or of Gianluigi Colalucci's team arduously restoring the ceiling of the Sistine Chapel. Instead, several of Wall's figures look off as if they were daydreaming, indifferent to the spectacle around them, which is not to say that they can entirely escape it, for even as we see them with their backs to the painting, their gaze is necessarily falling on another part of it on the circular wall. This restoration of a late nineteenth-century battlefield thus reproduces precisely the kind of distracted, semiattentive viewing that earlier students of the Napoleonic era located in firsthand witnesses to battles. Surrounded by the action they could not entirely miss, these onlookers were somehow never fully engaged by the all-consuming nature of the setting in which they found themselves. What remains to be asked is whether this observational posture is a symptom of total war, evidence of the degree to which the complete militarization of sociocultural experience has rendered impossible a more direct and, one presumes, "honest" engagement with the horrors of the battlefield. Alternatively, it may be that the picaresque posturing of a Fabrice, the bored spectatorship of a Pierre, or the casual "looking away" of Wall's curators is a form of resistance to the scopic logics of modern military power.

§ 3 Looking at the Dead

> Ironic that Mathew Brady would be the name most associated with the moment when photography supposedly brings war home since he rarely set foot on a battlefield since he purportedly could not stand the sight of dead bodies.
>
> — Alan Trachtenberg, *Reading American Photographs*

> Only the dead have seen the end of war.
>
> — George Santayana

During the course of the nineteenth century a transformation took place in the representation of battlefields. Established forms such as narrative prose, paintings, and drawings were gradually complemented by the products of new technologies, most prominently photography, a medium in which physical chemistry played a role not completely governed by the human hand or mind.[1] At first glance, the proliferation of photographic images seems to have hastened the erosion of the boundary between first- and secondhand encounters with combat, a boundary that was already becoming porous in the prephotographic age. From its inception, however, photography was also implicated in the idea—or fantasy—of an "external" perspective or overview from which even total war could be processed and evaluated. As much as photographs and later films of warfare became central to the notion that civilian life had become completely permeated by military experience, they also helped to preserve the belief that the onlooker could remain safely above the fray.

If the invention of photography profoundly altered the public's experience of war, it has nonetheless proven difficult to explain how war photographs differ from other photos and how photographs of war differ from other representations of combat. To some extent the problem lies in distinguishing between the violence that photos represent and the violence that the photographic medium itself visits upon its audience or its subject matter. Photography may also expose a violence at the heart of experience itself, revealing human perception to be innately marked by instability and trauma. These concerns come together in a deceptively simple question: What happens when one views a photograph of a soldier slain in battle?

Does such an image offer us any clues as to why people kill each other on such a large scale, or is it part of broader cultural systems designed to control or even erase the onlooker's consciousness of human beings' status as mortal?

The standard narrative of photojournalism describes a sharp break between the age of the camera and the period of human history prior to the mid-nineteenth century when noncombatants encountered phenomena such as battles only in the verbal or visual forms that would later come to be deemed less "reliable." As Peter Maslowski writes, "Photography forever altered the human vision of warfare by preserving, with a vivid immediacy, its images. Memories dim and ultimately die, but photographs remain clear and crisp. Pictures are time machines."[2] Even the most ardent proponents of photography's ability to impart knowledge of the past grant that the camera is anything but a docile purveyor of truth and that photos can be as misleading as any other medium—if not more so, given the authority customarily accorded to them on account of their supposed directness. Nonetheless, the fantasy of an objective battlefield image endures. In an article on photography in the American Civil War, Joel Snyder proposes the following:

> The modern way of making war photographs requires that the photographer be in the center of the action, and that the subject appear to be oblivious to his presence. The implication of this technique is that the "truth" of the situation is depicted by showing, in a relatively close-up fashion, a subject engaged in the business of war, which is usually the business of killing or being killed. The subject is too engaged in the activity to regard the camera. And this failure to respond to the camera assures us that there is no staging of the facts, no needless dramatizing of the situation. The drama is supposed to grow out of the un-tampered facts of the moment.[3]

The "objectivity" of photography is frequently said to be a factor of its production process since the laws of chemistry and optics combine to generate an image that is never entirely under the control of the individual who snaps the shutter, no matter how much care the individual may exercise in framing and timing the shot. In Snyder's account, however, it is the integrity of what the camera is recording that ensures the power of the image; the exigent situation—the danger of the battlefield—makes it impossible for the objects of the camera lens to pose. Here, the raw forces of life and death hold sway, leaving no room for vanity or posturing on the part of the combatants. What the photo depicts is thus "authentic" in the sense that it is not "made-for-the-camera." The artifice involved in capturing a specific shot from a certain angle at a particular moment does not completely occlude the genuineness of the recorded scene, which retains at least a trace of something not imparted to it by the photographer.

Snyder's argument is something of a straw man inasmuch as it is designed to highlight his claim that photographs of the American Civil War fail to conform to this conception of "truth in photography" and that in fact the very notion of capturing an image of "the action" was incompatible with the aesthetic paradigms under which early photographers such as Mathew Brady or Alexander Gardner labored. Their work was governed by the conventions of portraiture, they shot from a great distance, and they showed relatively little interest in producing what a contemporary viewer would regard as an action shot.[4] Snyder's straw-man argument is equally misleading, however, as a description of the century and a half of warfare and war photography that have followed the Civil War. Although there are unquestionably many close-ups of soldiers killing and being killed—blurred shots of beach landings, men with rifles shot from odd angles as they run forward on the field—the most memorable and influential war photos have tended to be staged scenes. Indeed, upon inspection, even many fuzzy images of combatants in motion turn out to have been pictures of simulated attacks. Whether they depict the raising of the Soviet flag on the Reichstag, infantrymen running across the rubble at Stalingrad, or General MacArthur wading ashore at the Philippines, posed war photographs have been the norm, and the popular visual imagination has been enthralled not by action shots but by carefully crafted representations that are anything but "un-tampered." Far from asserting its independence from classical aesthetic media, photography has repeatedly confirmed its debt to, even its continuity with, traditional painting, if not with comedy and melodrama as well. Some scholars have suggested that the photographs of a given war can be typed on the basis of the influential artistic paradigms of the era. Pictures of the First World War resemble Renaissance religious paintings, whereas those of the Second World War take their cue from the films of Alfred Hitchcock, and so on.[5] Even today, when the technology to produce "real" pictures of "the business of killing and being killed" is available to every soldier with a cell phone, the well-known images of recent conflicts are not graphic renditions of life-and-death combat or depictions of subjects oblivious to the photographer's presence.

It is by no means clear whether the dynamic of posing and posturing that insistently emerges in war photography is a product of the photographer's intentions and the aesthetic or journalistic trends influencing her or a symptom of formal or presentational parameters intrinsic to the photographic medium itself. Photography's unique perspective on warfare may lie in the way in which it exposes the play of simulation and dissimulation intrinsic to battle—something of which other representational media can offer only fleeting glimpses. This would suggest that the quest for an "un-tampered" or "unadulterated" war photo is a search for a photograph of something other than a war.

Nowhere are the implications of the posed battle scene more uncertain than with records of the most intimate aspect of wartime loss: the fallen soldier on the ground. For more than a century there has been widespread public access to journalistic representations of corpses.[6] During this period two countervailing factors have influenced the dissemination of such images. On the one hand, portable, inexpensive photographic equipment has become increasingly available. If initially only professionals working in teams had the means and expertise to produce pictures at the front, numerous photos were taken by individual officers during the First World War, and by the Second World War thousands (if not tens of thousands) of common soldiers defied regulations and carried cameras to record their experiences.[7] Today virtually all military personnel have a cell phone with a camera or video function.

On the other hand, governments have attempted to regulate the production and distribution of war photographs, a practice that has become essential to waging war. When U.S. Secretary of Defense Donald Rumsfeld appeared before the Senate Armed Services Committee in May 2004 to discuss the photos of Abu Ghraib prison, he wondered, with seemingly unfeigned confusion, whether it would still be possible to pursue military operations "in the information age, where people are running around with digital cameras and taking these unbelievable photographs and then passing them off, against the law, to the media, to our surprise, when they had not even arrived in the Pentagon."[8] Unfortunately, the images from Abu Ghraib have turned out to be only the tip of the iceberg. Many U.S. soldiers stationed in the Middle East use lightweight digital cameras to film combat operations as they take place and later craft the footage into MTV-style music videos by adding a soundtrack of songs from their favorite bands. Traded among servicemen and servicewomen and shown to astonished families at home, this ever-growing supply of photos and videos depicting live firefights and the graphic mutilation of bodies has also made its way onto Internet pay sites.[9]

The efforts of politicians and generals to control the production and distribution of war photos have led to extensive cooperation between the armed forces and journalists. Throughout the twentieth century Western news agencies actively collaborated with wartime governments, and the mass media were often more a part of the official war effort than external observers, much less watchdogs. Armies also deployed their own documentary units. During the First World War official military cameramen made numerous photos and compiled extensive film footage, although relatively little of this material involved "live" battlefield action, and censors carefully regulated its distribution.[10] British photographers were forbidden to take pictures of corpses, and the U.S. government largely censored photos of dead American soldiers, although it encouraged the dissemination of images of the enemy in the press.[11] Similar practices continue today as American media outlets have routinely been prevented from airing pictures of the coffins of American casualties returning from abroad, and many American television editors choose not to show gruesome scenes of civilian deaths to the public. Of course, such acts of censorship are now largely symbolic since Al Jazeera and European media services frequently run pictures of dead U.S. military personnel and civilians killed by U.S. forces, which immediately become globally available on the Internet.

During the Second World War official statements from both the Allied and the Axis powers described the camera as a weapon, an idea that was popularized in mainstream publications such as *National Geographic*, which declared that "cameras and film have become as essential in this war as guns and bullets, on some occasions more so."[12] The qualifying "more so" referred to the fact that some combat operations were specifically tailored to their visual reproducibility. Army cameramen were given invasion plans in advance so that they could coordinate their operations with the troops to maximize the spectacle, although the resulting images were still strictly censored.[13] The view that war was fought through as much as in front of the lens was advanced by John Steinbeck, who served as a Mediterranean correspondent for the *Herald Tribune*. In a report from the Allied landing at Salerno, he claimed that American GIs experienced the "real" event as if it were a film: "It didn't seem like men getting killed, more like a picture, like a moving picture."[14]

Reflecting on the American public's reception of war coverage in Iraq in the first decade of the twenty-first century, Nicholas Mirzoeff contrasts what he calls the official "war image" with commercial advertising, arguing that whereas the latter succeeds by engaging the spectator in doubt and unfulfilled desire—Does my hair look right? Would I be more attractive and successful in those shoes?—the war image functions properly "when its supporters simply accept it."[15] In these terms the key issue is the picture's ability to perform "the American victory" rather than its representational accuracy.[16]

Although many photographs appear to conform to this model, it is not clear that the performance of victory has ever been the exclusive function of even the most overtly propagandistic pictures. One of the most famous examples of wartime image management took place in 1943 when *Life* magazine ran a photo of several Americans killed in the assault on a beach in Papua New Guinea. Encouraged by President Roosevelt to break the prohibition against publishing pictures of dead GIs because he was concerned that the public had become complacent about the war effort, *Life* offered an image clearly designed to have a perlocutionary effect on its audience. Rather than seeking to prompt straightforward acceptance, however, the picture sought to influence its viewers by engaging them in doubt and desire. Perhaps the most distinctive feature of this photograph is that the bodies are shot so that the soldiers' faces are obscured, raising the question of how far the photographer was willing or encouraged to go in the pursuit of a representation of human tragedy. It is not clear whether the editors of *Life* or the federal government would have allowed a similar image with visible faces to be published.[17] Of course, the picture may be more provocative in this form since it invokes the ubiquitous threat of death that servicemen and servicewomen confront daily. Each soldier on the sand becomes a placeholder, and anyone can imagine that a friend or family member is or soon could be the figure lying there. Indeed, the implied universality of the scene may extend even further, for unless one knows something about helmets and uniforms,

FIGURE 3.1 George Strock, *Three Dead Americans on the Beach at Buna*, 1943. © 2000–2011 Getty Images Inc. From Vicki Goldberg, *The Power of Photography: How Photographs Changed Our Lives* (New York: Abbeville Press, 1991).

only the photo's caption makes it clear that these are U.S. soldiers. In this way the corpses uncertainly depict anyone, no one, or somebody's very particular "someone," be it a parent, sibling, or spouse.

The position of the bodies and their relationship to the ground leave little doubt that the figures are dead rather than asleep. Still, the question of whether they were arranged, as was customary with photographs of corpses in the American Civil War, hovers uneasily in the background. The sand offers no clues since it has been wiped clean of footprints or other marks, ostensibly by the tide. As much as the picture captures the indelible traces of wartime tragedy and loss—bodies sprawled as they fell in action—it also shows the inexorable erasure of such traces. Without intervention from someone outside the camera frame, the corpses will probably be swept away by the waves with the next tide. Underscoring the variability of the physical medium it records, the photograph also points toward the changeability of its own medium; another—hypothetical— picture taken just before or after might have shown something quite different. The immediacy of this record, the camera's supposed ability to exhibit physical devastation "as it was," exhibits its power as much through reference to what it does not illustrate as to what it does, calling attention to the labor that may or may not have gone into posing and timing the scene but is not discernible on the film.

In the midst of the Second World War, the publication of a picture of dead U.S. servicemen seemed to herald an end to the enormous divide that existed in the First World War between the horrific death and destruction the public read about in newspapers and the glaring absence of any photographic confirmation of such horrors.[18] Even with Roosevelt's encouragement, however, there was considerable unease about allowing the photographic image to have free rein. While *Three Dead Americans on the Beach at Buna* stretched across two full pages of *Life* magazine, it was not assumed that the photo could "stand on its own" or "speak for itself." The image was accompanied by a long editorial piece that sought to justify the decision to run it—a decision informed by the conviction that sometimes words are "not enough."[19] There is more than a hint of regress in this argument. Why should one need more words to explain that "mere words" are not sufficient to impart what the published picture conveys? What was really being excused in the editorial statement may have been the editors' embarrassment that they could not resist offering additional thoughts about what they were showing, although it remains unclear whether they were worried that the photograph alone said too little or too much. If Susan Sontag famously claimed that the "link between photography and death haunts all photographs of people," the editors at *Life* may have feared that photographs of dead people are less informative about death than one might hope.[20]

Only our provinciality as denizens of the photographic and filmic age allows us to forget that other kinds of images have laid claim to the accurate depiction of past events. History paintings of the Napoleonic era were often celebrated for their remarkable trueness to life, prompting the same double takes in audiences that photographs subsequently induced in eyewitnesses to events who saw the accuracy of their own memories confirmed on film. Louis François Lejeune was a French general who produced numerous canvases depicting his experiences in the Napoleonic campaigns, most famously *The Battle of Marengo*, which shows the 1800 clash between French and Austrian forces in northern Italy. Discussing the extraordinary popularity this painting enjoyed, Michael Marrinan observes the following:

> Perhaps most surprising to us today are the many comments concerning the crowd's enthusiasm for Le Jeune's picture (*The Battle of Marengo*), and the almost unanimous appreciation of it as astonishingly true. "You feel as if you are witnessing the action," wrote the *Mercure de France*; "one day, while looking at the picture, I found myself next to a young soldier. He could not contain his expressions of surprise and joy: *that's really it*, he said, *I was there and the action was hot*."[21]

For Marrinan, the complexity of these images is related to the fact that history painters of the era, "trained to render events visible, found themselves working against the grain of an information system designed to make events readable."[22] The art of this period had to accommodate the dictates of the reigning propaganda machine, which demanded an aesthetics of legibility. It was not enough to claim that the audience could "see" what was being depicted; a painter also had to inscribe the official interpretation into the visual field such that the viewer could "read" the government-sanctioned result of the battle in it.[23] Well before the advent of photography or film, the modern war picture offered a hybrid of the mimetic, the semiotic, and the performative, its semblance of legibility proving to be anything but transparent. Rather than resolving the potential ambiguities of the verbal order, the visual realm was exposed as highly unstable. The resulting pictures of battles, including those that elicited a chorus of testimonies to their representational accuracy, were far from unequivocal documents. If a canvas could produce a "that's how it was" effect, it could equally well perform in an entirely unexpected fashion. Scholarship on paintings of the Napoleonic battlefield has shown that even renditions of triumphant victory parades could subtly work against the official message while appearing to support it.

Did the advent of photography alter this complex dynamic of the visible and the readable or simply extend its vicissitudes to a new format? Although several wars were photographed in the 1850s—most notably the Crimean War—the American Civil War was the first to produce an extensive body of photographic images that were widely viewed both at the time and afterward. In contrast to the highly regulated system within which the well-known photographs of the Second World War were made almost a century later, the photography of the mid-nineteenth century was a decentralized praxis. Most of the tens of thousands of pictures made were taken not by government agents or news reporters authorized to visit the battlefields but by freelancers who aimed to sell them to ordinary citizens or to the soldiers themselves.[24] In a somewhat macabre fashion, commercial photography ended up recording the military career of many combatants from beginning to end. Upon enlisting, most soldiers donned their uniforms and sat for formal portraits in studios before heading off to their units; for those who did not survive the ensuing battles, these individualized, highly personal images might be complemented by their anonymous appearance in photographs of corpses strewn across the fields.[25]

As a medium of memory, photography was implicated in the preservation of destruction on two levels: it charted the decimation of individual bodies and the dismantling of the identity logic, according to which previous wars were about the exploits of known rather than unknown fighters. Much of the scholarship about Civil War photography has focused on this shift from paintings of immortalized heroes in the heat of battle to pictures that capture the daily activities of anonymous men at the front. Alan Trachtenberg argues that although most of the photographs of troops eating or putting up tents were staged, they were designed to create an impression of the quotidian and the informal: "The strength of the pictures lies in their mundane aspect—their portrayal of war as an event in real space and time—a different conception of the very medium within which war takes place: not the mythic or fictional time of theater, as in Benjamin West's famous *Death of General Wolfe*, but the real time of an actual camp or battlefield."[26]

It is less clear whether this transformation in the conceptualization and representation of war was the result of changes in the way battles were being fought or whether photography heralded a revolution in observation and representation that impacted military praxis. Steven Conn suggests that a transformation in war itself was at issue, maintaining that paintings of the American Civil War have enjoyed little acclaim either in the nineteenth century or today because grand-manner history painting could not find any "Washington-Crossing-the Delaware moments," topoi, or motifs to call its own: "The problem . . . was not that painters did not try to capture the Civil War in paint, but that they were unable, apparently, to use history painting to convey the large meanings and ultimate truths of the conflict whatever those might have been."[27] Interestingly, Conn maintains that photography made no effort to replace history painting on its own turf, choosing to avoid dramatic battles scenes and epic moments of life-and-death struggle. While there were technical constraints imposed by the cumbersome equipment and development process, he insists that "more than this, photography's purposes were entirely other. Rather than attempt to make narrative and moral sense of the war, photographs served as part of the apparatus of documentation."[28]

The question of whether changes in warfare originated with the media used to observe and record them continues to inform reflections on the documents of the Civil War and the advent of war photography in general. At times the novel character of the battles is treated as the decisive issue;[29] at other points, photography is said to have played an active role in changing the way war was understood, if not the way it was conceived of and waged by the men who fought it.[30] Trachtenberg sees the challenges presented by the spectacles of the American Civil War as the culmination of changes in fighting that occurred in the Napoleonic era, the theoretical force of which was canonized by Carl von Clausewitz's account of warfare as both rationality incarnate and the quintessence of haphazard chaos. In these terms the Civil War was the archetype of Clausewitz's "fog of war," a historical event "ruled more by chance than design, and occurring within battlefields thick with smoke."[31] The photographic report of such a series of occurrences would of necessity be fragmentary not because wide-angle lenses did not yet exist or because there were not enough photographers to capture the action but because no individual image can explain how the single scene it illustrates can or should be understood as part of a larger philosophical or political narrative—or even whether what it depicts is a product of comprehensible forces or a record of happenstance. If they appear to be poignant representations of human suffering, Civil War photographs may nonetheless fail to underwrite intelligible inferences about the nature of warfare or the human condition in general.

The question of whether a single war photograph can offer insight into larger cultural and historical forces, facilitating a transition from an individual scene to a broader account of the meaning of a battle, a war, or human existence as such, is the preoccupation of one of the best-known photographic studies of the Civil War period, Alexander Gardner's *Photographic Sketch Book of the War 1861–1865*. Beginning the American Civil War as an employee of Mathew Brady, Gardner soon struck out on his own. Published in 1866, his two-volume work contains a hundred photos, each accompanied by a detailed commentary. Gardner's discussions of his pictures have played a central role in their reception and interpretation. Although subsequent research has revealed that many of the statements he makes about these images are false, his narratives are so rich and detailed that the picture sometimes comes across as a supplement to the verbal text rather than the other way around.[32] The title alone of *A Harvest of Death* rivals the photograph it captions, and the accompanying commentary is a pastiche of different genres, beginning like the opening of a sentimental novel ("Slowly, over the misty fields of Gettysburg—as all reluctant to expose their ghastly horrors to the light—came the sunless morn, after the retreat of Lee's broken army"); quickly shifting gears to take the reader through a panoply of mythical motifs ("A battle has often been the subject of elaborate description; but it can be described in one simple word, *devilish!* and the distorted dead recall the ancient legends of men torn in pieces by savage wantonness of fiends"); and culminating in an interpretive conclusion about what the image means, a pronouncement whose summary tone raises more questions than it answers: "Such a picture conveys a useful moral: It shows the blank horror and reality of war, in opposition to its pageantry."[33]

Prefiguring the disclaimer made by the editors of *Life* almost a century later, Gardner announces in the preface that his book "is designed that it shall speak for itself. . . . Verbal representations of such places, or scenes, may or may not have the merit of accuracy; but photographic presentments of them will be accepted by posterity with an undoubting faith."[34] One might ask why Gardner complemented his photos with verbal narratives if doing so introduced the possibility of inaccuracy, a question that remains unaddressed, as does the related question of why the book needs a preface whose main theme is that a preface is unnecessary. As with Marrinan's account of paintings produced under the influence of the Napoleonic regime of propaganda and censorship, the relative primacy of seeing and reading—the simultaneity of both acts in the encounter with the battlefield, and the possibility that they may come into conflict or diverge in important ways—is at the forefront of Gardner's presentation of the nascent representational medium of photography.

FIGURE 3.2 Alexander Gardner, *Home of a Rebel Sharpshooter*, 1863. © The Museum of Modern Art, New York, anonymous gift. From Davis Art Images.

Gardner and his associates were the first photographers to arrive at Gettysburg in the aftermath of the battle, and the photograph *Home of a Rebel Sharpshooter* that he made there was to become one of the most enduring images of the Civil War. Gardner's commentary on the picture begins with an account of discovering the body: "The artist, in passing over the scene of the previous days' engagements, found in a lonely place the covert of a rebel sharpshooter, and photographed the scene presented here. The Confederate soldier had built up between two huge rocks, a stone wall, from the crevices of which he had directed his shots, and, in comparative security, picked off our officers."[35] The photographer describes his picture as though it reproduces a setting he had stumbled upon and begun to decode, like a detective at a crime scene. His ability to draw inferences based on the physical evidence at hand, as well as other information about the battle that he has garnered from the participants, ostensibly provides the resulting image with a degree of authenticity since Gardner is able to narrate a story that makes sense of the details we now view. This analysis of the facts of the scene slowly shifts to more existential ruminations that rely less on what was supposedly found on the battlefield, and ultimately Gardner becomes overtly creative with his reflections on what the deceased soldier must have endured:

> There was no means of judging how long he had lived after receiving his wound, but the disordered clothing shows that his sufferings must have been intense. Was he delirious with agony, or did death come slowly to his relief, while memories of home grew dearer as the field of carnage faded before him? What visions, of loved ones far away, may have hovered above his stony pillow! What familiar voices may he not have heard, like whispers beneath the roar of battle, as his eyes grew heavy in their long, last sleep![36]

Having explained how the photo was taken, Gardner instructs his viewer in how to read it, leading us through the issues that the image raises while stressing that certain aspects of the picture must remain a mystery. The exposition relies on conventional topoi: the dying man's death is figured as the advent of sleep, his last thoughts are assumed to be memories of home and his loved ones, and the horror of the carnage is quietly countered by the intimacy of the private experience of expiring. The picture is thus presented as if it invited us to speculate on the most personal features of the dead man and facilitated at least some basic insight into his interior existence, although obviously we cannot be sure of any of the conclusions we draw.

Given the complexity of these ambitious flights of poetic fancy, it may come as a surprise that contemporary scholars have concluded that what we see in *Home of a Rebel Sharpshooter* is a staged scene rather than a document of how the battlefield looked to Gardner and his associates directly after the storied clash. The gun is not a sharpshooter's weapon but a prop Gardner carried with him and used in several other photographs. Far from lying as he fell, the Confederate soldier's body was arranged with considerable care; another of Gardner's pictures shows the same corpse with its face turned away from the camera. Indeed, the dead soldier was moved to this site with a blanket that Gardner regularly used to shift corpses, indicating that the photographer-poet must have concocted the entire explanation of the shooter's vantage point, his putative identity as a sharpshooter, and his ability to pick off "our officers."[37] In short, Gardner's entire account of the photograph is a fiction.[38]

Intriguingly, Gardner extends the narrative of his photograph to include a second "encounter" with the rebel sharpshooter, claiming that, four months later, while attending the consecration of the Gettysburg Cemetery, he "chanced" to pass by the same site again:

> The musket, rusted by many storms, still leaned against the rock, and the skeleton of the soldier lay undisturbed within the moldering uniform, as did the cold form of the dead four months before. None of those who went up and down the fields to bury the fallen, had found him. "Missing," was all that could have been known of him at home, and some mother may yet be patiently watching for the return of her boy, whose bones lie bleaching, unrecognized and alone, between the rocks at Gettysburg.[39]

At this point Gardner's tale becomes markedly fanciful. In this fantasy of permanence in decay, the photograph serves as a hinge that articulates two different experiences of the artist. Yet as William Frassanito has convincingly argued, the notion that a corpse would have lain on the field at Gettysburg for four months after the battle is improbable.[40] It is far more likely that Gardner had to race in immediately after the fighting ended to arrange the body for his photograph before it was buried. It is even more likely that the rifle, if it belonged to the soldier rather than to Gardner, would have immediately been looted by Union forces or relic hunters.

More than fifty years before tombs of unknown soldiers emerged in the wake of the First World War, Gardner's story aims to turn his "sharp-shooter" photo into an emblem of the unknown warrior, the lost every-man whose dead body eludes interment, "the one who got away." Here, "lost" means not just that the rebel soldier is dead but also that he remains unidentified; he is "missing," and hence for his friends or family unclassi-fiable as either "living" or "dead." Contrasting sharply with the vast ma-jority of Civil War images of individuals, portraits of soldiers taken at a local photographer's studio long before they saw combat, *Home of a Rebel Sharpshooter* is an antiportrait, an image of anonymity. In this regard one must acknowledge the power of the picture's title and its archly ironic use of the word *home*.

The corpse Gardner depicts functions as a kind of remainder or excess—it is the lifeless body rather than the spirit that does the haunt-ing, proving to be the piece of the battlefield that refuses to go quietly. A tableau mort rather than a tableau vivant, it is staged not by living peo-ple posing as a "dead" painting but by a dead person posing as a dead person. In this representational logic, death is not a natural phenomenon that one can stumble across like a tree or a rainbow—if we are to "see" it, it must be carefully arranged and accompanied by an extensive verbal addendum. Otherwise, the fallen boy could always be asleep—or, given the artifice with which Gardner composed his photos, lying with his eyes closed until the cameraman tells him to stand up and pose some-where else on the field. In contrast to the many photos of the American Civil War that show troops engaged in daily activities, Gardner's image of the aftermath of Gettysburg resuscitates the traditional topos of the fallen warrior but in a new format, as a figure of unknown glory in defeat.

In the photographer's fantasy, the sharpshooter who picks off "our officers" from his carefully chosen "home" is the alter ego of the photogra-pher himself, taking his shot of the scene.[41] Although the photographer's work is not carried out quickly in the heat of battle but after the fact, with deliberation and care, he tries, like the marksman, to choose the perfect spot from which to espy his prey and succeeds or fails based on his ability to capture the scene before it escapes him. However, by giving the fallen rebel soldier a voice so that his inner thoughts and feelings can be told from the grave, the putatively "living" photographer invites us to ask from which side of the frontier between the living and the dead his own story is

being told. In presenting the camera as a weapon, Gardner hints that its
optic aggression is a force directed by the cameraman against himself as
much as against the object of his lens's gaze. In his identification with the
dead the photographer-writer triumphs as deceased.

Gardner's verbal account of his photograph thus coordinates two stories: a tale in which a young soldier, skillfully perched behind some rocks
where he could target his foes, was shot and died, and another in which
a photographer came upon a body—twice. Given the importance that
Gardner places on his "second" encounter with the dead soldier's remains, it is striking that he never addresses the question of why he failed
to make a photographic record of it. His narrative about his picture is
based on a fantasy involving two experiences, neither of which he actually had, yet this narrative is supposed to take precedence over the visual
document facilitated by the picture that was made. Gardner answers the
question of whether an individual photograph of a battle can offer a
meaningful view of a given engagement or insight into the nature of
military praxis as such by complementing his most famous image—one
of the most famous war photos of all time—with a story that undermines
the authority of photography as an evidentiary medium. It is as if he were
trying to confirm that his *Home of a Rebel Sharpshooter* was entirely consistent with the well-established medium of history painting and that
photography presented no new conceptual or representational specifici-
ties that might alter the way that his audience looked at or understood
warfare.

Haunted by a second photograph that was not taken and could not
have been taken, Gardner's image betrays a conflicted temporal structure.
On the one hand, Gardner presents it as one moment in a long sequence
of events—if it is not an "action" shot, it is part of a series of incidents that
transpired during and after the battle. On the other hand, the story about
a body remaining undisturbed over a period of months is designed to abstract the dimension of time from the photo so that what the viewer sees
in *Home of a Rebel Sharpshooter* is an enduring monument to death rather
than a representation of a particular moment on the field at Gettysburg.
By definition, the photo is a fixed image, but whether this image is in turn
an image of fixity is less clear.

William F. Stapp has proposed that Gardner, who was Scottish, was
the only Civil War photographer likely to have seen British photographer

Roger Fenton's pictures of the Crimean War and that he therefore had a richer sense than his contemporaries of the power of the new medium to explore the mysteries of the modern battlefield.[42] On the basis of my analysis of *Home of a Rebel Sharpshooter* it is far from obvious in what respects Gardner believed that photography "documented" warfare, as so many scholars have maintained, although this may be precisely the respect in which his work reveals its debt to Fenton. While photographs of wars in Mexico, the Punjab, and Burma predate Fenton's use of the camera in the Crimea, he is generally heralded as the "first" war photographer, having been sent to record events on the peninsula at the behest of Prince Albert in order to help counteract antiwar sentiment at home and especially the antiwar reporting of the British papers. The propagandistic nature of Fenton's excursion contrasted with the lack of official restrictions that journalists enjoyed during the conflict, which arguably saw the highpoint of freedom of the press in the modern era.[43]

Fenton took no pictures of dead soldiers, and in fact most of his photos were posed portraits of officers or scenes of troops behind the lines engaged in the mundane activities of daily life. What he is today largely remembered for, however, are two very different images, which do provide a useful point of comparison with Gardner's project. Fenton shot two photographs of a road from the same vantage point. In one, the road is clear, with cannonballs lying in a ditch to the side; in the other, it is covered with cannonballs. Viewed together, the two pictures testify to the intervention of one or more persons who are not visible, although it is not known whether it was Fenton who altered the scene or someone else, for example, soldiers moving cannonballs to the side as a first step toward collecting them for reuse. Much of the discussion of the pictures has centered on the question of which was made first. Art historian Ulrich Keller has argued that Fenton photographed the empty road and then put the cannonballs on it in order to make the second shot appear more dramatic and dangerous, a point endorsed by Susan Sontag.[44] Errol Morris has questioned Keller's logic, reminding us that many scholars have been unable to decide how to sequence the pictures. While Morris ultimately concludes that Sontag and Keller were right about the order in which the photographs were made, he maintains that it is impossible to know which of the two images Fenton thought was more ominous or whether he was responsible for rearranging the cannonballs.[45]

FIGURE 3.3 Roger Fenton, *Valley of the Shadow of Death*, 1855. Gernsheim Collection, Harry Ransom Center, University of Texas at Austin.

FIGURE 3.4 Roger Fenton, *Valley of the Shadow of Death*, 1855. Gernsheim Collection, Harry Ransom Center, University of Texas at Austin.

It is unclear why Keller and Sontag take it for granted that the photo-graph with the cannonballs on the road is more foreboding than its counterpart. Sontag herself appears to acknowledge that the location of the cannonballs is not the key issue. Treating the two pictures as comple-mentary facets of a single work, she emphasizes that the iconic status of "the" photo rests on the fact that it did not need to be staged since there were no people or corpses involved. "Fenton's memorial photograph," she writes, "is a portrait of absence, of death without the dead."[46] This claim builds on Gardner's fantasy of the rebel sharpshooter's skeleton, a photo-graph he claims to have seen but never taken, by suggesting that the power of the modern battlefield is captured not by a picture of living or dead soldiers but by an image of a barren terrain in which the human form is lacking. Photography comes into its own as a medium of war representation by revealing that, in the age of total war, the quintessen-tial military spectacle is defined by the absence of combatants. Death and destruction are left to the viewer's imagination.

Do Fenton's and Gardner's photographs testify to the power of fantasy, or do they demonstrate that even the most active imagination can never be creative enough to capture the post-Napoleonic battlefield? English photographer Richard Pare, who has written extensively about Fenton, acknowledges the difficulty of determining which of the two pictures of the road was made first, but he is content to leave the issue unresolved. Following Sontag, he treats the images as two versions of the "first iconic photo of war," which gains its significance from the fact that "it is devoid of any topographical detail that defines a particular place; it becomes instead an image about the horror of all war and the mundane business of destruc-tion. It suggests only the potential for sudden and indiscriminate death."[47] Pare complements Gardner's everyman logic with the figure of an "every-place," a generic site on which people kill and are killed, an abstract place-holder for the omnipresent potential for slaughter. If *Valley of the Shadow of Death* is a complex title, rich in specific and potentially contradictory allu-sions, Pare reads it as a figure for the entire planet.[48] Fenton's photo is an invitation to the viewer to acknowledge the permanent threat of war at any place and time—the picture achieves the impossible by capturing the totality of total war in a single view. It is a bounded scene of unbounded strife.

The problem with this argument is the uneasy presence of the cannon-balls. Their change of location between the two shots introduces a specificity of time and sequence into Pare's generic topos, reminding us that there is something fundamentally paradoxical in contemplating two distinct representations of "everyplace." It is not by chance that Fenton and Sontag must collapse the two images into one in order to make the claim that they exhibit an abstract space. The very fact that there can be dueling depictions of the topos suggests that it is in fact *a* place, not *any* or *every* place, just as the appearance of a twin to the unknown soldier would compromise his status as unknown. Set side by side, Fenton's photographs force us to ask whether one must always understand an individual photo with reference to a "before" and "after" that it articulates in virtue of its claim, however minimal, to represent a moment in time. Fenton's photographs demand to be sequenced irrespective of how one orders them or how one explains the circumstances that led to the cannonballs being moved. Although photography was only in its infancy in 1855, it is not just the possibility of death that is present in its absence in these pictures but the possibility of movement, as well. Fenton photographed several decades before Eadweard Muybridge designed his zoopraxiscope or developed his famous sequence of a galloping racehorse, but the use of magic lanterns to create the illusion of motion with still images was already well established by the end of the eighteenth century.[49] The scenes of *Valley of the Shadow of Death* owe much of their iconic status to the fact that they constitute a protofilmic event, revealing more about the battlefield than the many pictures Fenton took of soldiers posed with their weapons by casting the scene of combat in temporal terms and reminding us that fighting takes time. The "iconic image of war" reveals itself to be a photograph of the failure of any photograph to win a total view of the battlefield. It invites its viewers to complete it by putting its parts in order or explaining the circumstances that gave rise to the scene(s) it depicts, although the effort to do so may only be able to repeat without entirely mastering the inherent changeability at work.

Like the ghost of the photograph that Gardner did not take, the claim of *Valley of the Shadow of Death* to present a generic space of loss and death is haunted by a potential for change that compromises the abstraction that Sontag and Pare identify in it. In this regard Gardner is Fenton's inheritor. His picture of the rebel sharpshooter betrays the challenges that attend any effort to realize photographically the timeless monumentality for which a sculpture or painting of a fallen warrior strives. The fact that Gardner felt compelled to complement his shot of the rebel marksman with an account of another scene that never took place, the fantasy of an antiphotograph that would record the fact that his subject matter had not moved in months, bespeaks an unease about the stability of the image that he did produce, as if the fallen figure might get up and walk away—as if, despite all appearances to the contrary, the next photograph of that spot would have been a version of Fenton's portrayal of the modern battlefield (i.e., a rock wall with nobody there). In the end Gardner's picture presents itself as an image that is both complete in its own right and radically fragmentary. Exhibiting transformation and change rather than the constancy and solidity for which a monument aims, it asks to be integrated into a larger story while simultaneously resisting that very gesture.

Our analysis suggests that early war photography was a volatile discourse, a medium experimenting with new representational standards while continuing to rely on the conventions that had long governed painting and narrative prose. With regard to the documentation of war's human costs, the question is whether these presentational dynamics changed as advances in technology and shifts in cultural mores gradually made it possible to confront an audience with an image that seemed to leave nothing to the imagination. In the "instant-of-death" photo the unique ability of the photographic medium to capture a moment in time and the horrific suddenness with which life is regularly lost in warfare are united in the ultimate record of the "un-tampered facts of the moment."[50] If Sontag argues that the quintessential picture of death shows "no body," the instant-of-death image purports to capture a human being on the verge of passing over to "the other side." At once the ideal humanist work of art and a graphic demonstration that people are composed of flesh and blood, such a picture appears to distinguish photography from history painting definitively and finally. The best-known examples of the genre include Robert Capa's illustration of a soldier in the Spanish Civil War, *Death of a Loyalist Militiaman, Cerro Muriano, Córdoba Front, Spain, September 5, 1936*, commonly known as *The Falling Soldier*, which shows an infantryman collapsing to the ground just after being struck by a bullet, and Eddie Adams's picture of the South Vietnamese general Nguyen Ngoc Loan executing a Viet Cong officer in Saigon during the Tet Offensive, which was taken just after the trigger was pulled and exhibits the physiological torsion in the victim's face as the bullet rips through his head.[51]

In their representation of instantaneity and "perfect" timing, these photos are presumably compelling evidence for the inadequacy of "mere words." Nonetheless, what they purport to achieve is far from simple. They claim not just to depict a singular moment but also to do so in such a way as to establish its absolute consequentiality within a series of events, i.e., on the basis of what Adams's photograph shows us, we are to know with certainty that the figure on the right fell dead to the street a second later and that the figure on the left had pulled the trigger a second earlier. The instant-of-death image seeks to realize what philosophical skeptics regard as impossible: a tangible illustration of cause and effect. In this regard, such a picture is a testimony to stability and predictability in the spatiotemporal realm as much as it is evidence of the arbitrary whims of fate. Ulrich Baer has written that "photographs can capture the shrapnel of traumatic time. They confront us with the possibility that time consists of singular bursts and explosions and that the continuity of time-as-river

FIGURE 3.5 Robert Capa, *The Falling Soldier*, 1936. © International Center of Photography/Magnum Photos.

FIGURE 3.6 Eddie Adams, *Saigon Execution*, 1968. © AP/Wide World Photos.

is another myth."[52] With instant-of-death photos, however, it is unclear whether the "shrapnel of traumatic time" is ever fractured or singular enough; such a picture may achieve its forceful presentation precisely because its viewer incorporates the instant it exhibits into a coherent causal chain that respects a unidirectional sequence. If there were anything in the image that suggested that time was interrupted, frozen, or running backward like a cartoon, the tone of the photograph would immediately change from tragedy to farce.

The instant-of-death photograph purports to be a permanent record of a transitory instant, although an instant whose consequences were graphically permanent. The traumatic impact of such a picture may have to do with the way in which it isolates a particular moment, monumentalizing it as absolutely meaningful while still demanding that its viewer coordinate this moment with a "before" and an "after." Shuttling between the ephemeral and the fixed, the image testifies to the photographer's skill in enshrining an arresting scene for posterity as much as it illustrates the fragility of the human condition or the possibility for cold-blooded murder. But does the force of the photograph lie in what it records or in the precision and skill with which it was made? This question acquires a particular urgency when we remember that even photographs of this sort cannot avoid the charge of being misleading representations, if not elaborate ruses, rather than "un-tampered" traces of an empirical past. *The Falling Soldier* has repeatedly been labeled a fake, the staging of an instant of death captured on film rather than the documentation of a death that actually occurred.[53] The claim is less that such a photograph could not have been taken than that this picture is not such a photograph. A celebration of the existence of a "real" instant-of-death photograph is thereby deferred until an authentic exemplar can emerge.

Capa responded to these charges with a remarkable story about how he captured the image. As recounted by his friend John Hersey, he claimed that he was crouching in a trench as the men around him charged an enemy position, and he "timidly raised his camera over the top of the parapet and, without looking, at the instant of the first machine gun burst, pressed the button."[54] To emphasize that he had scarcely participated in the picture's production, Capa added that it was only months later, when he happened to look at an old roll of undeveloped film, that he realized what had been recorded. In response to the accusation that the photograph is a fake, Capa answers with a tale of pure mechanical happenstance in which his only contribution was to press the shutter release during a live firefight. His vision—what he could see, much less what he could see through the viewfinder to "frame" the shot—was not involved at all. This is the opposite of Gardner's sustained (and possibly equally fictional) encounter with the dead soldier and his skeleton. In contrast to Gardner's narrative about a lengthy viewing and reviewing of a body complete with a hypothetical reconstruction of its final living seconds, the story Capa tells about his photograph suggests that it represents less danger or death than chance, although not a chance killing—since for all we know the soldier who fired at the loyalist militiaman took careful aim at his subject—but a chance recording of the event. Unlike Gardner, Capa cannot relate the experience of coming upon the scene of the falling soldier because he never did. We must therefore abandon the assumption that a photograph replicates or immortalizes an experience someone once had of looking at something. Not only is what a viewer sees in the picture something that no one ever saw, but if Capa had been looking through the viewfinder of his camera, it would have been more difficult, if not impossible, for him to have taken the picture. If this is the ultimate war photo, it is because it offers a testimony to the battlefield observer's blindness, or at least to the stark separation of the photographer from the camera, which functions "best" when it is left to its own devices. At the same time, Capa's explanation of the photo's production finds no confirmation in the image itself, which is powerless to reveal whether it is a product of chance or human design. To this day skeptics continue to mount new evidentiary assaults against it.

Allegedly "un-tampered," Adams's photograph of an execution in Vietnam would appear to be an even more compelling record of an "instant of death." Still, this image was produced under very specific circumstances. Sontag describes the theatrical quality of the scene: "[I]t was staged—by General Loan, who had led the prisoner, hands tied behind his back, out to the street where journalists had gathered; he would not have carried out the summary execution there had they not been available to witness it. Positioned beside his prisoner so that his profile and the prisoner's face were visible to the cameras behind him, Loan aimed point-blank."[55] Far from passively documenting the shocking reality of warfare, this famous photograph was arguably a cause of the execution it depicts.[56] At the very least, the fact that the scene between the general and his prisoner took place in front of members of the press corps starkly influenced the way in which it unfolded. Analyses of the picture have tended to focus on the relationship that developed between the general and Adams in the aftermath of the incident, as if their subsequent behavior toward one another might shed some light on what transpired that day in the street. Attempting to clarify his role in this grisly drama, the photographer stresses that he had not anticipated what he was about to record: "It was common to hold a pistol to the head of prisoners during questions. . . . The man just pulled a pistol out of his holster and shot him in the temple. I made a picture at the same time."[57] Adams indicates that he believed that he was going to witness a routine interrogation like many others that had been played out in front of him in the course of the war, only to discover too late that this was not a threat but the real thing. The true horror of the picture would thus be that it captures the exact moment at which the officer stops playing executioner and starts being one, the point at which there is suddenly no difference between the simulation of the intent to kill and killing itself.

But who, exactly, was doing the killing? "I killed the general with my camera," Adams declared melodramatically, literalizing Gardner's notion of the photographer-sharpshooter by concluding that just as General

Loan shot the prisoner, so he, Adams, destroyed the life of the individual who would forever after be vilified as "the evil man in that picture."[58] As if taking the photograph rather than shooting the prisoner in the head were the real crime, Adams went to some lengths to defend Loan's actions, explaining that just prior to the execution the general had been told about a terrible atrocity committed by the Viet Cong and was in an agitated state of mind when he confronted the prisoner, who might have taken part in the massacre. At one instant-of-death extreme (Capa's photo), the photographer disavows any role in the production of the picture; at the other extreme (Adams's photo), he seeks to usurp the shooter completely, maintaining that photography, as the cause in this instance of two deaths, is the problem and that the resulting image is intrinsically misleading when it comes to understanding why what happened took place and what it means.

Comforting Adams when he apologized for having ruined his life, Loan told his counterpart that if he "hadn't taken the picture, someone else would have"—the remark of a true Napoleonic warrior, who assumes that combat takes place in an absolutely public space.[59] In the photograph itself, however, the general does not reign supreme in the visual logic. The face of the third prominent figure in the picture, the soldier on the left, stands out due to its violent mien, which serves as a sort of surrogate expression for the aggression one assumes must have been motivating the general, whose face is not visible. The sense that the full significance of what we see involves more than just the shooter and his victim is compounded by the fourth figure in the foreground on the right. He is also faceless and, even more important, seemingly oblivious to the momentous scene being played out beside him, giving no indication that he has started at the sound of the pistol and is about to turn around. It is as if the improvisational quality of the drama captured by the camera localized the reach of the spectacle so that even a bystander immediately next to it could miss it. In this sense what Adams's picture illustrates is not the precision or immediacy of photography's reproductive powers but the fact that even a depiction of one man blowing another man's brains out becomes an internally fractured scene, as if even the most basic unit of consequential experience contains within itself a diversionary logic such that the brute presentation of cause and effect—"a man with a gun kills another man"—cannot be concretized in a univocal image.

The instant-of-death photo forces us to consider the relationship between the violence depicted in an image that a camera captures and the violence involved in abstracting an instant in time from its temporal or causal continuum, shifting it from an experiential flux to a new forum in which it can be studied as a fixed, even independent referent. Such a photograph, far from merely documenting the existence of people, actions, or objects (e.g., guns), becomes a shocking object in its own right, an object whose production is as much of an event as the event it exhibits. Photography thus reveals something about the violence inherent in perception and its surrogates. In an age of total war, human beings faced with images of the battlefield are not simply beset by disturbing data that confront them from without; experience *is* a sustained series of shocking encounters with different forms of violence that never permit of simple localization or compartmentalization and are always potentially rehearsed and repeated by the media that process and record them.

In the twentieth century the two most important theorists of photography as shock perception were Ernst Jünger and Walter Benjamin, contemporaries who stood at different ends of the political spectrum. In his essay *On Pain*, written in 1934, Jünger made an often-cited claim that photography is "a weapon of the [modern] worker-type. For him, seeing is an act of assault."[60] Jünger does not just draw an analogy between looking and fighting or claim that observation is an important part of any battle since ideally one would like to catch sight of one's foe before one's foe can do the same. Rather, he insists that photography has come to exemplify "our specific manner of seeing," a form of vision that observes the world with "an insensitive and invulnerable eye."[61] Our gaze is a version of Adams's camera in Vietnam, which, as Jünger says, "records the bullet in mid-flight just as easily as it captures a man at the moment an explosion tears him apart"; it is a gaze that is, Jünger leaves no doubt, "a peculiarly cruel way of seeing . . . a kind of evil eye."[62]

This perceptual posture is part of the larger picture Jünger paints in *On Pain* of a society whose members are distinguished by self-detachment and indifference to the sight of suffering and death, a condition that presages a "new way of life" characterized by discipline and the abandonment of bourgeois sentimentality. Jünger's text is often read in conjunction with his essay *The Worker*, written in 1932, and its utopian image of a new breed of men organized through militaristic Fordism. As political theory the two pieces betray a virulent conservatism; viewed historically, Jünger seems to be diagnosing the transition from democracy to fascism. When these works are juxtaposed with his 1931 *The Dangerous Moment*, a collection of photos of imminent injury and death (catastrophes, accidents, and scenes of political upheaval), it is hard to escape the conclusion that Jünger fetishizes the instant-of-death image as the ultimate testimony to the power of the forces he sees gripping society.[63] Importantly, he does not conceive of shock as something one chooses to indulge in, as though it were a predilection of an adrenaline junkie pursuing extreme sports. Jünger's claim is rather that modern experience *is* a shock experience.[64] As he makes clear in his essay "On Danger," which was written as an introduction to *The Dangerous Moment*, danger is no longer an exception but is "constantly present" throughout social life.[65] If the militarization of European society between 1914 and 1918 spawned this form of perception, in the Weimar Republic it had become the norm.[66]

Walter Benjamin, who saw his own work as a critique of the fascist aestheticization of war and politics he identified in thinkers such as Jünger, also described the repeated exposure to shock as characteristic of the modern era. Invoking Freud's conception of consciousness as a shield against stimuli, Benjamin proposes that memory traces are formed precisely when something does not enter consciousness: "[O]nly what has not been experienced explicitly and consciously, what has not happened to the subject as an isolated experience [*Erlebnis*], can become a component of *mémoire involontaire*."[67] To the extent that consciousness successfully defends against shock, the sight of a soldier executing a prisoner with a pistol does not fully impact the psyche and produce traumatic reverberations. Benjamin believes that media such as photography and film facilitate a unique engagement with dynamics of discontinuity, disruption, and repetition, exposing the psyche to extreme stimuli while at the same time training it in shock defense, allowing for quasi experiences of what can be known only insofar as it has already been forgotten.[68] For Benjamin, the photographic image is an inherently conflicted exhibition that depicts the retreat of exhibition itself. Every photo is a tacit betrayal of the presentational claims of its own medium, offering a glimpse of something that can manifest itself only in its failure to be directly encountered.

In contrast to Jünger, the photographs that Benjamin discusses are not scenes of imminent death. Still, he is equally interested in the kinds of images Capa or Adams made because for him the distinctiveness of photography has as much to do with the mechanics of taking a picture as with the impact of the resulting photo. Considering the ways in which technology has changed human experience so that now a tiny motion of the hand can have enormous ramifications, Benjamin writes: "With regard to countless movements of switching, inserting, pressing, and the like, the 'snapping' by the photographer had the greatest consequences. Henceforth a touch of the finger sufficed to fix an event for an unlimited period of time. The camera gave the moment a posthumous shock, as it were."[69] In "capturing" the moment in which General Loan shot a Viet Cong officer, Adams's photo unsettles the very notion of the momentary; his image illustrates the singularity of its subject matter, a unique instant, by negating its essential fleetingness through the claim to fix it permanently as one point in a chain of causes and effects.

Benjamin's description of the technologically enhanced power of the "touch of the finger" applies equally to Loan's decision to pull the trigger of the gun. Adams's photo is a depiction of the alignment of two touches of the finger, which complement each other not as mirror opposites but as disjunctive alternatives embroiled in a play of action and reaction. It thus becomes unclear precisely what "moment" the photograph captures: the point at which the trigger is pulled, the shutter release is pressed, or the victim's head contorts. "Posthumously shocked," the moment cannot hold still, and for this reason Adam's photo veils rather than exposes what the general intended to do with the gun and what the correspondent intended to do with the camera such that we no longer know whether the image is evidence of Jünger's "cruel" gaze or of the most heartfelt humanist regard. Adams's photograph documents the instability that arises when the event of an execution can no longer be distinguished from the allegory of photographic memorialization, which fixes the event permanently in obscurity. This is a photograph about the way in which any image that makes a claim to documentation must make a visual argument for what constitutes a "real" reproduction of reality even as the very mechanics of that argument inexorably undermine the presentation of what is supposedly most authentic about what is being exhibited. The resulting picture is a testimony to what is experienced most profoundly insofar as it is *not* experienced; and the soldier in white pants on the right strides along undisturbed, as if he were in another scene altogether.

Eduardo Cadava has emphasized Jünger's preoccupation with the air raid as a forum in which photography, light, and destruction are graphically conjoined in a spectacle, observing that, for Jünger, the key connection between photography and war was speed: "[T]here could be no lightning war without the flash of the camera. No blitz without photography—and in part because both are a matter of speed. Like the rapidity of the blitz, the technology of the camera also resides in its speed. Like the instantaneity of a lightning flash, the camera, in the split-second temporality of the shutter's blink, seizes an image."[70] The difference between nineteenth- and twentieth-century war photography would appear to lie in the advances in the medium that made a true "action shot" possible as exposure times began to be measured in fractions of a second. As the camera shutter sped up, it presumably left painting—and posed scenes such as *Home of a Rebel Sharpshooter*—further and further behind, heralding the almost perfect fusion of weapons with observation and recording devices that has today become the norm.

In fact, the aesthetic ideology Cadava identifies in Jünger is a Napoleonic doctrine, a connection that comes to the fore in the work of French photographer Henri Cartier-Bresson, often regarded as the father of modern photojournalism. Cartier-Bresson espoused a philosophy of photography based on the idea of the "decisive moment," the term Napoleon used to describe the ability to act at the crucial juncture in the battle: "In war there is but one favorable moment, the great art is to seize it."[71] Transposing this notion to the visual arts, Cartier-Bresson argued that success in producing an image is predicated on the rapidity with which one can seize a moment with the camera such that the resulting document becomes a record of a "precise and transitory instant" that can never be recovered.[72] This doctrine reaffirms the idea that the photographic medium is first and foremost an exhibition of loss, a re-presentation of something that does not permit of repetition. It also underscores that, for the modern artist, the distinction between taking a photograph and painting a picture, still blurry in the case of Fenton or Gardner, could not be clearer: " 'Photography is not like painting,' [Cartier-Bresson] told *The Washington Post* in 1957. 'There is a creative fraction of a second when you are taking a picture. Your eye must see a composition or an expression that life itself offers you, and you must know with intuition when to click the camera.' "[73] As in Jünger, the essence of this philosophy is speed. "In photography," Cartier-Bresson declared, "you've got to be quick, quick, quick, quick.

Like an animal and a prey."[74] In linking Napoleon's ideology of the timely seizure of a moment—the seizure of time itself—to the brutality of a hunting animal, Cartier-Bresson's aesthetic reveals its debt to Jünger's and Benjamin's common emphasis on the inherent violence of the modern gaze.

As our analysis of Adams's documentation of the execution in Saigon reveals, the difficulties involved in photographically "seizing the moment" are considerable, if not insurmountable. It should therefore come as no surprise that Cartier-Bresson's disciples have sought to illustrate the tensions inherent in his doctrines. French photographer Luc Delahaye worked as a photojournalist in the 1980s and 1990s and was a member of the photo cooperative Magnum, which Cartier-Bresson had founded with Capa. Covering major conflicts around the globe, Delahaye built a reputation for being able to take pictures for which the viewer was all too willing to believe he had risked life and limb. Since leaving journalism, he has continued to explore similar subject matter, although his more recent work suggests an interest in producing a different kind of picture. In 2001 Delahaye switched to shooting with a wide-angle, medium-format handheld camera and began displaying panorama-like prints in four-by-eight-foot color. The first project he embarked on, his History series, comprised scenes of battle zones and political events. Often blending multiple shots electronically, Delahaye created precise digital images that included pictures of refugee camps, a mass grave in Bosnia, and people at a rally for an opposition presidential candidate in Belarus.[75] He has referred sarcastically to this change in his work as the point at which he "officially" became an artist.[76]

At first glance, the photos in the History series appear to be overt reactions against Cartier-Bresson.[77] Delahaye's expansive views in which landscapes, buildings, and masses of people or the sky predominate seem like history paintings that require study and reflection—one certainly cannot get the gist of the pictures in an instant, as with Cartier-Bresson's famous photo of a man caught in midstride as he leaps over a puddle or his equally well-known picture of a woman in postwar France denouncing a Nazi informer in front of a crowd. While technology now allows photojournalists to take vivid action shots, capturing "reality" millisecond by millisecond, Delahaye appears to make use of modern digital and computer media to restage old-fashioned idioms. In *Baghdad IV*, taken in the Iraqi capital in 2003, it is difficult to determine whether one is seeing a noteworthy

FIGURE 3.7 Luc Delahaye, *Baghdad IV,* 2003. C-print, 245 cm × 111 cm. Courtesy of the artist / Galerie Nathalie Obadia.

incident on the street or an ordinary urban terrain like any other in the battle-ravaged city on that day. The scene lacks an implied narrative or even an obvious focal point, as if it were simultaneously an action shot, a landscape portrait, and a poorly-timed mistake showing some people who just happened to wander in and out of the frame. The smoke that hovers in the foreground is potentially ominous, threatening to obscure the view entirely, although it may just be incidental and on the verge of dissipating. The human figures present are not all looking in the same direction or preoccupied with the same thing, and the elegant shapes of the buildings that line the street contrast starkly with the trash strewn on the right side of the photo, as if this were an architectural shot prior to being airbrushed.

Nonetheless, there are some similarities between Delahaye and Cartier-Bresson that warrant consideration. No less than his predecessor, Delahaye stresses the importance of precise timing, arguing that the pace at which he shoots his pictures is crucial to preventing his own gaze from dominating the scene he captures. He sounds much like Cartier-Bresson when he describes his ambition to "show the event at the very moment it takes place. . . . My body must be anchored to the ground and must seek the best point of view, without any visual taboos."[78] Photographing from ground level as a photojournalist might, Delahaye highlights the limited position of a camera that has no pretensions to offering a god's-eye view of the proceedings. He emphasizes that "no matter how complex or ob-

scure a picture can be, it will always show the nature of the photographer's
relation to the real with a degree of clarity."[79] This relationship, however, is
not the core of the photographic experience but only a prelude to the artist's withdrawal. "At the heart of the event," Delahaye continues, "my effort
is to disappear; I introduce a distance that borders on indifference."[80] This
double motion, culminating in the retreat of the artist, ostensibly distinguishes Delahaye's pictures from Cartier-Bresson's "decisive-moment"
photos, although it is by no means obvious how the two-part sequence is to
be realized.

While almost all of the photographs in Delahaye's History series display multiple human figures at various degrees of remove, *Taliban* shows
a single individual shot at close range. As his most overt experiment in
rendering death beautiful, this picture has proven to be Delahaye's most
controversial work to date, and he has had a good deal to say in interviews about the circumstances surrounding its creation: "I was staying
since two weeks with a small group of Northern Alliance fighters in a
farm on the frontline, waiting for the offensive. It eventually happened
and in great confusion, on foot, we crossed the no man's land and reached
the Taliban lines. That's where I made this image. The morning after,
we reached Kabul."[81] The phrase "great confusion" is typical of Delahaye's
comments about the picture, which seem designed to give the impression
that he came upon the body, photographed it immediately, and then
moved on—very different from Gardner's narrative about photographing

FIGURE 3.8 Luc Delahaye, *Taliban*, 2001. C-print, 237 cm × 111 cm. Courtesy of the
artist / Galerie Nathalie Obadia.

the rebel sharpshooter, which is deliberately vague about what the photographer means when he says that he "passes over" the scene. Given the profound stillness the *Taliban* picture presents—it shows an inert figure, untroubled by live comrades or any other trace of the combat that felled him—Delahaye seems to be trying to inject the act of capturing the image with a dynamism that the picture itself lacks, as if he were seeking to shoot the scene as Cartier-Bresson would have yet somehow produced a completely different result.

In another interview Delahaye offered a different description of the experience of taking this photograph:

> He was dead a few minutes lying in a ditch. This is an example of fast. In my head I am thinking only of the process. Do I have enough light? Is the distance good? Speed too? This is what allows me to maintain an absence or distance to the event. If I impose myself too much, look for a certain effect, I'd miss the photo. This happened very fast; I need to make it slow. I see the two crossing in my mind.[82]

Responding to Cartier-Bresson's demand that one "show the event at the very moment it takes place," Delahaye suggests that the road to success is not necessarily the speediest one, but he acknowledges that he does not have the luxury of sustained reflection since to dwell too long would be to "miss the photo."[83] His emphasis on showing the "event" invokes one of Cartier-Bresson's well-known statements about his artistic practice: "To me, photography is the simultaneous recognition, in a fraction of a second, of the significance of an event as well as of a precise organization of forms which give that event its proper expression."[84] However, Delahaye makes reference to this idea of recognizing an event's significance in order to use it against the ideology of "quick, quick, quick." The process of photographing the dead soldier required a number of rapid decisions, but in the midst of the "great confusion" of their advance across no man's land to the Taliban front line, speed was enlisted in the service of slowing things down. The result was a "slow" snapshot that is not an instant-of-death picture but rather a photograph of the posthumous shock that photography has visited upon the instant of this—and every—soldier's fall.

Given Delahaye's stress on the precarious crossing of fast and slow that defined his experience of taking his picture, we must return to his opening claim that the soldier "was dead a few minutes lying in a ditch." Exactly how did Delahaye know this? Did he stop to check the temperature of the corpse? The body looks a little too tranquil, and what the viewer sees in the photograph is less evidence of the recentness of the soldier's demise than a rich catalog of what has transpired since. The deceased man's boots and weapon have been looted, and the corpse is surrounded by a network of traces of the comings and goings of others in the sand. Where Cartier-Bresson imagined capturing the decisive moment on film, Delahaye's photo shows not the blitz of war but its spectral aftermath.

Cartier-Bresson's ideology of speed should not be conflated with Jünger's fetish of images of imminent injury and death. For Cartier-Bresson, the need to take photographs in a precise manner was so central to his practice that it began to displace his interest in the resulting pictures. Indeed, Delahaye maintains that Cartier-Bresson was basically a performance artist using the camera as a prop: "The essence of Cartier-Bresson is photographic performance. He didn't really need to put the film in the camera— the importance for him is the act of taking pictures . . . being in the right position and being fast."[85] For Delahaye, the image itself is undoubtedly critical, although in his comments on *Taliban*, the act of capturing the image begins to occlude the event being documented. What, then, does his photograph ultimately record: a dead body? The encounter of a passerby with a dead body? A patch of landscape that happens to include a dead body? In contrast to most of the other pictures in the History series, time is not a factor for the objects in the viewfinder since nothing in the image is animate or immediately unstable. Delahaye's commentaries on the picture emphasize the peripheral sense of danger on the field of combat— the photographer has to work quickly and move on as the troops advance. However, from the perspective of what the picture exhibits rather than how it was made, it is anything but an action photo.

In trying to shoot the picture such that he does not impose his subjective gaze on the scene, Delahaye has produced an image that renders the viewer's perspective more dynamic. When one looks at the photo, it may at first appear as if one is hovering above the corpse in the air, but this intuition is gradually complemented by the impression that one is looking down on the scene from a small ridge somewhere to the side, a levitation effect typical of devotional pictures of Christ descending from the cross, which often have a similar telephoto feel about them. This sense of participating in a quasi-disembodied gaze contributes to the intimacy of the encounter, as if the viewer were part of a private meeting between souls or engaging with an icon, a devotional image that would serve as a

FIGURE 3.9 Benjamin West, *The Death of General Wolfe*, 1770. National Gallery of Canada, Ottawa, Ontario. Image from Helmut von Erffa and Allen Staley, *The Paintings of Benjamin West* (New Haven, CT: Yale University Press, 1986).

portal to the transcendent. Such details recall the long tradition of battle-field paintings in which fallen warriors are portrayed in a variety of New Testament poses. Of course, as with Benjamin West's well-known picture of the British general James Wolfe dying at the battle of Quebec in the Seven Years' War, these are generally group scenes, whereas Delahaye's Taliban fighter is alone, with the posture of his body ambiguously in a state of grace—some have even likened it to a lyrical dancer—or contorted in agony.

Delahaye's picture may seem to exemplify the classical aesthetic topos of the beautiful death or to offer a traditional humanist presentation of the fallen enemy as the noble "other" who is a substitute for our own selves. However, when we look more closely at the soldier's face, we encounter neither the closed eyes of a sleeper nor a riveting look back, but a quasi-disembodied stare that half returns our gaze in a dreadful fashion. The sense of repose surrounding the corpse is further complicated by the stray piece of straw on his face, which may either confirm or refute the suspicion that the scene was arranged depending on whether one assesses it as genuinely or artificially "random." In either case the straw highlights the reduction of the human form to lifeless matter while forcing the viewer to consider the extent to which the photo's rich colors and the coordination of the tones of the body and its clothing with the surrounding landscape recall the beauty of a history painting. In an interview with Delahaye, Jörg Colberg comments on the similarity between *Taliban* and traditional battlefield painting: "Maybe we're now at a point where photography creates our contemporary version of paintings of old masters?"[86] However, rather than constituting a new version of a painting, Delahaye's photograph takes its viewer through a range of experiences of different media and aesthetic paradigms. While the deceased body modulates from a randomly found object to an icon, emblem, or even a synecdoche for the humanist ideal of the self, the scene shifts between a close-up of a lovely natural setting, a contemplative portrait of a staged figure, and a realistic depiction of the horrific costs of war. At the same time, the shock the picture gives to the traditional idea of the photograph as a preservation of a moment never culminates in a confirmation of the image of the dead soldier as nondecisive. An echo of the fleeting lingers, a hint that the picture has captured a trace of something that was almost never there.

By trying to introduce a degree of indifference into the process by which he takes a photograph, Delahaye seeks to ensure that he does not produce images dominated by a subjective viewpoint. What guarantees, however, that the resulting photos will not create a similar indifference in their viewers? This is a pressing question in the case of the *Taliban* image because the affective tone it imparts to its audiences is one of security. There is no intimation that the bullet that felled this young man might have hit us, which is not to say that Delahaye is simply aestheticizing violence since, as I have already noted, his Taliban combatant reveals himself on closer inspection to be anything but a serene exemplar of a beautiful corpse. In playing the conventions of art and art history against the documentarist ideologies of photojournalism, Delahaye explores the ambiguous posture of death, a problem similar to the one Gardner confronted in fashioning an illustration of the difference between a deceased human being, a sleeping body, and someone obediently lying on the ground in an arranged pose—an illustration that turned out to be impossible until the photographic image was complemented by a lengthy verbal narrative. If Delahaye's depiction of the fallen warrior confronts us with the most concrete, tangible evidence of the price of battle—a young man killed before his time—*Baghdad IV*, arguably the rightful inheritor of Fenton's *Valley*, may be Delahaye's most ominous war photograph because it potentially includes us in its space of uncertain possibility, a ghostly arena in which something tragic may happen, whereas *Taliban* keeps us safely outside the fray.

With all of the photographs considered thus far, visual evidence of the demise of our fellow human beings has prompted questions about fakery or stagecraft. As if Cartier-Bresson's performance art with a camera were the norm rather than the exception, an abstract or artificial element seems to haunt even the most stridently documentary impulses. The moment the photographer activates the photographic apparatus with Benjamin's "touch of the finger," a host of rituals and representational logics are set in play that are not reducible to the "un-tampered facts of the moment." From Fenton to Delahaye, an image of war's human toll must posit its own standards of reality each time it purports to present an instance of the fearful costs of combat, but this gesture invariably compromises the picture's claim to immediacy. We thus return to the original question of this chapter: What happens when we look at photographs of dead soldiers? Do we witness the tragedy of their demise or its inevitability and thus ultimately its banality? Do we see death as something to fear in our own future, or do we register such a scene as an irreducibly artificial or foreign scenario, something that only happens to other—possibly "hypothetical"—people?

In her 1973 *On Photography* Susan Sontag famously proposed that war and photography were "inseparable" because photographs allow people to satisfy their curiosity about pain and death while strengthening "the feeling that one is exempt" from such horrors, which seem to menace others' lives rather than our own.[87] The narcissism of personal immortality is thereby complemented by a depersonalization of the world, which at least in this respect is not made in our image. This is why Sontag goes on to argue that "photography's realism creates a confusion about the real."[88] To her it is clear that Roosevelt's attempt to galvanize the public during the Second World War by allowing magazines to publish pictures of dead American servicemen could never have enjoyed lasting success: "An event known through photographs certainly becomes more real than it would have been if one had never seen the photographer—think of the Vietnam War. (For a counter-example, think of the Gulag Archipelago, of which we have no photographs.) But after repeated exposure to images it also becomes less real."[89] Read today, such remarks appear to be a version of the habituation argument frequently repeated in the press, as when the *New York Times* declared that "no conflict has ever been as instantly and closely covered as the Iraq War, but access spurs complacency."[90] Yet Sontag's position is more complicated than this would allow. She treats reality as something that approaches or recedes—an event becomes "more" or "less" real—but never quite arrives, as if reality were "really" an ideal with which actuality could never completely coincide.[91] When she writes that "as much as they create sympathy, photographs cut sympathy, distance the emotions," she is describing a more negative force than mere acclimatization: "The vast photographic catalogue of misery and injustice throughout the world has given everyone a certain familiarity with atrocity, making the horrible seem more ordinary—making it appear familiar, remote ('it's only a photograph'), inevitable."[92] The closing conjunction of "familiar, remote, inevitable" is cacophonous unless one treats the uneasy juxtaposition of concepts as a symptom of psychological tensions, in which case contradiction becomes the gold standard for insight. The coupling of "remote" with "inevitable" suggests that a mechanism of denial or repression is at work. Similarly, the pairing of "familiar" and "remote" constitutes a precise description of the uncanny. However its contradictions are understood, this concatenation of psychophotographic effects suggests a volatile emotional dynamic in which photographs engage, excite, and even interrupt or confuse the onlooker, who does not enjoy the luxury of being an "objective" or "disinterested" spectator. Indeed, Sontag argues that photographs both abstract feelings from something that might impact us if we encountered it firsthand and arouse feelings that are "not those we have in real life."[93] Photographs create emotions that would not otherwise exist, producing an affective reality that is no less real than real life, to the point that "the real thing" is frequently a disappointment. Photography thus effects nothing less than a wholesale unsettling of the emotional realm of human experience, undermining the integrity of feelings, which are suddenly divided between those one has in "real life"—which are always at risk of being taken away by a photograph—and those facilitated by the photographic medium and therefore arguably not one's own at all.

It is difficult to reconcile this view of photography as both an aggressive producer and a usurper of emotional reality with another of Sontag's most controversial claims about the radical passivity that photography imposes on its viewers: "Photography implies that we know about the world if we accept it as the camera records it. But this is the opposite of understanding, which starts from *not* accepting the world as it looks. All possibility of understanding is rooted in the ability to say no. Strictly speaking, one never understands anything from a photograph."[94] This position seems to be refuted by Sontag's own argument about photography's disruption of the self-evidence of our affective life. By making us feel closer to or further from the reality from which they alienate us, photographs comment on their own reality effects and make it impossible for us to accept the world "as the camera records it." If anything, photography's primary achievement is its articulation of a "no."[95]

Aware of this tension, Sontag returned to the discussion three decades later in her final book, *Regarding the Pain of Others* (2003), in which she reconsiders two commonplaces that she defends in her earlier writings: the notion that the public's attention is shaped by images in the mass media and the notion that the public is saturated with images and thus inured to their effects.[96] At first glance this reassessment is limited in scope. She echoes her earlier position on photographically induced passivity, suggesting that a photo alone is never an interpretation and that photos "haunt" but do not facilitate understanding and must therefore be supplemented by captions or verbal analysis. Ultimately, however, uncertainties emerge. At the conclusion of the book Sontag considers a photo by Jeff Wall in order to ask what happens when contemporary artists use photography itself to explore the extent to which the modern spectator is saturated by war images.

Wall's *Dead Troops Talk* (1992) is a picture of a "battlefield" constructed indoors on a stage set. It shows, as its parenthetical subtitle explains, *a vision after an ambush of a Red Army Patrol, near Moqor, Afghanistan, winter 1986.* The Russian soldiers killed in the ambush have come back to life and are interacting with one another while Afghan soldiers nearby are looting corpses, seemingly unaware of their revivified counterparts. The image is a digital montage of a number of different shots. Although Wall went on to use digital technology in many subsequent works, this was his second piece produced through extensive computer editing and was therefore something of an experiment.[97] The result, a meticulously planned scene, is pure Hollywood, combining the zombie aesthetic of George A. Romero with the pictorial conventions of history painting and

FIGURE 3.10 Jeff Wall, *Dead Troops Talk (a vision after an ambush of a Red Army patrol, near Moqor, Afghanistan, winter 1986)*, 1992. Transparency in lightbox, 229 cm × 417 cm. Courtesy of the artist.

the visual iconography of war films. Sontag notes that Wall references Goya as an inspiration for the work, and she describes the photo as "the antithesis of a document," an instance of photography as antievidence.[98] An ironic "action" shot, the picture begs to be read as a commentary on the entire tradition of war photography.

Precisely what in *Dead Troops Talk* is (re)animated, what remains dead, if not buried, and what is revealed to have been neither alive nor dead all along? In an interview Wall states that he conceived of the new possibilities afforded by digital technology for "photographing things that could never have happened" as "kind of a release of all the constraints of the actual photography."[99] *Dead Troops Talk* is to be a photo that exhibits photography's newfound freedom from any reliance on what is empirically "given" to the lens to record. Pressing the shutter release, the act whose traumatic implications preoccupied Benjamin and Jünger even as it remained the central event in the practice of Cartier-Bresson, loses its paradigmatic status when the image—as a montage—requires many different snaps of the shutter. While the resulting picture may depict a "moment" in time, this moment is no longer coincident with the moment or moments in which the photograph was taken. The double touch of Adam's execution picture or Gardner's cameraman-as-sharpshooter motif has been abstracted out, and the image no longer serves as a testament to war photography's status as the "other" killer alongside the killings it records.

Is it accurate to call *Dead Troops Talk* a war photograph? One can readily identify analogs for Wall's image, pictures of empirical battlefields that vividly depict the suffering of soldiers. Much of Sontag's early thinking about photography was influenced by the fact that during the Vietnam War the images of the dead circulating in the public sphere were for the first time complemented by graphic pictures and videos of the severely wounded. If one of the first war photos, Fenton's image of the road in the Crimea, did not need to be staged because it involved no human figures, it could be assumed that the photographic images of the 1960s and 1970s finally achieved the same degree of self-evident authenticity because they displayed too many battered and maimed bodies to have been posed. *Dead Troops Talk* questions such an inference by reminding us that Hollywood has long been skilled at simulating gruesome physical destruction. At the same time, Wall's photograph does not comment on existing shots of "real" battlefields in an entirely serious, much less tragic, mode. Discussing the freedom that digital technology seems to afford

FIGURE 3.11 Larry Burrows, *Reaching Out*, 1966. © 2002 Larry Burrows Collection.

him, Wall observes that in facilitating "hallucinatory," "otherworldly 'special effects,'" the new process suggests the possibility of developing "a kind of philosophical comedy."[100] In *Dead Troops Talk*, he elaborates, "three characters [top center of the picture] are clowning [laughing as two try to force one to eat a rat], a kind of comedy. I didn't want the picture to be too serious; if it would be too serious, I would feel it would be monotonous and in the end would be pompous."[101]

In playing with the established idioms of war representation, Wall stages the nightmare of the battlefield by turning it into something even more dreamlike. His approach bespeaks insight into the performative dimensions of soldierly existence, as well as an acute awareness of the fine line between playacting and killing. Wall's photo asks what would happen if troops broke character and, ignoring their script, started kidding around on the field—although the picture also reminds us that this is an impulse best kept in check until one is dead. Still, Wall's remarks about his photograph may be misleading insofar as they suggest that comedy is its exclusive or even predominant mood. The two individuals tormenting a third for sport are only a small part of the scene. There is nothing light or playful about the dazed figure with a bloody head, the zombie consumed

FIGURE 3.12 *Dead Troops Talk* (detail).

by rage, or the shell-shocked men, not to mention the bodies of dead Russian soldiers sprawled on the ground. If the photograph has elements of the carnivalesque or the absurd, this is only one tone among several. In fact, the overall effect of the photo has to do more with the lack of inter-action between the different elements of the scene, as if by juxtaposing the various pictures he took separately, Wall never quite created a single image, leaving us with a display of disjointed fragments, a parody of the powers of digital photography. While Wall himself has referred to the scene as a "dialogue of the dead," the dialogue one sees in the photograph is exclusively between the dead; the Afghans and the (un-)dead show no interest in each another. The Russian soldiers are not zombies who attack the living—the scene is more like a still from a fantasy film in which one group is blithely unaware of the other's presence in the same field.

Although Sontag uses this photo as the centerpiece for her closing re-marks in *Regarding the Pain of Others*, she never acknowledges its comic features because for her the major, if not the only question presented by the picture is whether in looking at it the viewer enters into a dialogue with the dead.[102] Consequently, she dwells on the indifference of the dead to the living:

> These dead are supremely uninterested in the living: in those who took their lives; in witnesses—and in us. Why should they seek our gaze? What would they have to say to us? "We"—this "we" is everyone who has never experi-enced anything like what they went through—don't understand. We don't get it. We truly can't imagine what it was like. We can't imagine how dread-ful, how terrifying war is; and how normal it becomes. Can't understand, can't imagine. That's what every soldier, and every journalist and aid worker and independent observer who has put in time under fire . . . stubbornly feels. And they are right.[103]

With these remarks Sontag, who often goes out of her way to highlight the ways in which the photographic medium problematizes our ability to make apodictic statements about the truth of human existence, interrupts her theory of photography to offer a theory of war. Her insistence on the singular terror of "being there" and her assertion that those who have been under fire are convinced that their experience cannot be imparted to others is markedly—one might even say "violently"—normative, not least since she claims to speak not just for herself and for all those who count themselves among the living but for the dead as well.

The conception of experience Sontag sets forth is fundamentally negative since what the one who has "put in time under fire" ends up feeling is that those who have not cannot know what such an experience entails. The most powerful dimension of the experience of war is not the experience of combat itself (which becomes "normal") but the metaexperience of the fact that the experience cannot be shared. In this sense Wall's photo does say "no"—it says, "No, you do not understand what we have experienced." In Sontag's terms this may be tautological since for her experience is always the experience of a "no," an assertion of a feeling of ownership over one's experience. At the same time, her claim that the specificity of a firsthand encounter with warfare lies in how "normal" the horrors become implies that those who endure it end up having the same relationship to it as those who, in the logic of *On Photography*, become desensitized to the horrors of battle through the media's excessive coverage of them. Whether it is first- or secondhand, for Sontag the experience of war is an experience of saturation that renders the singular ordinary. Given that she elsewhere insists that photos never lose their power to haunt us, one might even propose that for her not being under fire may be the best way of maintaining an appreciation of war's uniqueness and staying focused on its horrors rather than on one's sensation of owning a memory of them that others do not. Once again, the basic paradox of the Napoleonic war watcher imposes itself: the need to make a case for the authority of an ostensibly immediate encounter with combat—the need, that is, to bear witness to one's status as a witness—compromises both the immediacy of individual experience and the priority of the immediate over the mediated.

Although Sontag made a public spectacle of putting herself under fire when she spent time in Sarajevo during the Bosnian War in the early 1990s, her argument is not simply grounded in her own empirical experience.[104] She writes from the impossible position of having "put in time under fire" and not having done so. It is as if she cannot decide whether her visit to the front does give her insights into the conflict that others do not enjoy. As a consequence she declares that what soldiers, journalists, and aid workers share is not unique knowledge of the specificity of battle but the sense that those who were not there cannot imagine what it was like. This is an odd transformation of the Napoleonic war imaginary, under whose auspices the ideal war watcher was someone with a powerful imagination rather than a superior vantage point or a powerful telescope.

For Sontag, to watch a war is not to garner sensory data about a series of events or to envision what these events must have involved but to embrace the fantasy that one can see the difference between what others can and cannot confabulate.

Although this uneasy differentiation between and conflation of what can be imagined and what one imagines that someone else can imagine is the kernel of Sontag's analysis, it also marks the point at which it becomes most difficult to know whether Wall's photo is saying "yes" or "no." This tension is most legible in a shift in her analysis such that "we" are no longer opposed to "the dead" but to their living substitutes, "every soldier, and every journalist and aid worker and independent observer who has put in time under fire." The answer to the rhetorical question "What would the dead have to say to us?" turns out to be "A great deal." Despite Sontag's declaration that the dead are "supremely uninterested in the living," in her argument they do not, as in Wall's photo, remain content to talk among themselves but rather speak to us, enumerating everything they understand that we do not.[105] Moreover, if what "we" do not "get" is the experience of being a corpse, this means that Sontag claims to write from the position of Wall's zombies, situating herself on the border between the living and the dead, since if "we . . . can't understand, can't imagine," she *can* imagine, or at least she can imagine that she can imagine enough to understand that "they [who died under fire] are right."

Sontag's conflicted reevaluation of her claim that photos cannot facilitate understanding perceptively reveals the way in which the modern mass audience to war finds itself uneasily perched between the living and the dead—unable to identify with or to speak on behalf of either order and uncertain whether battlefield spectacles are best grasped with the eyes or in the imagination. This vexed relationship between battlefield photos and figures of human agency—both in front of the lens and behind the camera—has haunted war photography from its very inception. Whether in the work of Fenton, who abstracted human forms entirely from the scene he recorded; Capa, who withdrew his own gaze from the viewfinder; or Wall, who shattered the identity between the instant of pressing the shutter release and the instant represented in the resulting image, it is difficult to distinguish between a first- and secondhand photographic "experience" of a scene of battlefield casualties. No individual image can articulate a coherent standard with which to evaluate the authenticity or power of its representations of human mortality. If photographs of fallen soldiers invite an onlooker to participate in an intimate encounter with the plight of a fellow human being, they do so by reminding the viewers that they are being confronted with something entirely outside their realm of experience, at which point the pictures' genuineness, legibility, and even their relevance have become suspect. In the end, war photography's audiences are compelled to judge each individual spectacle of destruction as something irreducibly foreign. Far from extending, augmenting, or intensifying the human gaze, the camera under fire asks why we ever thought that a gaze—human or mechanical—would help us understand war.

§ 4 Visions of Total War

In a recent American newspaper cartoon, three generals stand around a table covered with a model battlefield, complete with miniature soldiers and tanks. "No matter how long I stare at this map and these toys," one of the commanders says to his colleagues, "I just cannot understand why these people won't cooperate." At first glance the joke seems obvious: military leaders refuse to accept that people are not pawns to be manipulated, whether by a child or a godly puppet master standing above the game board. Still, the generals are not wrong to believe that force can compel the inhabitants of a village, city, or nation to obey the dictates of those with superior firepower. Human history is rife with examples of organizations, governments, and entire peoples who have been "persuaded" by such means to endure the most radical transformations in their lives. The darker side of the joke may be that those who "won't cooperate" may soon be less animate than the game pieces on the board. In this respect the more basic question the cartoon raises is whether the personal relationship a soldier or civilian has to the events and agents of warfare invariably retains a trace of the abstraction that is depicted here—indeed, whether what we call "war" is conceivable at all in the absence of some degree of formalization.[1]

On one level this line of inquiry may seem trivial, if not fundamentally misguided. How can a diagram capture the horrific physical and emotional trials that compose the traumas of combat? Surely this is the fantasy of someone condemned to a perpetual childhood of waging wars with chessboards of various sizes and colors. In fact, war's uniqueness among human endeavors has to do with the way in which it demands a new understanding of the concrete consequences that abstractions have

FIGURE 4.1　Dan Piraro, *Bizzaro Comic Strip*, 2006. Courtesy of the artist.

in the physical world. Warfare constantly imposes rapid modulations between ideas and reality, between intelligible visions and sensible phenomena; at the same time, a military program unfailingly presents itself as
a straightforward means to an end, ostensibly indifferent to the violent
conflation of the physical and the metaphysical it demands. War seems
to necessitate a reconsideration of every standard and measure of cost-
benefit analysis, leaving some observers incredulous as to the madness of
its existence, others relieved, if not pleased, by its practical utility. War
creates a vexed relationship between actual and imagined violence while

presenting the corporeal realm of suffering and death as one part of a system of means and ends that can be evaluated economically, in terms of prices paid and goals realized, and ethically, in terms of just and unjust acts. To declare that such an account of military praxis "dehumanizes" the true tragedy of warfare is to fail to recognize that militarism achieves its totalizing violence as much through the force of its abstractions as through the accuracy of its bullets and missiles.

In the Napoleonic era, at the very moment when clashes of troops were assuming unparalleled levels of destructiveness, laying waste to thousands of men by the hour, battles came to be understood as phenomena best grasped in the imagination. Although this tension left its mark on efforts to conceptualize the major European and American conflicts of the nineteenth century, it was not until the First World War that the uncertain relationship between the ideals and material actualities of warfare became the central focus as military commanders in effect became office workers. Rather than leading cavalry charges or rallying their forces to hold a crucial hillside, generals began spending their time pouring over diagrams and managing shipping plans, seeking to forestall the inevitable chaos of engaging with the enemy through endless preparation.[2] Along with the maps for the prospective clashes came detailed scripts. While Wellington had no written notes for the Battle of Waterloo, one corps of the British army had a thirty-one-page plan for the first day of the Battle of the Somme, and, as Stephen Kern relates, "one of the most widely discussed pieces of literature in British military circles before the war was a short story, 'A Sense of Proportion,' about a general . . . who made such elaborate preparations for a battle that just before its commencement he was confident enough of the outcome to spend the time fly-casting for trout."[3] The defining conceit of the Napoleonic war imaginary, the belief that one was best situated to share what a battle had been like if one had not actually seen it, reached its logical end point in the exhaustive detailing of the battle before it could take place, in the description of what it would have to be. This was not a process of articulating a hypothesis and then confirming it through experimentation. Many of the army commanders never visited the front for any length of time, if at all, so their relationship to the fighting was not dissimilar to that of the public on the home front following the story in the newspaper.

Over the past century, the Great War has been accorded enormous cultural significance as "the moment in which the new sensibility of

English—and international—modernism [came] fully into existence," indelibly altering society, consciousness, and artistic praxis.[4] These claims consistently arise because the events of 1914–1918 constituted the first major war in which the gap between "being there" and understanding something about battle by creatively conceptualizing its aims and parameters was explicitly part of day-to-day military operations, to the point that imaginative expression became as much a feature of a soldier's life as gas masks and muddy trenches.[5] Of course, if this was a war that was waged largely in and through the imagination, it was also an instance of a sublime collapse of the authority of the imagination, for there has rarely been a set of short-, medium- or long-term plans that failed so completely in their execution. In the final analysis, the First World War's cultural and aesthetic significance stemmed from the way in which it championed the creative faculties of its participants while exposing them as incomplete, insufficient, even inhumane.

When military commanders began to conceive of warfare as an activity explicitly predicated on the imaginative powers of the mind, they found that the intelligible order proved to be far more difficult to control than the material one. Ideas for battles that had not yet been realized or were not yet possible took center stage as both standards and goals, confounding the generals' ability to reflect on the implications of the battles that were taking place or had been fought. The First World War thus became the impetus for the modern theorization of total war as an exercise in imagining conflicts that could be realized in the future. Central to this discourse was the work of the German general Erich Ludendorff. Although he did not publish his book *Der totale Krieg* until 1935, he wrote as early as 1919 that "it was impossible [in the First World War] to distinguish where the sphere of the army and navy began and that of the people ended."[6] Ludendorff's concern in reflecting on the freshly concluded struggle was to demonstrate that the German war effort—which he had largely directed from 1917 to 1918—had not been absolute enough, and he sought to make the case for a still broader mobilization of Germany's human resources if the next war was to result in victory rather than defeat.[7] Recent failures were cast as the impetus for conceiving of something even more extreme, and the term *total war* came to serve as the name for a missed opportunity rather than for the conflict that had just transpired.[8] If total war was explicitly understood as an ideal that might never be realized in practice, this has not prevented several generations of historians from debating which previous wars—the Second World War, the First World War, the Franco-Prussian War, the American Civil War, the Napoleonic Wars, the Wars of Reformation—are most genuinely deserving of the title, suggesting that another cultural "achievement" of the First World War was the way in which it pitted theoretical and historical analyses of modern militarism against one another, a rift that has yet to be resolved.[9]

Ludendorff's vision of a total war was paralleled by other theorists of the interwar period, most notably Giulio Douhet, the Italian advocate of airpower and strategic bombing. In 1921 Douhet proposed that "the prevailing forms of social organization have given war a character of national totality—that is, the entire population and all the resources of the nation are sucked into the maws of war. And since society is now definitely evolving along this line, it is within the scope of human foresight to see now that future wars will be total in character and scope."[10] A century earlier Carl von Clausewitz had warned that "in the field of abstract thought, the inquiring mind can never rest until it reaches the extreme, for here it is dealing with an extreme: a clash of forces freely operating and obedient to no law but their own."[11] Clausewitz thus cautioned against trying to wage battles on the basis of assumptions about "the pure concept of war" since one was likely to lose oneself in the "play of the imagination issuing from an almost invisible sequence of logical subtleties."[12]

When such "subtleties" are allowed to run free, the results are alarming. In his 1930 essay "Total Mobilization," Ernst Jünger echoed Douhet's convictions about the power of mass social organization, declaring that "in this unlimited marshalling of potential energies, which transforms the warring industrial countries into volcanic forges, we perhaps find the most striking sign of the dawn of the age of labor."[13] Jünger's remarks indicate that the discourse of total war was grounded in the notion that soldiering had been normalized as a day-to-day economic activity, while factory and farm work had become forms of soldiering:

> [F]ollowing the wars of knights, kings, and citizens we now have wars of *workers*. [T]he image of war as armed combat merges into the more extended image of a gigantic labor process. In addition to the armies that meet on the battlefields, originate the modern armies of commerce and transport, foodstuffs, the manufacture of armaments—the army of labor in general. In the final phase . . . there is no longer any movement whatsoever—even that of the homeworker at her sewing machine—without at least indirect use for the battlefield.[14]

Stressing the everyday quality of war, Jünger sees total war as the name for a situation in which labor in the service of international conflict is no longer regarded as an unusual activity and, if anything, has acquired a permanence that makes it the norm. From this perspective the legacy of the First World War is less its extraordinary destructiveness than its enshrinement of state-sponsored combat as an integral feature of the workplace. Henceforth, the complete militarization of existence is routine.

A conflict waged under the authority of the Napoleonic war imaginary invariably manifests itself as a threat to existing concepts of war. When the hierarchy of actual over envisioned battles is upended, both the theory and the practice of war become a struggle against the systems in terms of which a war's identity and legitimacy, as well as its dreadful consequences, are understood. In the military-economic ideologies that emerged after the Great War, the paradigm of the soldier-laborer transcended any particular manifestation of work such that the material praxis of war superseded the very opposition between production and destruction, as a result of which war could no longer be distinguished from peace by the presence (or absence) of violence. Twentieth-century militarism thus unsettled the very social and cultural paradigms that aimed to judge it ethically or to explain what it meant. What a war "is" threatened to become unknowable either as an abstract philosophical matter or, practically, on the level of recognizing one when one had seen one.

If the First World War confirmed that future battles would be waged as much in the boardroom or the newspaper as on the proverbial field of combat, many of the enabling abstractions of 1914–1918 were as simple as a child's game, although they made it difficult to know what there was to see on the battlefield. The central schema was the concept of the line. As Allyson Booth describes it:

> Lines provided one of the most powerful methods of organizing the war, dictating the topography of its landscape and the imaginative habits of the men who engineered it. Both systems of defense and conceptions of offense adhered unwaveringly to an ideal of the line; men and materials were installed on the landscape according to its inevitable simplicity, and, for most of the war, muscle and guns invested the ideal with bulk and firepower.[15]

Far from simply an idea, the concept of the line influenced every level of the campaign and became the principal standard by which success or failure was to be evaluated as any given operation sought to hold the line or move it forward. As Jünger, himself a soldier at the front, explained, "[T]he tactics of the line were pursued to their logical conclusion" as men advanced in rows as if on parade and were summarily mowed down.[16] In this simple geometric realm one could counter a given line segment only by confronting it with others.

The ascendance of the line signaled that the more venerable metaphor of the theater of war was no longer functional insofar as there was nothing left to see. As Booth stresses, the journalists of the period had a sophisticated understanding of their own reliance on geometric abstractions, openly acknowledging that their reports based on linear schemas confirmed the impossibility of winning a clear view of the proceedings: "Newspaper accounts of battles used the geometry of the line to structure their accounts of what was happening at the front even while they admitted that it was almost impossible to discern what *was* happening and that what was actually being described was the visual obstructions themselves."[17] If reports about Napoleonic-era combat still relied on some minimal claim of battlefield visibility, the trench warfare of 1914–1918 saw this fiction dispensed with entirely. In *Storm of Steel*, a text based on his diaries of life at the front, Jünger describes something well beyond the mere obfuscation of one's line of sight by the smoke of weapons: "I had taken part in a major engagement without having clapped eyes on a single live opponent. Only much later did I experience the crash of the modern battle with the appearance of infantrymen on the open plane, which for decisive, murderous moments interrupted the chaotic emptiness of the battlefield."[18] In this war of attrition, in which opposing armies lived for months alongside their foes in parallel trenches a few hundred yards apart, the intermittent assaults rarely brought the combatants face to face. The British publication *War Illustrated* confirmed Jünger's impression when it attempted to excuse the absence of gripping action photos of the struggle across the Channel by explaining that "modern warfare lacks much which the battlefields of the past provided. Soldiers today are fighting enemies on the continent whom they never see."[19]

In *Storm of Steel*, Jünger searches for a narrative form with which to impart the story of what was, like the Napoleonic Wars, thought to be the most horrific war ever experienced, a conflict in which thousands of soldiers fought and died in a struggle with invisible opponents. His text lurches between vivid accounts of disaster and the inexorable reassertion of normalcy. Relating his initial brush with death, Jünger spares no details in describing his first comrade to fall, the mummified French corpses around him, and the sight of a headless torso, but his account of events quickly shifts as the ordinary preoccupations of a more leisurely life reimpose themselves. Observing a "midmorning lull" in the fighting, Jünger uses it as an opportunity "to take a good look at everything."[20] Characterizing the trenches as junk shops, he proceeds to do a little shopping, picking up some French ammunition, considering and then discarding a canteen wrapped in blue cloth, and then settling on a real find:

> The sight of a beautiful striped shirt, lying next to a ripped-open officer's valise, seduced me to strip off my uniform and get into some fresh linen. I relished the pleasant tickle of clean cloth against my skin. Thus kitted out, I looked for a sunny spot in the trench, sat down on a beam-end, and with my bayonet opened a round can of meat for my breakfast. Then I lit my pipe, and browsed through some of the many French magazines that lay scattered about.[21]

Like a dandy in the park who has just come from the tailor, Jünger is not about to let the grim reminders of human finitude around him disturb the comfort of his morning repast. He does shudder a little when he recalls that, while eating, he was attempting to unscrew what he thought was a lantern and only later realized was a live hand grenade, although the story seems designed to suggest that there is no contradiction between the dreadful business of killing and the banal experience of idly passing the time with consumer fripperies. As much as the battlefield offers a unique scene of death and destruction, it also constitutes an extension of the café or the department store. To call this tension—if it is one— feigned nonchalance or the narrator's indifference to his own mortality is too limited; nor is it just a green recruit's naïveté since the dual character of his military environment does not change as Jünger garners more experience in the course of the book.

In *The Great War and Modern Memory*, Paul Fussell proposes that Jünger's memoir is typical of first-person accounts of the First World War, which are riddled with descriptions of darkly ironic events, weird coincidences, and near-death experiences that in retrospect assume a humorous pall. Fussell catalogues a number of such incidents that sound as if they have been lifted from pulp fiction—a private recalling that the worst torture of the war was being ordered to heat water for the officers but being forbidden to gather fuel to make a fire to heat the water; another soldier remembering that the pitiful death throes of an officer's dog seemed to overshadow the human losses all around. For Fussell, these narrative schemas function as form-giving figures: "By applying to the past a paradigm of ironic action, a rememberer is enabled to locate, draw forth, and finally shape into significance an event or a moment which otherwise would merge without meaning into the general undifferentiated stream."[22] The modern industrialized battlefield seems fated to remain inchoate unless one can impose upon it a series of inversions that serve to organize what would otherwise prove impossible to share since there would be no way to figure it as a meaningful occurrence. At the same time, the irony employed to ensure that war stories remain a viable discourse risks trivializing the soldiers' trials by reducing them to humorous anecdotes rather than enshrining their ghastly specificity for posterity.

Despite what Fussell claims, the conception of war as a series of ironic vignettes was not something added to individuals' memories after the fact but rather a tension that informed life at the front as it was experienced. No longer respecting epic conventions of time, space, and pacing, the conflicts of the First World War were distinguished by their radical discontinuity, as if with each subsequent day, hour, or minute the proceedings began anew with no regard for what had just taken place. This sense of permanent disjunction jeopardized both the possibility of establishing a coherent battle narrative and the very integrity of experience as a sequential process unfolding within a combatant's interior life. The Napoleonic dilemma of how to tell a war story when there was no longer an outside to the war grew even more vexing as it ceased to be clear whether one could speak of an "inside" to the participants. The ultimate threat of the forces of schematization and formalization that defined the Great War was thus their challenge to the notion of the human being itself, which was constantly on the verge of being exposed as an outmoded abstraction, irrelevant to the day-to-day mechanics of modern military praxis.

Nowhere was this challenge more far reaching or potentially damaging to traditional conceptions of "our common humanity" than where the need to make sense of the ubiquity of death was concerned. In his 1915 essay "Thoughts for the Time on War and Death," Sigmund Freud grappled with the notion that industrialized slaughter had become a giant show threatening to consume Europe. Although it would be five years before Freud developed his theory of the death drive in *Beyond the Pleasure Principle*, he had already begun to suspect that the aggressivity that impels people to kill each other could not fully be explained by libidinal dynamics. In the first part of "Thoughts" he poses what would appear to be a simple question, asking why Europeans had become so profoundly discouraged with a world in which governments and their peoples were demonstrating a daily capacity for brutality. Rather than adding another voice to the chorus of laments about the human potential for barbarism and self-destruction, Freud claims that what was most disappointing was the depth of the disappointment that gripped society. It should not, he suggests, be surprising to see one's fellow humans sinking so low because they have never risen very high in the first place—people make a good show of keeping their instinctual impulses in check, but such drives are always present, and they can and will manifest themselves in violent forms. Although ostensibly prompted by the horrific nature of the battles that he and his compatriots were witnessing in 1915, this aspect of Freud's argument was not specific to the First World War or even to war in general. The first section of his essay thus ends on a vague note with the suggestion that a more widespread awareness of the human potential for destruction could help to dispel some of the "logical bedazzlement" that the mass violence was producing.[23]

Freud goes on to assume a more commanding tone as he refocuses on human beings' beliefs about their own mortality. The problem with a war such as the one taking place in 1915 was not that it revealed that people were capable of killing one another on a mass scale but that it undercut the customary conception of death without replacing it with a new one. Because "in the unconscious every one of us is convinced of his own immortality," it is impossible, Freud maintains, "to imagine one's own death [*der eigene Tod ist ja auch unvorstellbar*]," and "whenever we attempt to do so, we can perceive that we are in fact still present as spectators."[24] Any representation we might hazard of our own demise is fundamentally a ruse; we are depicting someone else's fall rather than our own. Under normal circumstances we cannot help but notice that people die, but Freud argues that we tend to emphasize the fortuitous quality of death, its accidental character—we transform death from a necessity into a contingency. Even soldiers on the battlefield in the midst of slaughter continue to regard themselves as secure bystanders rather than real participants in a carnage that may fell them at any moment, which is to say that the ambition to represent oneself as a spectator above the fray is nothing less than a desire to cast oneself as immortal.[25] In these terms, the mixture of sincere

curiosity and distraction that Jünger assumes in the face of efficient militarized slaughter offers evidence of what was for Freud a fundamental psychological truth about one's inability to treat oneself as an entity in need of
mourning.

In his reflections on the spectatorial dimensions of war in the cinematic age, Paul Virilio argues that threatening postures, the ability to
cow the opponent prior to defeating him, are an integral feature of warfare and that "to fell the enemy is not so much to capture as to 'captivate'
him, to instill the fear of death before he *actually* dies."[26] Freud's claim
that one cannot acknowledge the possibility of one's own demise implies
that instilling the fear of death in one's foe may be more difficult than it
first appears since no matter how convincingly one menaces one's enemies, they can understand one's threats only as a representation of someone else's impending death rather than their own. By the same token, one
tends to turn a blind eye to the illustrations one's foe has to offer of one's
own ruin. Virilio's conception of war as a clash of threatening spectacles
is thus fated to be a competition between performers who operate in parallel, each without an audience. Hobbes's account of waging war as the
demonstration of one's willingness to fight thus reaches its paradoxical
conclusion: battles are fought through efforts to make manifest a will to
kill, yet however many people die, the reality of this intent cannot be felt
by the intended recipients of the warning.

This discord at the heart of the spectacle logic of modern warfare suggests a new way to conceive of the peculiar relationship to the enemy depicted in the memoirs of the First World War. Insofar as a soldier's goal is
to force his opponents to recognize their own finitude, the soldier must
fashion a representational mode that will neither memorialize the adversaries nor allow them to live on indefinitely as the subjects of a history. In
other words, one must avoid representing one's foes in a manner that will
implicitly confirm their immortality or betray the fact that one's conviction of one's own immortality rests on the same fiction that one's opponents entertain about themselves. However perilous or traumatic combat
may be, taking part in it or describing it after the fact potentially jeopar-
dizes something that one's unconscious values far more than one's physical
well-being: its commitment to its own status as immortal. The fact that
soldiers in the trenches of France would experience the repeated threats to
their person in the form of detached, ironic vignettes that involved others'
confrontations with the haphazard but deadly whims of fate confirms the

resourcefulness of the unconscious in deflecting challenges to its fundamental conviction that death is something that happens only to others.[27]

Still, Freud was skeptical that the unconscious could maintain this
fantasy of immortality under all circumstances, arguing that in the bliz-
zard of violence that was the mechanized slaughter of the First World
War, death had begun to lose its grip on its own haphazardness:

> It is evident that war is bound to sweep away this conventional treatment of
> death. Death will no longer be denied; we are forced to believe in it. People
> really die; and no longer one by one, but many, often tens of thousands, in a
> single day. And death is no longer a chance event. To be sure, it still seems [*es
> scheint*] a matter of chance whether a bullet hits this man or that; but a sec-
> ond bullet may well hit the survivor; and the accumulation of death puts an
> end to the impression of chance [*dem Eindruck des Zufälligen*]. Life has, in-
> deed, become interesting again; it has recovered its full content.[28]

These remarks situate Freud squarely within a complex facet of modernist
discourse in which technology is first and foremost understood as a man-
ufacturer of accidents.[29] Thanks to the democratization of assembly-line
death, there is more than enough random mishap and misfortune to go
around. With so many bullets in the air, chance (*Zufall*) becomes the
norm or the general case (*der allgemeine Fall*) from which exceptions de-
viate. Freud does not claim that chance is thereby completely obliterated,
only that its scope is restricted. The decision about which bullet will hit
which soldier is still left to Fortune; the fact that a bullet will hit a soldier
is not. Viewed in the aggregate, accidents are no longer "merely" accidents,
although considered independently each one remains accidental, just as a
city full of people driving fast cars will witness more crashes than one full
of horses and buggies.

There is some ambiguity in Freud's claim that the accumulation of
bullets that find their marks ends the "impression of chance" since it is
unclear whether it is semblances of randomness or determined connections that accumulate. The ubiquity of chance events heralds the retreat
of chance, but since this retreat is itself predicated on what "seems" to be
the case, any appearance of determination may in fact be a manifestation
of contingency. This is why Freud must acknowledge that things could be
otherwise. The implied close of his sentence is that "a second bullet may
well hit the survivor"—*or not*. Suspended between the old conception
of death that we have begun to challenge and a new notion of death we

cannot entirely embrace, we struggle with and against the negation of the semblance of death's randomness as our unconscious flounders, uncertain whether it is the simulation or the faux simulation of chance that best serves its purposes in confirming its immunity to being felled in combat.[30] From this perspective Jünger's *Storm of Steel* or the memoirs Fussell describes should be seen as attempts to reassert the power of accident in the face of the predicament that Freud describes. The irony that emerges from these accounts of soldiers' brushes with death comes from a similar uncertainty as to whether the impression of luck is any evidence of its actual existence.

Throughout the first half of the twentieth century, the spectacles of mass death that characterized the First World War served as the impetus for a host of new ideas about the human being and its status as an intrinsically individual, social, or historical agent. The protofascist conceptions of the warrior-soldier that became prominent in military theory after 1918 were an attempt to respond to the material and ideological conditions that had unsettled the most basic humanist convictions about the sanctity of human life.[31] In contrast, many modernist authors reflected on the progressive potential inherent in the rethinking of liberal humanism prompted by the Great War. A writer whose work has received less attention in this context is William Faulkner.[32] In his novel *A Fable*, set in western France late in the First World War, Faulkner examines the interplay between totality and permanence that defines the experience of a world continuously at war, offering a new perspective from which to reconsider the militarized society of the twentieth century in which the human subject does not necessarily enjoy a stable vantage point from which to contemplate internal or external events. *A Fable* provides a provocative exploration of the power of abstraction and its place in modern militarism, suggesting that the warfare of 1914–1918 came to threaten the sanctity of the human being as an avatar of praxis, whether as a combatant under fire or a bystander watching from the wings. Central to this discussion is the figure of the unknown soldier, presented by Faulkner as the exemplar of wartime agency, as if the modern fighter were best understood with reference to an indefinite and ultimately unidentifiable entity.

As the title of Faulkner's novel suggests, war stories in the era of total war are distinguished by their allegorical indirection. From the outset, it is by no means clear that *A Fable* is primarily concerned with the war it overtly depicts. In proposing that nations depend on a deadlocked stalemate with their foes for their very existence, the book, written between 1944 and 1953, situates itself in the American political climate that followed the Second World War, when the interdependence of military and industrial interests became quasi-official government policy. As Noel Polk has argued:

> Though set during World War I, *A Fable* is really a meditation on the state of the world following World War II—it is a Cold War novel which dramatizes the inextricability of the military hierarchy from the political and economic and cultural hierarchies that run the world's nations, hierarchies that know no political boundaries and often connive with each other to insure [*sic*] their own survival, no matter the cost in blood to the expendable grunts who form the teeming masses of those whose lives are in their control.[33]

The suggestion that *A Fable* should be read as an allegory of the Cold War is persuasive, given the frequency with which its characters, primarily soldiers, identify an abstract entity termed "greed" as the controlling force in their lives. Human combatants are presented as existing solely in order to serve the war machine, which in turn obeys the injunctions of a military-capital logic that demands ceaseless conflict.

Still, given the thematic prominence of the First World War in Faulkner's corpus, rivaling even his interest in the Civil War, it is striking that Polk does not reflect further on the underlying reasons for aligning the First World War with the Cold War.[34] At first glance they appear to be quite different phenomena, the former's large-scale, assembly-line slaughter contrasting with the latter's uneasy coupling of localized conflicts and the constant threat of unbounded violence.[35] Common to both events, however, is the constitutive role of fantasy. Grounded in the mutual threat of two superpowers to initiate a nuclear exchange that neither would likely survive, the Cold War was the radicalization of Hobbes's conception of war as a willingness to fight rather than armed clash per se. If the ability to imagine what a battle would be like played a key role in the First World War, it became even more crucial in the Cold War, which saw the establishment of a military landscape in which possible and actual combat, threatened and realized aggression, were equally central to the military effort.[36] Representing the ultimate "nonshooting" war by the ultimate "shooting" war, Faulkner reveals that the legacy of the Great War was not its status as the standard of pure destructiveness, against which all subsequent conflicts were to be compared, but its affirmation of an imaginative logic according to which all future military triumphs or defeats would have to be assessed with reference to the fantasy of a "super conflict," which might never come to pass. This shift in the evaluation of militarism came to fruition after the Second World War and the detonation of the atomic bomb, when visions of apocalyptic scenarios became a medium of combat in their own right. By juxtaposing a period of relatively indirect conflict with the full-blown slaughter of the First World War, Faulkner exposes the degree to which modern military praxis is as much a virtual as an actual struggle. Clausewitz's ominous claim that the theory of warfare always leads to practical extremes thus finds a twentieth-century parallel in the perceived need for all war machines to establish a vision of what the ultimate war might look like.[37]

A Fable confronts the Hobbesian relationship between threatened and actual violence directly, asking whether inactivity in war is potentially as significant as even the most systematic forms of killing. The story, which takes place during a week in France near the end of the First World War, focuses on the circumstances surrounding a mutiny and its unexpected consequences. The narrative is punctuated by a series of conversations between combatants who ponder the loss of individual volition within the broader military-industrial complex that governs their existence. At first glance the characters appear to affirm the idea that clashes between nations are driven by the overarching interests of wealth. Guided by greed, war takes priority over the people who fight it, the ideals they may hope to protect, and even the notion of the enemy itself. As one officer explains, "It's not we who conquer each other because we are not even fighting each other. It's simple nameless war which decimates our ranks."[38] In these terms war is not an act of destruction but the perpetuation of life: "'The Boche doesn't want to destroy us,' said the Corps Commander, 'any more than we would want, could afford, to destroy him. Can't you understand: either of us, without the other, couldn't exist?'"[39] This delicate balance between mutually assured survival and mutually assured destruction conditions the plot throughout and forces us to ask whether the most important events are the ones that happen or those that do not.

Whether writing about the American Civil War or later conflicts in Europe, Faulkner has been seen as more interested in the repercussions of war on the home front and in war's aftermath than in the travails of modern combat themselves.[40] Consistent with this observation, *A Fable* has relatively little to say about machine guns, the disease-ridden life of the trenches, or poison-gas attacks. Scenes set on the front lines unfold as if they are taking place in a stable, almost dreamlike environment, and even the accounts of artillery fire raining down on infantrymen assume an abstract tone. Given the totalizing nature of the military arena that the book presents, there is no reason to assume that the narrative should focus on the gory details of battle, but in fact the plot is based on a bizarre event that interrupts the drudgery of the quotidian routine. On the first day of the story, a solitary French regiment refuses orders to leave the trenches and charge across no-man's land. As a consequence of this decision, the entire Western front comes to a standstill. "By simply declining to make an attack," one soldier explains, "one single French regiment stopped us all."[41] The realization that armed combat can stop—that is, that the constant fighting that is the very essence of total war can be interrupted—shocks the characters, not least because this unexpected event appears to occur both effortlessly and instantaneously. Officers and enlisted men alike struggle to come to terms with it by attempting to punish the mutineers, to celebrate or repeat the original ceasefire, or simply to recount what has transpired in new ways in an effort to conceive of the act as part of a teleological scheme that they could then treat as they would any other program. Ultimately, no one is sure whether the soldiers' nonattack should be considered an act at all. "At dawn yesterday," one officer relates, "a French regiment did something—or failed to do something which a regiment in a front line is not supposed to do or fail to do, and as a result of it, the entire war in Western Europe took a recess."[42] In declining to follow the instruction to attack, the regiment seemingly undermines the very distinction between heeding orders and ignoring them. Moreover, the single unit's behavior proves contagious, spreading to encompass the entire army. In sum, a group of soldiers institutes a local strike that quickly becomes the grounds for a general strike, fulfilling, at least momentarily, the pacifist fantasy that a war is declared to which no one comes.

If this impromptu strike seems to suggest that the rank and file have the power to interrupt the business of modern assembly-line killing, it is nonetheless far from evident that the mutiny is disruptive of the dynamic of total war, regardless of the degree to which this recess in battle unsettles any simple opposition between combat and a ceasefire. The historical analogs for the central event of Faulkner's tale certainly do not bespeak a potential to effect real peace. In the so-called Christmas Truce of 1914, soldiers from both sides spontaneously met in the no-man's land between the trenches to exchange gifts and drink toasts. This pause in the fighting is said to have grown from its original manifestation near Ypres to other areas along the front, eventually expanding to include football matches between British and German troops.[43] In April of 1917 enormous French casualties precipitated a mutiny in a regiment that spread to units in more than half the divisions of the French army; as in *A Fable*, the soldiers did not retreat but simply refused to obey orders to continue the assault.[44] Faulkner's vision of a wartime recess exploits the threat implicit in these incidents: the notion that the inactivity of a mutinous regiment could be so infectious as to contaminate the entire front and paralyze the war machine itself. It is this logic of transmission, the communicable quality of the paralysis that emerges rather than the failure to act per se, that suggests that something fundamental has gone awry with the dynamics of military agency.[45]

One of the first things we learn about the mutiny is that if the refusal of a single regiment to attack could paralyze the entire Western Front, this was not due to the crucial role played by this unit in the campaign. According to the commanding officer, the rebels' mission was "a sacrifice already planned and doomed in some vaster scheme, in which it would not matter either way, whether the attack failed or not: only that the attack must be made."[46] Given the empty nature of the operation, the commander chooses his most expendable regiment for the task, knowing that the enemy will repel them almost immediately. The mutinous soldiers' crime is not their refusal to do anything vital but their rejection of an act that will be worthwhile only insofar as it is a sham. Those who defy orders unwittingly decline to *simulate* an attack; they opt out of a plan whose success does not rely on their ability to meet or to fail to meet a goal. Neither a "real" thrust nor a real "feint," the decision to stay put when given the order to go over the top unsettles the opposition between action and inaction in war, if not the distinction between action and mock action. The regiment is called on to sacrifice itself, but in going on strike rather than striking out against their foes, the soldiers sacrifice only their own ability to serve as a sacrifice, whether in the name of their own interests or the army's.

To grasp the status of this event in Faulkner's account of the paradoxes that plague military agency in a time of total war, we must recognize that the initial mutiny gains its full significance only at a point later in the book when other soldiers attempt to repeat Monday's bizarre act of resistance but instead bring about a bloodbath. As troops from both sides venture unarmed into no-man's land, believing that they are restaging the spontaneous truce of a few days earlier, they are blown to pieces by artillery set in place by the powers that be. Throughout the novel, both the illegal act of the mutineers and the unexpected consequences of their crime receive an efficient response on the part of the army commanders. As if the top brass had been anticipating the crisis for years, one character notes, the shells at the front lines are replaced with duds immediately after the unscripted pause in fighting so that a German general can safely fly over for a conference with his French, British, and American adversaries in which they consider how best to continue the war, laying the groundwork for the annihilation of the soldiers who subsequently attempt to repeat the ceasefire. In disrupting the relationship between military action and its simulation, the spontaneous truce by the common soldiers exposes a further level of dissimulation in which the dueling military hierarchies are foes in name alone. In the larger logic of this war, genuine combat, real killing, can continue only after a failed effort has been made to repeat the original inaction (the "nonact") of Monday.

For Faulkner, this fundamental discord between agency, act, and telos is central to the events of 1914–1918, which force us to consider the "totality" or "permanence" of conflicts not simply in terms of ammunition expenditures and body counts but also as a dynamic in which any given act—active or passive—is consequential only once it has been shown to have gone beyond the limits of what was possible when it occurred. Taking Hobbes's distinction between war and combat to its extreme, an act becomes part of a total war by embodying an idea of conflict that is not yet conceivable; hence, the Monday mutiny becomes significant only with the failed effort to repeat it, which reveals that the original was merely the semblance of a ceasefire all along.[47]

This basic sequence—(dis)simulation, pseudorepetition, then destruction—dominates the novel on all levels, from local scenes to the broader chapter-to-chapter trajectory. One consequence is that each major figure in the story is accompanied by an imperfect counterpart, a faux double who supplements the incompleteness of the original subject. The most important example involves the two leaders who are punished for the Monday mutiny. The division commander, who was nominally in charge of the disobedient regiment, is shot, although in a typical rehearsal of the book's dynamic of dissimulation and destruction, he has to be shot twice, once in the back and once in the front. (In between, the first bullet wound is covered up to make the execution look more honorable.) The second leader to be punished is named the corporal. *A Fable*, an overtly allegorical work that contains few proper nouns, leaves no doubt that this young man is Jesus Christ. After he has finished scrounging up wine for a wedding and raising money to heal a blind woman, the corporal and the band of twelve mutineers he heads are executed in a ritual that follows the Gospels to the letter, complete with a barbed-wire crown of thorns. Since the novel is set in the week before Easter Sunday, we correctly anticipate the corporal's resurrection, which occurs through a series of mishaps in which his body is lost in the process of being buried, only to reappear when it is picked up by chance by some soldiers who have been instructed to find an anonymous corpse that can be interred in the Tomb of the Unknown Soldier.

Tombs of unknown soldiers first appeared in a number of nations immediately after the First World War, initially in France and Britain, then later in the United States, Italy, Belgium, and Portugal.[48] With the unprecedented casualties of 1914–1918, the task of keeping track of the fallen bodies became impossible, but the war witnessed a new degree of bureaucratic efficiency in the form of records listing the names and deployment details of every soldier. For each field littered with unidentifiable human remains, there was a precise paper trail indicating who should have been there to be found.[49] For those on the home front reading daily accounts of the horrific battles in the news, this disjunction was intensified by the sheer absence of bodies. In addition to censoring photographs of dead British servicemen, the British government decided in 1916 that deceased combatants would not be returned for burial in the United Kingdom. Most American casualties were also interred in Europe. After the 1918 armistice, this led to a host of innovations in public mourning, novel social exercises in the management of mortality designed to cope with the new forms of absent loss. In addition to inspiring the construction of tombs of the unknown soldiers, the First World War marked the first time that entire cemeteries were devoted solely to fallen soldiers so that the act of commemorating those killed in battle was overtly separated from the memorialization of other kinds of death.

A Fable identifies the dynamic of the unknown soldier as the key to the disruptions in military praxis that total war effects. In a personal letter

Faulkner explained that friends in Hollywood had suggested to him that a story about the unknown soldier might work in a film script.[50] He went on to describe the evolution of what was to become the central plot detail of the novel:

> The notion occurred to me one day in 1942 shortly after Pearl Harbor and the beginning of the last great war: Suppose—who might that unknown soldier be? Suppose that had been Christ again, under that fine big cenotaph with the eternal flame burning on it? That He would naturally have got crucified again, and I had to—then it became *tour de force*, because I had to invent enough stuff to carry this notion. . . . That's right, that was an idea and a hope, an unexpressed thought that Christ had appeared twice, had been crucified twice, and maybe we'd have only one more chance.[51]

As melodramatic as such a scenario may sound, Faulkner's comments about the novel's construction are provocative in several respects. His reference to "the beginning of the *last* great war" points toward the way in which any account of a war after the "war to end all wars" confronts the curious irony that although every war since Waterloo has presented itself as a kind of corrective to the conflicts that have preceded it, no war has convincingly brought the implied developmental sequence to a close. Each post-Napoleonic war poses as the crowning achievement of a trend toward ever-greater destructiveness without ever completing the process. In this regard Faulkner concludes the earlier quotation not by proposing that a second opportunity to recognize the messiah has been missed but by suggesting that although this second chance was not taken, there may be "another" one. The pattern of repetition is open ended. If there is always one more "last" war, there is always one more savior, or rather, one more chance to miss the savior. If total-war theorists after the First World War called for the formulation of increasingly horrific scenarios of destruction, from the perspective of Faulkner's "other chance," a "total war" is distinguished by the way in which it simultaneously avers its own absolute character and implies that the acts that constitute this absoluteness may at some future point prove to be repeatable.

With the introduction of this unorthodox messianic logic, *A Fable* upends a crucial feature of the iconography that governed the burial of dead soldiers during the First World War. As George L. Mosse has argued, "the basic design of the English war cemetery brought to life the link between the fallen and Christian sacrifice with its hope of resurrection."[52] Indeed, Mosse continues, "the design of the war cemeteries of most countries symbolized this relationship [between the fallen soldier and Christ] just as it is shown in the wall painting that . . . depicts a fallen soldier literally sleeping in the lap of Christ."[53] In *A Fable* it is not possible to rely on the figure of Christ as the salvation for every fallen man because Christ himself is lost, although nobody knows that this has happened. When Faulkner's corporal leads a mutiny, is executed, and then reappears as a corpse randomly chosen to be *the* unknown soldier, we witness not the return of the repressed but the return of the unrecognized. In this drastic reversal, the leader of the people—this nobody who becomes known throughout the entire army as somebody who led a mutiny for everybody—is reborn not as the Son of God, who ascends to the heavens, but as the material exemplar of the unidentified, i.e., as the body in the Tomb of the Unknown Soldier. Once again we encounter the book's insistent sequence of simulation, pseudorepetition, and destruction, but in this case the destruction occurs first, leaving in its wake only the simulation of a nonidentity and the repetition of a negation. Far from shedding his status as mortal in being resurrected as the Son of God, the corporal messiah returns—or apparently returns—as an unknown man, or rather as the archetype of the unknown, as any nameless man. The logic of this strange turn of events cannot be characterized as a transition from a general term to a particular one or vice versa. Neither everyman nor no man, the corporal is not really *a* man at all, and yet he is no more than *a* man, either, much less *the* man.

In Faulkner's novel, the disruption of subjective agency effected by total war turns Christ, the ultimate figure of salvation for the fallen warrior, into a generic emblem, the unknown soldier, someone with whom everyone can identify precisely because nobody knows who he is.[54] In this respect the corporal distinguishes himself as a paradigmatic agent only insofar as he functions as a figure in permanent flight from his own status as unique or ideal. In this "Great Cold War," everyone—combatants and noncombatants alike—unwittingly works toward the goal of making the unknown soldier the model of military agency. It is therefore not enough to say that the symbolic sacrifice of the corporal, the heroic leader of the resistance to war, is himself sacrificed. His loss becomes the memorialization of another kind of loss, the loss of individuality wrought by war. The failed sacrifice of the corporal to the idea of subjectivity becomes a memo-

rial to the collapse of symbolization, and the very plan of dealing with
death by making monuments to the unnamed dead becomes a testament
to the radically incomplete form that military agency has assumed. The
novel thus suggests that modern war is unique because it undermines the
illustrative function of exemplarity and the very notion of using a standard (e.g., heroism) to judge particular instances of human action. The
most pernicious "achievement" of total war may therefore be the way that
it hinders the ability of any individual agent to be representative of agency
as such.

In focusing on a curious interruption in battle, *A Fable* demonstrates
not that people are puppets of a capitalist juggernaut pulling their strings
but that modern war, far from constituting a forum in which people can
confirm their status as entities capable of shaping the parameters of their
own historical existence, has suspended the paradigms of individual and
collective agency within a virtual space in which human beings have lost
the ability to reflect on their own finitude and thus the very possibility of
coming to terms with loss. If the First World War generates unique medi-
ums of memory—military cemeteries and tombs of unknown soldiers—it
also unsettles the structures of self-determination that would allow such
memorials to facilitate a social engagement with the dead or even with
death as such. In Faulkner's vision the monuments to the fallen mark the
loss of an unknown loss (the missed messiah) rather than the catastrophic
annihilation of millions of soldiers. In this respect *A Fable* is first and
foremost an allegory of the social inability to mourn the loss of the abstraction that is the human being.[55] Instead of inviting us to take the horrific conflicts of the First World War as an opportunity for individual re-
demption or as a warning of the greater destruction that humankind may
inflict upon itself in the nuclear age, Faulkner reveals that wars are characterized as much by breakdowns in the symbolic logic of cultural self-
insight—for instance, our failure to recognize Christ ("again")—as by a
loss of control over the exercise of violence. In *A Fable*, total war—whether
in the form of the First World War or the Cold War—is not first and
foremost a folly of politicians, generals, or businessmen; it is the moment
when subjectivity itself is suspended or goes on strike. If we do not learn
from our mistakes in war, it is because war is an assault on our systems of
self-understanding.

Freud's studies of the experience of loss suggest that it is only through
pathological and ultimately failed forms of mourning that we can do

justice to an absent Other without simply forgetting it or transforming it into a version of ourselves. In other words, a "successful" process of mourning is one that does not culminate in getting over what has been lost.[56] Only by not coming to terms with death can we treat the demise of an individual or group as something other than a by-product of our fantasies of our own immortality. This is not, however, what happens in *A Fable*. Insofar as the corporal's body is interred in the Tomb of the Unknown Soldier, the failure to identify the messiah becomes the grounds for a memorial to anonymous loss, but this event is neither the end of the book nor, structurally speaking, a scene of resolution or closure. Continuing the twisted logic of near doubles, *A Fable* ends with a second ceremony for a corpse that is far from anonymous. This final scene is the funeral, ten years after the armistice, for the old general, the supreme commander of the Allied forces during the war—and, as it happens, the father of the mutinous corporal. From the perspective of this curious bond between buried father and buried son it becomes clear that the decisive confrontation in the novel occurs neither on a battlefield nor in a cemetery but in an officer's chambers, when the corporal, just prior to his execution, is brought to a hearing with his father, whom he has never met. In the book's lengthiest meditation on the long-term viability of human agency in the face of total war, the old general insists to his offspring that it is only folly that will save humanity: "[I]t's not I but you who are afraid of man, not I but you who believed that nothing but a death can save him. I know better. I know that [man] has that in him which will enable him to outlast even his wars; that in him more durable than all his vices. . . . His deathless folly [will save him]."[57]

It is far from obvious what is meant by the suggestion that human survival will be ensured by thoughtless excess or extravagance rather than by rationality or any capacity for sympathy. The old general goes on to describe a future war in which machines will have taken over as man retires from the field, too weak to continue to participate in battle:

> It will not be someone firing bullets at [man] who for the moment doesn't like him. It will be his own frankenstein which roasts him alive with heat, asphyxiates him with speed, wrenches loose his still-living entrails in the ferocity of its prey-seeking stoop. So he will not be able to go along with it at all, though for a little while longer it will permit him the harmless delusion

that he controls it from the ground with buttons. Then that will be gone too; years, decades then centuries will have elapsed since it last answered his voice; he will have even forgotten the very location of its breeding-grounds and his last contact with it will be a day when he will crawl shivering out of his cooling burrow to crouch among the delicate stalks of his dead antennae like a fairy geometry, beneath a clangorous rain of dials and meters and switches and bloodless fragments of metal epidermis, to watch the final two of them engaged in the last gigantic wrestling against the final and dying sky robbed even of darkness and filled with the inflectionless uproar of the two mechanical voices bellowing at each other polysyllabic and verbless patriotic nonsense. Oh yes, he will survive it because he has that in him which will endure even beyond the ultimate worthless tideless rock freezing slowly in the last red and heatless sunset, because already the next star in the blue immensity of space will be already clamorous with the uproar of his debarkation, his puny and inexhaustible voice still talking, still planning; and there too after the last ding dong of doom had rung and died there will still be one sound more: his voice, planning still to build something higher and faster and louder.[58]

There is nothing particularly original about the suggestion that human beings may lose the capacity to control the technological dynamics they have set in motion. As has often been observed, industrialized warfare evolved in the First World War such that "men now battled machines."[59] More than thirty years before Faulkner's novel, Thomas Edison declared that "if the United States engages in [this war], it will be a war in which machines, not soldiers, fight. . . . The soldier of the future will not be a soldier, but a machinist."[60] Beyond the simple replacement of human combatants by mechanical surrogates, modernist aesthetics described a fusion of the corporeal and the automated. As Klaus Theweleit has written, modernism's "new individual" was "a man whose physique had been mechanized, his psyche eliminated—or in part displaced into his body armor."[61] In stark contrast to such familiar models, Faulkner presents a future in which the *corps humain* remains profoundly fragile. Hardly cyborgs, the people envisioned by the old general are even less mechanized than at present. These denizens of the future do not change in response to technocratic forces they no longer control—they simply hide. Far from facilitating a refashioning of the human physique, technological know-how threatens to replace people entirely.

In the extended exchange between father and son that follows, it becomes difficult to discern who is saying what. At times the two finish each other's sentences, as if some grander script were being played out in which both were merely reciting their lines. In this vein the old general's "two mechanical voices bellowing . . . polysyllabic and verbless patriotic nonsense" can be read as a description of his encounter with his illegitimate child. In fact, the general's image of mechanical voices could be said to characterize most of the conversations in the novel, in which military men of various ranks bully and bluster their way through debates that sound as pro forma as the names of the book's characters. On the basis of this scene, *A Fable* begins to look like a story of machines rather than people, as if the military economy of 1918—and indeed of 1954—were already at risk of becoming too complex to be left in human hands.[62]

In the messiah as unknown soldier and the old general's critique of military nonsense, we have two approaches to the fundamental crisis of agency effected by the ideology of total war and its assaults on the representational logics of the human being. Still, it is by no means clear what the old general means by man's "folly." Exactly where in this monstrous mechanical din is one to hear the "enduring inexhaustible" human voice "planning still to build something higher and faster and louder"? In 1950, six years after he had begun working on *A Fable*, Faulkner accepted the Nobel Prize in Stockholm, proclaiming:

> I decline to accept the end of man. It is easy enough to say that man is immortal simply because he will endure: that when the last ding-dong of doom has clanged and faded from the last worthless rock hanging tideless in the last red and dying evening, that even then there will still be one more sound: that of his puny inexhaustible voice, still talking. I refuse to accept this. I believe that man will not merely endure: he will prevail. He is immortal, not because he alone among creatures has an inexhaustible voice, but because he has a soul, a spirit capable of compassion and sacrifice and endurance. The poet's, the writer's, duty is to write about these things. It is his privilege to help man endure by lifting his heart, by reminding him of the courage and honor and hope and pride and compassion and pity and sacrifice which have been the glory of his past. The poet's voice need not merely be the record of man, it can be one of the props, the pillars to help him endure and prevail.[63]

The Nobel address and the old general's speech are in dialogue with one another. At first glance one might assume that the novel ironizes the meaning of the address simply by citing it. The specific target of *A Fable*, however, is the inexhaustibility of voice celebrated in the acceptance speech, in particular the claim that the poet's voice can be both "the record of man" and "one of the props . . . to help him endure." Faulkner's corporal, the messiah, the spokesman for the faceless masses who long for nothing but the end of the war becomes a "prop"—a cornerstone of a memorial—only through a gross mistake that in a sort of antitransubstantiation converts his body into something to be commemorated as forgotten. In wartime the sacred and the singular (e.g., Christ) cannot be referred to as more or less than an anonymous corpse. An "inexhaustible voice," then, is what the old general would term "folly." It is a voice that mistakes itself for something more foundational than it can actually be, a voice that is permanently divided from the image it projects of itself without ever becoming a memorial to loss.

According to the total-war theorists who emerged in the wake of the First World War, the principal task of the modern warrior is to be victorious in the trenches *and* in the imagination, to rule both actual wars and the visions of more horrible wars yet to come. In *A Fable* such a power appears to be won only at the price of giving up on the ability to distinguish a singular event from one that is fated to be repeated again and again—be it the return of the messiah or the killing of a nameless, faceless infantryman. Does this mean that the novel offers an alternative to Jünger's fantasy of total mobilization, in which the "surging forth of the masses" reveals "a new form of armament . . . one which strives to forge its weapons from purer and harder metals that prove impervious to all resistance"?[64] Or should this blurring of the generic and the unique be viewed as a confusion that renders society vulnerable to the emergence of precisely the kind of collectivity that Jünger or Ludendorff celebrated? Alternatively, is *A Fable* ultimately no more than an endorsement of individualism, its presentation of the messiah corporal serving as a reminder that war's fundamental horror is its disruption of the dynamics of the liberal self?

In fact, *A Fable* does more than any of these conclusions would suggest. By challenging the notion that humankind's best defense against total war is its "inexhaustible voice," the novel warns that a critique of militarized society must go beyond simple condemnations of the permanent war economy if it is to avoid becoming one more mechanical outlet babbling "verbless, patriotic nonsense." The modern war machine wages material struggles to coordinate bodies, machines, and fantasies; to this end it must constantly articulate visions of unthinkably destructive conflicts. In response, *A Fable* asks us to pursue a conception of humanity's future that is not based on the imaginative prophecies of impossible battles yet to come. The search for "total" conflict structures our models of subjectivity just as much as it sets the agendas of military and industrial planners. Ideologies of war spectatorship have as much to say about who we are as we do.

When Faulkner began *A Fable* at the close of the Second World War, the logic of Napoleonic spectatorship remained in full force. The catastrophic destruction of 1944–1945 appeared to be the result of the predicament Walter Benjamin described in the late 1930s in his famous essay "The Work of Art in the Age of Its Technological Reproducibility": " 'Fiat ars—pereat mundus,' says fascism, expecting from war, as Marinetti admits, the artistic gratification of a sense perception altered by technology. This is evidently the consummation of *l'art pour l'art*. Humankind, which once, in Homer, was an object of contemplation for the Olympian gods, has now become one for itself. Its self-alienation has reached the power where it can experience its own annihilation as a supreme aesthetic pleasure."[65] In *The Iliad* the warring Greeks and Trojans are observed by the gods on Mount Olympus, but in the mid-twentieth century, human beings come to enjoy the spectacle of their own destruction. Did people savor the show from safely above the fray, like Homer's deities, First World War generals in their war rooms, or Freud's ever-confident unconscious? Or were the spectacle's viewers always at the front in a grisly pageant in which they were both onlookers and participants?

Twenty years after the publication of *A Fable*, Thomas Pynchon's *Gravity's Rainbow* continues Faulkner's reflections on the relationship between total and cold warfare and its implications for the battlefield audience. Offering an extreme vision of modern warfare as a struggle for information, Pynchon follows Faulkner in devoting little attention to scenes of combat as he explores the latter part of the Second World War in Europe, with particular emphasis on the mythologies of military technology embodied in the Nazi V-1 and V-2 rocket programs. Working with a series of motifs from mechanics, optics, and electricity, *Gravity's Rainbow* radicalizes the venerable figure of the theater of war into an all-encompassing military cinema, a forum so comprehensive that it allows one character to claim that the conflict with Hitler's Germany was ultimately not political in nature: "It means this War was never political at all, the politics was all theatre, all just to keep the people distracted . . . secretly, it was being dictated instead by the needs of technology . . . by a conspiracy between human beings and techniques, by something that needed the energy-burst of war."[66]

Against a backdrop of modernist topoi that includes the mechanization of chance and the concern that wartime technology may hijack what would formerly have been a clash between human beings, *Gravity's Rainbow* obsessively introduces details of German expressionist and classical Hollywood cinema, identifying the history and culture of the film industry as the true heart of the Western war machine.[67] The book interpellates its reader as a member of a film audience, particularly in the closing pages, when the narrative makes a jump forward to the 1970s and describes an audience in a Los Angeles movie theater at the instant that a falling missile is about to make contact with the ceiling above them. The projectile is both an impossible blast from the past—a V-2 rocket, the preparations for whose mid-1945 launch have been extensively detailed—and a present-day atomic bomb, whose impact will bring to a close the metaphorical trajectory of weapons technology that unfolds throughout the book, from Nazi missile programs to the Manhattan project and beyond. The novel does not, however, end in apocalypse, for the narrative suspends us at the moment at which the missile "reaches its last unmeasurable gap above the roof of this old theater."[68] Perched at an infinitesimal remove from the completion of our journey down the road to nuclear holocaust and *total* total war, we, the readers as audience members, are informed by the narrator that "there is time, if you need the comfort, to touch the person next to you."[69] We are then invited to participate in a sing-along and helpfully offered the text of a hymn composed by an ancestor of the novel's main character. The book concludes with a dash as we are called to join our voices in unison: "Now everybody—."[70]

Established as both the novel's narrator and the principal object of its narrative at the moment just prior to decimation, the readers of *Gravity's Rainbow* become the true viewers of modern warfare only at the instant that they find themselves on the brink of disappearing in a mushroom cloud hand in hand with the film industry itself—the ultimate made-for-Hollywood catastrophe. The coincidence of media and spectatorial destruction is ambiguous in both tone—uncertainly tragic, comic, or tragicomic—and consequence, since we are either annihilated with the city or reminded that we are only reading a book about watching a film about the annihilation of books, films, and audiences. Whatever the future holds, it is present only in its permanent deferral. The close of *Gravity's Rainbow* delivers a "posthumous shock," not to a moment from the past captured in a film still but to the "next" moment—the moment of a detonation that is never quite at hand. In Pynchon's Cold War we do not experience our "own annihilation as a supreme aesthetic pleasure"; rather, we find ourselves perpetually confronted with a miniscule—and possibly entirely imaginary—border that divides certain death from a death that can never arrive. Insofar as fantasies of planetary destruction have become a key feature of warfare, it is difficult to know what forces—human or technological, political or aesthetic—require "the energy-burst of war" and whether the spectacle-intensive threats of modern weapons are to be feared or embraced as evidence that our imaginative capacities, what Faulkner's old general called our "deathless folly," will save us after all.

At the end of his "Work of Art" essay, Benjamin declared that "all efforts to aestheticize politics culminate in one point. That one point is war."[71] Faulkner and Pynchon suggest that to respond, as Benjamin insists we must, by "politicizing art" means understanding that the spectatorial dynamics of militarized culture are as crucial to its termination as they are to its perpetuation.[72] In modern warfare, fantasy and abstraction have profound material consequences as social, economic, and technological forces. Absent some acknowledgement of the powers of simulation and irony that shape the battlefield, our efforts to bring the era of total war to a close are condemned, as the old general warns, to verbless patriotic nonsense.

Conclusion

Old Wars, New Wars

> In fact, the peace of which most men talk . . . is no more than a name; in real fact, the normal attitude of a city to all other cities is one of undeclared warfare.
>
> — Plato, *Laws*

> I just want you to know that when we talk about war, we're really talking about peace.
>
> — George W. Bush

In May 2008, a couple checking their voice mail discovered a message from their son, a U.S. soldier serving a tour of duty in Afghanistan. During a firefight, the redial function on the soldier's phone had accidentally been triggered, and for several minutes a connection was established with his parents' home line. The resulting recording consisted primarily of the sounds of gunfire and calls for ammunition, with an ominous "Incoming!" just before the link was cut.[1] With no warning, a war almost seven thousand miles away had invaded their home. This story illustrates the odd predicament that confronts us in the twenty-first century as we find ourselves only one haphazard push of a button away from audio or video contact with a firefight. The dissolution of the battlefield's boundaries seems to be complete; even at the farthest remove from a hostile engagement, the would-be civilian is unable to escape war's sights and sounds. At the same time, the very accuracy with which modern technological convenience imposed a record of sensory data on these parents—this was not a "wrong" number—calls attention to the mediated nature of their encounter with the battlefield. What these parents received was not "live" physical data from the engagement but a digital reproduction that existed only because of an accident involving a poor keyboard-lock function. Having "missed" the chance to hear the sounds of the event as they took place, they had to wait to learn what the transmission meant. Listening to the message, they had no way of knowing whether it had outlived their son.[2] Whatever this communiqué imparted, it was not the gist, much less the details, of what had taken place in Afghanistan.[3]

While the erosion of battlefield boundaries in the modern era has seen the advent of periods of widespread violence and destruction, it has also meant that combat's very ubiquity in the public sphere has rendered it less pressing, even invisible. This is not to discount the substantial transformations in information technologies that today alter the mass audience's relationship to the spectacle of warfare on an almost daily basis. With each new controversy surrounding the dissemination of photographs, videos, or classified documents via the Internet, there is a surge of optimism as members of the press corps and whistle-blowers declare that it has become possible to monitor a war "live," as it happens, and that the public will finally be able to grasp what it really means for soldiers to kill one another. An equally vociferous chorus of detractors laments such changes, arguing that in an age in which secrecy has become obsolete, military operations may no longer be possible. Despite the passion that informs these clashing perspectives, there is little evidence that heightened access to images and information about contemporary battles has led to a more intensely engaged viewing audience. Studies of the media's coverage of recent warfare in the Middle East suggest that the Western news consumer treats videos of embedded reporters or live exchanges of machine-gun fire with no greater interest than stories about bloodless election frauds or the antics of political leaders on vacation, and as combat operations drag on and ratings drop, the media respond by sharply curtailing their reporting.[4] A similar situation prevails with independent documentary films, which have drawn notoriously few viewers—the U.S. war in Iraq, for example, has proved itself to be "hell on the bottom line at the box office."[5]

One explanation for this disconnect between supply and demand is that the public has been conditioned by the entertainment industry to expect a particular kind of visual spectacle that only Hollywood can provide. Recent fictional films about the U.S. military presence in the Middle East have fared considerably better than their documentary counterparts, continuing a tradition by which the movie industry has dictated the standard and format of how the horrors of war's realities are to be packaged, sold, and consumed. As Thomas Doherty has argued, the Second World War saw "the motion picture industry become the preeminent transmitter of wartime policy and a lightning rod for public discourse. . . . Hereafter, popular art and cultural meaning, mass communications and national politics, would be intimately aligned and commonly acknowledged in American culture."[6] Given the degree to which the news media now participate in almost all areas of popular culture, this observation seems obvious, but its implications are far from self-evident. While the audience for *Saving Private Ryan* (1998), Tom Hanks's film about D-day and the Allied invasion of Europe, was at least a hundred times larger than the combined audiences for all the documentary footage of the same events viewed in the previous half century, this was a testament neither to the ingenuity of Hanks's production nor to its fidelity to the historical record. The firsthand experience of battle has become such a fluid, volatile commodity that it is difficult to identify the origin of any putative "reminiscence," whether one examines the psyches of individual war veterans or the editing room of a cinema studio. Like most of the movies of the last fifteen years that have been celebrated for their realistic depictions of combat, the firefights in *Saving Private Ryan* were based on the perspectival logic and graphic design of video games, the very games now used by the military to train army recruits. Completing the circle, these soldiers evaluate the severity and authenticity of their time on the battlefield by deciding how closely it resembles their prior experiences with PlayStation. Far from an irreducibly personal ordeal, absolutely singular in its particularity and specificity, "being under fire" has become a generic electronic good that is shuttled between various broadcasting and consumption formats, from films and news clips to computer readouts on tanks or military command centers, Xbox cartridges, and wartime video diaries.

If an increasingly broad array of traditional and nontraditional media outlets have access to battlefields and the means to transmit audio-video information about the events that take place there, it should not be assumed that a larger number of civilians are consequently now privy to what is "really" going on. Reporters and military censors craft journalistic representations of combat, although less to protect state secrets than to make their shows conform to audience expectations. Popular taste demands not so much that the news about current military operations comprise fearful spectacles of destruction but that it change regularly and be presented in a neatly organized narrative with a well-defined conclusion.[7] As NBC's former Baghdad correspondent Mike Boettcher puts it: "Americans like their wars movie length and with a happy ending. If the war drags on and there is no happy ending, Americans start to squirm in their seats. In the case of television news, they began changing the channel when a story from Iraq appeared."[8] A successful war story is distinguished by the absence of anything unexpected or out of the ordinary or at least the absence of anything unexpected or out of the ordinary to which the audience is not already accustomed.[9] In surveying the ostensibly "nonfictional" representations of combat on offer, it becomes difficult, if not impossible, to distinguish the production and reception of news about battles from the processes of standardization and commercialization that inform the treatment of any current event. War reporting lacks an aesthetic to call its own. Documentary footage from the Middle East tends to be cut and narrated as if it were part of a tourism infomercial, while the presentation of scenes of devastated cities or villages on the evening news mimics the Weather Channel's coverage of hurricanes and tornadoes. In theory, the battlefield is a unique conjunction of power and tragedy, design and chaos; in practice, it has become anything but a paradigmatic spectacle and is routinely subordinated to other representational dynamics.

Even the media's attempts to develop "something new" for their war coverage often rely on time-tested motifs. In the 1991 Gulf War, the much-vaunted CNN video transmitted from the nose of a bomb as it fell from a plane onto a building graphically completed the fusion of military and surveillance forces by miming a quarter-century-old scene from Stanley Kubrick's *Dr. Strangelove*, in which a bomber pilot has a front-row seat to the destruction of the world as he rides his atomic payload to the ground like a rodeo cowboy on a bucking bronco. Popular reaction to the CNN clip was tepid, primarily limited to the comment that it "looked like a video game." A little more than a decade later, efforts to sell the Second Gulf War were similarly disappointing. As Nicholas Mirzoeff has suggested, despite the boasts of the major news services that they would provide the public the most complete access to soldiers under fire imaginable, in the 2003 U.S. invasion of Iraq,

> more images were created to less effect than at any other period in human history. What was in retrospect remarkable about this mass of material was the lack of any truly memorable images. For all the constant circulation of images, there was still nothing to see. The relative anonymity of the war images must then be understood as a direct consequence of the media saturation. To adapt a phrase from Hannah Arendt, the war marked the emergence of the banality of images. There is no longer anything spectacular about this updated society of the spectacle.[10]

Building on the observation that the entertainment and advertising industries have long set the standards for reality itself, Mirzoeff proposes that in the current global media culture, a superabundance of visual data fails to produce even a few distinguished exemplars since people "use images as they do other commodities: as needed, and without reverence."[11] Dominated by issues of utility, the individual observer's relationship to photographs or video clips tends to be highly ironized and is only secondarily influenced by an assessment of their referential reliability. This dynamism and fluidity of digital capital means that distinctiveness is now a side effect of a larger economy in which a generalized substitutability and anonymity predominate.

Mirzoeff's argument is the latest in a long line of observations about the saturation of the social realm by images. Since the Vietnam War, when color photos and videos of severely injured and dying American servicemen first became widely available on the evening news, the public's blasé attitude toward the daily dose of horrors-on-tap has been explained by the notion that an excess of information about the suffering of others desensitizes its audience, which becomes so familiar with scenes of atrocity that it no longer finds them arresting. Repetition breeds complacency, and finally indifference. The same question that preoccupied Wordsworth and Coleridge at the turn of the nineteenth century as they witnessed the emergence of mass media culture continues to impose itself: In the midst of a triumphant schlock culture, do the information media still retain the power to shock?

Some social scientists have seen the lukewarm success of recent conflicts as media products in a very different light, as a confirmation of war's declining significance. They argue that over the past twenty years we have entered a new epoch in which governments no longer have a monopoly on deployments of armed forces. Such operations are now waged on a smaller scale by terrorists, guerilla organizations, and corporate mercenaries. To the extent that nation-states continue to be the principal agents in armed engagements, it is because they are involved in police operations or ridden by civil war, not because they are pursuing international aggression.[12] "War," as John Mueller bluntly formulates it, "is in the process of . . . disappearing altogether."[13] On this account, the centuries during which countries were pitted against one another in formal clashes with clearly defined beginnings and ends (winners and losers, creditors and debtors) were an anomaly, a brief period of exception preceded, and now to be followed, by centuries of poorly defined strife.[14]

Considered positively, this obsolescence of war as it was conceived of during the past two centuries marks nothing less than the disappearance of one of humanity's worst nightmares, leaving us with the comparatively minor problem of responding to a host of criminal operations. Supporters of such a view defend their optimism by pointing to the supposed triumph of democracy around the globe and touting the now popular view that governments that come to power through free elections do not wage war against each another.[15] Considered negatively, the disappearance of the nation-state's monopoly on war is seen as the beginning of a backward slide into a world no longer governed by the social contract, if not a Hobbesian war of all against all. Rather than regarding "irregular wars" as a collection of limited conflicts scattered around the globe that have relatively little to do with one another, these ongoing—potentially intractable and interminable—struggles can be characterized as symptoms of an underlying systemic violence that makes a mockery of claims for the rationality and stability of civilization.[16] In this context the Thirty Years' War is sometimes invoked as an analog for contemporary events, a conflict in which a variety of different groups saw the instigation of hostilities as a superior option to peace. Since the sociopolitical order of the existing states had not yet acquired a fixed form, the result was a lengthy mix of clashes between protonational groups, religious entities, and private enterprises that continued with no logical endpoint because no warring party saw its cessation to be in its interests.[17]

Critics of this bleak view respond that the nation-state's loss of its monopoly on large-scale armed violence is the first step in the emergence of a stronger international rule of law based on the enforcement of human rights treaties and the Geneva Conventions.[18] They also suggest that the globe is becoming more peaceful. While the cooperation between governments and multinational corporations characteristic of post-1945 "military Keynesianism" has been described as a permanent war economy, U.S. military spending as a percentage of the GDP was lower in the first decade of the new millennium than at any time since 1940. This point can be complemented by the coldest of evidence, body counts. In *The Better Angels of Our Nature: Why Violence Has Declined*, Steven Pinker amasses a host of statistical data to argue that today a smaller percentage of the world's population falls victim to violent death than ever before and that "we may be living in the most peaceable era in our species' existence."[19] If an upsurge in the documentation of armed combat in the form of graphic photos and videos seems to contradict this claim, Pinker counters that the modern media's tendency to focus on suffering and death has created a misleading picture of the human social condition, which is anything but inherently bellicose.[20] The public's reluctance to engage with news reports about war as if they were deserving of its undivided attention would thus be evidence of its ability to make informed decisions about the relative significance of the material available for its consumption. If people do not obsess about such representations of violence, it is because they are aware, whether consciously or unconsciously, that they are not of paramount importance. In this vein, many contemporary academic analyses of both still and moving images of battlefields have become more concerned with the specificity of the informational medium—photography, television, the Internet—than with what it imparts, treating war as merely one object of representation among others rather than as the defining phenomenon of the age.[21]

Pinker's statistical evidence for social stability can be viewed in a different light, as the product of an Enlightenment control fantasy that is fundamentally militaristic in nature. As Michel Foucault has written:

> Historians of ideas usually attribute the dream of a perfect society to the philosophers and jurists of the eighteenth century: but there was also a military dream of society; its fundamental reference was not to the state of nature, but to the meticulously subordinated cogs of a machine, not to the primal social contract, but to permanent coercions, not to fundamental rights, but to indefinitely progressive forms of training, not to general will but to automatic docility.[22]

If declining military spending and mortality rates can be invoked as evidence of an emerging reign of peace, they may also be a sign of the automatic docility Foucault describes, the military's dream of a perfectly regulated biosphere. In these terms, an exclusive focus on the suffering and death precipitated by war is misleading not, as Pinker surmises, because it makes human societies appear more warlike than they actually are but because it takes for granted that war's force and influence manifest themselves solely in the form of the physical violence that is effected by bullets and bombs. War's complete permeation of social experience means that it is no longer possible to isolate a battlefield image from everything else.[23] Broadcasts from webcams held by correspondents atop tanks in the Middle East fail to enthrall or shock because they are no more or less gripping, horrifying, or run-of-the-mill than what the Western information consumer encounters everywhere on a daily basis at home, in the streets, or at the office. In this view war is no longer a part of culture—it is the culture.

These divergent accounts of warfare's omnipresence or obsolescence bespeak a fundamental uncertainty about whether war should be conceptualized by analogy with peacetime social and political processes or whether sociopolitical dynamics must be seen as products of a more fundamental military praxis. The ostensible ubiquity of war spectators does not in itself resolve the dispute because recent history suggests that even in circumstances of the most extreme physical and psychological privation, it is difficult to decide what the modern war audience is or is not seeing and why. To some degree, watching war seems possible only insofar as one can continue to maintain the illusion of safety enjoyed by turn-of-the-nineteenth-century Britons, the notion that as terrible and all-consuming as war may be, it is somehow still somewhere else and thus someone else's problem.

One of the contemporary authors who has most extensively explored the relationship between individual and collective memory and the psychosocial dynamics that inform a population's experience or nonexperience of unchecked violence is the writer and academic W. G. Sebald. In a series of lectures he delivered in 1997, Sebald observed that "people's ability to forget what they do not want to know, to overlook what is before their eyes, was seldom put to the test better than in Germany" at the close of the Second World War.[24] At issue was not simply the difficulty of accepting moral responsibility for the crimes of the Third Reich but also the failure to acknowledge that the city in which one lived was no longer standing: "People walked 'down the street and past the dreadful ruins,' wrote Alexander Döblin in 1945 after returning from his American exile to southwest Germany, 'as if nothing had happened, and . . . the town had always looked like that.'"[25] If this degree of denial was possible in the face of near total desolation, the twenty-first-century war watcher's seemingly casual, if not indifferent, regard for contemporary battlefield spectacles may be a less pronounced form of disavowing reality—a willingness, in the simplest terms, to look the other way.

Is it possible to distinguish between true indifference and the self-protective defensiveness of simulated indifference that bespeaks concern rather than the absence thereof? Sebald entertains several explanations for the German public's seeming lack of interest in the devastated landscape in which it found itself in 1945, including the feelings of shame experienced by the survivors, the forces of collective repression that abstracted any affective reaction to the surrounding desolation from the public sphere, and, finally, trauma: "Obviously, in the shock of what these people had experienced, their ability to remember was partly suspended, or else, in compensation, it worked to an arbitrary pattern."[26] This last point explains the dearth of firsthand accounts of the Allied bombing raids that leveled Germany's cities, as *Trümmerliteratur* (rubble literature) "proves on closer inspection to be an instrument already tuned to individual and collective amnesia, and probably influenced by preconscious self-censorship—a means of obscuring a world that could no longer be presented in comprehensible terms."[27] If this were the full extent of Sebald's argument, it could easily be situated within the traditional line of sociological and psychological analyses of posttraumatic stress disorder. However, his diagnosis of individual and collective trauma, dynamics over which people by definition have no conscious control, is only one strand of an argument that is equally driven by a need to condemn German writers of the postwar period for their failure to overcome the forces of denial and describe what life in Germany was really like: "When we [Germans] turn to take a retrospective view, particularly of the years 1930 to 1950, we are always looking and looking away at the same time. As a result, the works produced by German authors after the war are often marked by a half-consciousness or false consciousness designed to consolidate the extremely precarious position of those writers in a society that was morally almost entirely discredited."[28] As the slide from "half-consciousness" to "false consciousness" in explaining the "inability of a whole generation of German authors to describe what they had seen" suggests, the psychological paradigm on which Sebald relies is uneasily paralleled by an ethico-political one.[29] At once judging and not judging his compatriots, Sebald attributes the blindness to history of his fellow Germans to forces both within and outside their control, as if he cannot entirely renounce the military dream Foucault describes of a machinelike society that soldiers on under any circumstances, even when the destructive powers of the military have pushed that society to the brink of disappearing altogether. While Sebald leaves no doubt that many traumatized survivors were simultaneously beset by the impossibility of recollection and the recollection of impossible experience, he remains intrigued by the fact that we cannot know what, if anything, Germans in 1945 or 1946 saw when they took stock of their immediate environment. In the end he is unable to relinquish his conviction that some of them should have at least written about their experiences *as if* they had seen more.[30]

In the post-Napoleonic era, the incomplete transition from a society of spectacle to a society of surveillance means that the values of both visual orders constantly vie for preeminence. Sebald's mix of psychological and ethical paradigms typifies the uneasy coexistence of these systems. The fact that for him war is as much about what one is supposed to see or experience as what one does see or experience in no way contradicts the realities of personal trauma, whether they be mental, emotional, or physical. Nonetheless, Sebald does implicitly posit a standard, a "trained" gaze, as Foucault would have it, that can be enthralled by the spectacle of a nearly obliterated society without being overwhelmed, witnessing the destruction of almost everything without thereby being reduced to nothing.

Bearing in mind Mirzoeff's account of our contemporary society of the unspectacular, the most important aspect of Sebald's analysis may be its invitation to look with a new eye at what the term *banal* means when it is used to describe scenes of wartime destruction. Sebald emphasizes that the firsthand accounts of the air raids over major German cities that did emerge were ridden with clichés: "The reality of total-destruction, incomprehensible in its extremity, pales when described in such stereotypical phrases as 'a prey to the flames,' 'that fateful night,' 'all hell was let loose,' 'we were staring into the inferno,' 'the dreadful fate of the cities of Germany,' and so on and so forth. Their function is to cover up and neutralize experiences beyond our ability to comprehend."[31] The startling thing about this passage is that Sebald does not ask how one can represent the unrepresentable or fail in trying but instead speaks critically about the domesticating force of misrepresentations of the unrepresentable. Despite the avowed impossibility of coordinating perception, memory, and conscious reflection when faced with "the reality of total-destruction," he implies that in grappling with the unfeasible one can err in different ways, some of which are more laudable than others. Each time Sebald accords a psychological explanation decisive authority (e.g., with the claim that the abundance of clichés in these reminiscences is symptomatic of the psychic defense mechanisms of those who endured the bombings), he tempers its explanatory power by hinting at the presence of an alternative paradigm, in this case with the implicit suggestion that a different language would more powerfully express the extremity and incomprehensibility under discussion, as if the ultimate standard were an aesthetic form rather than the degree of suffering. Describing the terrible costs of war inexorably raises methodological issues about representation that begin to "neutralize" the original terms of the argument.

Most interdisciplinary studies of trauma narratives over the past twenty years have explored the disjunction between events and the experience of them by focusing on people impacted firsthand by overwhelming horrors such as child abuse, war, or genocide. In assessing the legacy of the Napoleonic war imaginary, however, it is precisely the uncertain delimitation of "firsthand" that is at issue.[32] While few, if any, psychiatrists would regard the mediated forms of military experience transmitted through written accounts, photos, or videos as a major cause of posttraumatic stress disorder, the clinical diagnostic criteria for PTSD, which include witnessing such events, do not rule out such a possibility.[33] In this vein, a critical text such as Mirzoeff's, which sees the society of the spectacle replaced by the society of the unspectacular, may be performing the indifference it identifies in others, mistaking the traumatic bifurcation of consciousness and memory for the unremarkable—a traumatized theory rather than a theory of trauma. Even casual war spectatorship may have real psychic costs.[34]

Although he flirts with such a conclusion, Sebald does not ultimately need to endorse it for the simple reason that the psychological complexities of the narratives of postwar German survivors are thrown into relief by the overwhelming physical evidence of the devastation the German populace endured. No inhabitant of Germany's cities could claim to have had a purely "mediated" relationship to the fiery horrors. In contrast, contemporary observations about war's violent impact on those who never come within a thousand miles of a battlefield have no comparable backdrop of decimated cityscapes on which to rely. Inspired by Foucault's diagnosis of the fundamentally militaristic nature of Western society, some scholars nonetheless argue that warfare completely permeates the fabric of

our culture. Following Paul Virilio in highlighting the near identity of
military and civilian communications and representational media, Friedrich Kittler maintains that it has become increasingly difficult to distinguish between the experience of armed combat and the experience of
daily life. The question is whether such a position expands the concept of
warfare to the point of negating its uniqueness. As Geoffrey Winthrop-
Young writes:

> When media scientists use the term [*war*], it is often not clear whether they
> are talking about a military scenario—ranging from mobilization to actual
> combat—or whether they are trying to find an expression that adequately
> conveys the sensory overload and its long-term psycho- and sociogenetic
> impact we now experience on a daily basis. Reading Kittler, it appears that
> these days we are all exposed to what Jünger could only witness in the heat
> of the battles of World War One. Seated in front of terminals, movie screens,
> or loudspeakers, equipped with microphones, headphones, or VR headgear,
> we all experience—to quote the Jünger title Kittler is fond of quoting—
> "combat as inner experience (*Kampf als inneres Erlebnis*)." At this point, the
> theory busily shuttles to and fro between the literal, the more extended, and
> the clearly metaphorical meanings of war or combat; it therefore is necessary
> to understand how exactly the theorists in question deal with the overlap-
> ping of war and mediated sensory overload.[35]

The suggestion is that Kittler's argument may remove the grounds for
distinguishing between types of violence or even between violence and
nonviolence. On this account, to aver war's ubiquity is to elide its dreadful specificity. Kittler might respond that far from trivializing the severity of modern war, he identifies its profound impact on every aspect of
daily life, whereas the effort to preserve an account of the unique horrors
of "actual combat" may in fact achieve the opposite by characterizing
omnipresent violence as something that can be delimited and compart-
mentalized. Wherever one's sympathies lie in this debate, Winthrop-
Young's commentary is revealing in its insistence that we must take care
not to shuttle "to and fro" between the literal and metaphorical meanings of war without regard for their differences. In chiding the theoretician for being too theoretical, Winthrop-Young shifts the discussion
from the daily experience of violence to an argument about controlling
words. This new field of inquiry is difficult to navigate, not least since
any account of the force that might allow one to take charge of one's
terms and systematically distinguish the literal from the "more extended"

or the "clearly metaphorical" meanings of war will prove theoretical in the extreme.

In the introduction to this book we saw that, for Clausewitz, military praxis, conceived of as a programmatic program with a predictable grammar and logic, was invariably haunted by rhetorical forces, "friction" and "fog," that it did not entirely control. With this insight, *On War* uncannily anticipated the enduring conflict between a belief in the privileged nature of battlefield experience and the inherently mediated, even virtual quality of the spectacles of modern war. Clausewitz suggested that to describe the forms of activity peculiar to military praxis, it was necessary to take stock of a metaphorical violence whose relationship to the military enterprise would not be easily explained. In his rejoinder to Kittler, Winthrop-Young unwittingly confirms Clausewitz's thesis that war is always a struggle over what will count as war, and in this sense it is always a contest about the meaning of metaphor. To say that the concept of war is being used too broadly or too metaphorically is to forget that in Clausewitz's terms no definition of war is ever literal enough.

Nowhere are the implications of this insight clearer than when scholars intent on fashioning a new understanding of war that will capture the uniqueness of twentieth- and twenty-first-century military praxis attempt to embrace or reject Clausewitz's lapidary pronouncement that war is "a mere continuation of politics by other means."[36] For authors of all ideological stripes, coming to terms with this canonical proposition is never simply a matter of deciding whether Clausewitz "got it right." Whether seeking to applaud the truth of his insight or to correct his errors, Clausewitz's readers consistently aim to rival his stylistic virtuosity by recasting his elemental formula in even more striking terms. Beyond the obvious inversion ("politics is a mere continuation of war by other means"), the literature abounds with catchy glosses and parodies ranging from Baudrillard's "war is the absence of politics pursued by other means" to Virilio's "the cinema is war pursued by other means."[37] If these gestures were merely products of mimetic rivalry, they would be of only marginal interest. For Clausewitz, war is always a struggle over words and the forces that enable a given theoretical pronouncement about war to acquire the rhetorical and conceptual authority that his dictum enjoys. The desire to interpret this famous sentence by rewriting it implicates one in a hermeneutic militarism that is not easily assimilated to the very model of pragmatic statecraft the sentence ostensibly expounds.

Even efforts to demonstrate the transparency of the Clausewitzian mantra raise more questions than they answer. The political philosopher Michael Walzer, who has written extensively on the distinction between just and unjust wars, argues that

> Clausewitz's famous line, that war is the continuation of politics by other means, was probably meant to be provocative, but it seems to me obviously true. And the claim is equally obvious the other way around: politics is the continuation of war by other means. It is very important, however, that the means are different. Politics is a form of peaceful contention, and war is organized violence. All the participants, all the activists and militants, survive a political defeat (unless the victor is a tyrant, at war with his own people) whereas many participants, soldiers and civilians alike, do not survive a military defeat—or a victory, either.[38]

The suggestion that Clausewitz's pronouncement is "obviously true" is ambiguous, an affirmation that doubles as a criticism or at the very least as a reminder that we should not devote a lot of time to worrying about the claim since it is self-evidently accurate. Why, then, is it necessary to revisit it at all? And what does it mean to claim that the famous line is "equally obvious" when read in reverse? Walzer's view that the difference between war and politics is that the former is violent and the latter peaceful rests on a notion of violence as the taking of life, a limited conception of the term that may not account for some of the most hurtful consequences of either war or politics—indeed, there are areas of contemporary political theory in which the claim that politics is peaceful would be considered "obviously" false. Moreover, the self-evidence Walzer ascribes to the interchangeability of war and politics seems to belie the simplicity of his proposed distinction between them, pointing to the need to explain their relationship with reference to a more basic term. If the means of war and politics are absolutely different, what force or dynamic—violent or nonviolent, as the case may be—ensures that each is the "obvious" surrogate of the other? Do these fields have an essential connection, and, if not, why do they emerge together time and again?

Walzer's analysis of Clausewitz's definition of war misses the tension in the conjunction of a "*mere* continuation" with the open-ended "*other* means." Whereas the first phrase downplays the specificity of what is being described, as if it were part and parcel of a known operation, the latter expands the discussion into uncharted realms. For Walzer, who takes the word *continuation* as an affirmation of a comprehensible connection, the beauty of Clausewitz's statement about war is that it does not change what we already understand by "war" or "politics"—the claim is "obviously true" for Walzer because it has nothing to teach him. He reads Clausewitz's dictum by not reading it; he inverts it by not inverting it. If we instead take Clausewitz's definition of war seriously as a determination of the relationship between two or more concepts that articulates something essential about both, we must entertain the possibility that war "continues" politics by making us less certain that we know precisely where—for example, on which side of the violence/nonviolence divide— politics begins and war ends. Walzer's desire to exert absolute control over the meaning of the word *war*—"it *is* organized violence"—is itself a kind of violence that is dangerous precisely because it is not clear whether the impulse belongs to war or politics. Correspondingly, the violence of Clausewitz's claim may lie in its reliance on the word *continuation*, which now seems even foggier than "other."

In *A Thousand Plateaus*, Gilles Deleuze and Felix Guattari address the widespread desire to revise Clausewitz's canonical sentence about the relationship between war and politics. They argue that "it is not enough to invert the order of the words [*war* and *politics*] as if they could be spoken in either direction; it is necessary to follow the real movement at the conclusion of which the States, having appropriated a war machine, and having adapted it to their aims, re-impart a war machine that takes charge of the aim, appropriates the States, and assumes increasingly wider political functions."[39] Deleuze and Guattari acknowledge that the authority won by inverting Clausewitz's definition is a power peculiar to war, which is always in part a campaign to do things with words, but they quickly shy away from this insight and oppose "the words" to something "real." One might counter that, where warfare is concerned, verbal movements are as "real" and potentially violent as anything else. The problem is that such a response may simply repeat their interpretive gesture by extending the series of reversals without clarifying the underlying dynamic at work.

In his lecture course "Society Must Be Defended," Foucault takes a different approach to the authority won by inverting Clausewitz's famous line. He argues that the reversals began not with the commentators but with Clausewitz himself, who inverted a thesis in circulation since the seventeenth century that declared politics to be the continuation of war by other means.[40] Foucault's observation comes in the midst of a reflection on whether war is not simply the extreme case of relations of force laid bare but the paradigm for all power relations as well.[41] His key insight is that asserting the conceptual primacy of warfare does not produce a stable, unambiguous formula about its relationship to the political. Declaring the "original" claim—"politics is the continuation of war"—to be at once "diffuse and specific," he suggests that when the terms *war* and *politics* are aligned in a sentence, the resulting formulation will either betray contradictory tendencies or turn out to be tautological.[42] In the former case, the definition of war (or politics) remains ambiguous. In the latter case, the difference between war and politics vanishes ("war is politics," "politics is war"), but the dissolution of the distinction obscures rather than clarifies their allegedly common properties.

In the first volume of *The History of Sexuality*, Foucault again considers whether Clausewitz's maxim is confounding because it is simultaneously too diffuse and too specific:

> Should we turn the expression around, then, and say that politics is war pursued by other means? If we still wish to maintain a separation between war and politics, perhaps we should postulate rather that this multiplicity of force relations can be coded—in part but never totally—either in the form of "war," or in the form of "politics"; this would imply two different strategies (but the one always liable to switch into the other for integrating these unbalanced, heterogeneous, unstable, and tense force relations).[43]

Foucault tries to understand Clausewitz's account of the relationship between war and politics by taking the step that Walzer does not and postulating a third, more fundamental dynamic, a field of "force relations" of which war and politics are two different manifestations. This argument sidesteps the question of how literally Clausewitz's canonical maxim should be taken, decoding it by recasting it as a theory of coding whose specificity—or inherent violence—is never clarified. Both in this text and in the "Society Must Be Defended" lecture course, Foucault's invocation of Clausewitz is marked by a hesitancy in tone as he has repeated recourse to rhetorical questions and conditional formulations. In the end he remains uncertain whether it is actually in our power to choose to maintain or discard the distinction between war and politics or whether Clausewitz's philosophy enjoins us to challenge the very control fantasy in which "war" and "politics" are classificatory concepts to be used or discarded as we see fit.

In their 2004 *Multitude*, Michael Hardt and Antonio Negri invoke Foucault's reading of Clausewitz when they claim that war "is becoming the primary organizing principle of society, and politics merely one of its means or guises."[44] Affirming Foucault's assertion that it is no longer possible to speak of a clear distinction between war and politics, they declare that war is now an interminable condition, a "permanent social relation," the "general matrix for all relations of power and techniques of domination, whether or not bloodshed is involved."[45] This is a world in which "lethal violence is present as a constant potentiality, ready always and everywhere to erupt."[46] Since this destruction is primarily possible rather than actual, Hardt and Negri worry that the dangers they are characterizing may be confused with "merely rhetorical" strife, and they go out of their way to distinguish their proposed expansion of the concept of war from the common practice of speaking of sports, economics, or domestic politics as warlike activities, observing that in such realms "one has competitors but never really enemies properly conceived."[47] Given their rejection of bloodshed as the basic criterion for "real" war, the qualification is confusing, especially when they offer a historical review of the shift from Lyndon Johnson's war on poverty—in which the means to combat penury are "nonviolent," as a consequence of which the "war discourse . . . remains merely rhetorical"—to the subsequent emergence of campaigns against drugs and terrorism, where "the rhetoric of war begins to develop a more concrete character" since armed combat and lethal force are now involved.[48] As restricted as a focus on the last several decades of American social policy may appear in the context of a book that declares that we are in the midst of a global civil war, it is the vocabulary of "merely rhetorical war discourse" and a "more concrete" rhetoric that stands out. What ensures that the thesis that war is the "general matrix for all relations of power and techniques of domination" itself remains "concretely" rather than "merely" rhetorical? The concept of a matrix—a vexed term in structuralism and poststructuralism, gender theory, and media studies— is an odd notion on which to ground a distinction between metaphorical and nonmetaphorical wars. Hardt and Negri acknowledge the problem, opposing "metaphorical and rhetorical invocations of war" to "real wars," which they characterize as "not *so* metaphorical."[49] In attempting to

rework Clausewitz's canonical statement about war and politics, they redis-
cover his insight that any theory of war must account for an instability—
"friction" or "fog"—within language itself. This is why their move to
expand the concept of war to encompass politics lapses into a series of
qualifications about the relative literalness of any given concept of war
without confirming that war has its own model or "matrix" that can explain its relationship to or subsumption of the political. This is also why
the first task in interpreting *On War* is to decide how best to alter it, how
to read it by rearranging what Clausewitz says about war and politics.

If it is almost impossible to resist the temptation to try one's hand at
inverting Clausewitz's canonical statement about war and politics, his
readers inevitably find that the gesture is more complex than it first appears, and in pursuing it they encounter a host of difficulties that force
them to rethink their understanding of war's dynamics and the scope of
its influence. Some political philosophers have taken a different approach
and tried to distinguish war from other forms of sociocultural praxis by
affirming its uniquely violent character. On this account, whatever war
is, it is *not* politics. In an extremely influential argument Hannah Arendt
insists on the inherently nonviolent nature of the political, which for her
is primarily a realm of meaningful communication in which language,
understood as a medium that facilitates cooperation through reciprocal
comprehension, constitutes the condition of possibility of collective agency.
By contrast, violence, she argues, "is incapable of speech," effecting no "articulations" that political thought might register.[50] As the other of politics
so other that it cannot be referred to as such, violence is a means beyond
the means and ends of policy, an alternative to which there can be no
recourse. As open-ended as Clausewitz's reference to "politics by other
means" may sound, it does not include this domain.

This violent other nonetheless finds its way back into the conversation
when Arendt returns to these problems in her 1970 book *On Violence* and
confronts the question of why, in an age in which generations of the public have borne witness to the unparalleled costs of warfare, nations continue to fight. Arendt's unexpected answer is that war is not obsolete because there is no pragmatic alternative to it:

> The chief reason warfare is still with us is neither a secret death wish of the
> human species, nor an irrepressible instinct of aggression, nor, finally and
> more plausibly, the serious economic and social dangers inherent in disarma-

ment, but the simple fact that no substitute for this final arbiter in international affairs has yet appeared on the political scene. Was not Hobbes right
when he said: "Covenants, without the sword, are but words"?[51]

Having argued that violence was less than a blip on the radar screen of
politics, Arendt now presents it as a necessary supplement. In designating
war as the final arbiter of decisions between states, she implies that the
very boundary between speech and violence is articulated through the
military enterprise as a product of the violence it effects. War rules over
the distinction between war and politics because, without war, words
"are but words." Setting out to negate Clausewitz's basic claim that war is
politics, Arendt concludes by all but endorsing it, thereby conferring
upon war the very paradigmatic authority she sought to deny it.

The instability in Arendt's argument stems from the way in which she
bases her distinction between war and politics on a more fundamental opposition between language and violence. For Clausewitz, by contrast, the
theory of war begins with an effort to decide whether the claim of language
to effect violence, even "absolute violence," is a symptom of its power or its
impotence. With his exposition of friction and fog, Clausewitz's principal
concern is not whether linguistic "violence" is invariably metaphorical and
modeled on physical violence, as Winthrop-Young's "metaphorical wars"
might be modeled on literal notions of combat. Instead, Clausewitz asks
whether the very notion of expression—the expression of force, ideas, or
communal consensus—may be a by-product of the sadomasochistic impulses of language, the disfiguration of words by words that precedes any
instrumental use of them as a means. In this sense the language of war
names not a particular vocabulary or set of rhetorical strategies peculiar
to soldiers or political leaders but an intralinguistic conflict that emerges
whenever one tries, as Arendt does, to coordinate a model of communication with a theory of power. To the extent that this dimension of strife
is not explicitly identified, we are condemned to articulate distinctions
that will subsequently prove untenable. This is well illustrated by Arendt,
who distinguishes between power (the human ability to act in concert)
and violence (pure instrumentality, the multiplication of strength with
the aid of various implements), then almost immediately grants that
"nothing . . . is more common than the combination of violence and
power, nothing less frequent than to find them in their pure and therefore extreme form."[52]

Whether it tries to redefine the physical contours of the battlefield and the destruction it visits upon human beings or the conceptual parameters of the term *war* itself, modern military theory finds its object of study at once too abstract and too concrete, as ephemeral as it is destructive. The result is a host of epistemological and ethico-political dilemmas that first made their appearance at the turn of the nineteenth century, as the public became a mass audience of virtual bystanders who followed campaigns remotely through news reports and government bulletins. As the idea of what war should be like became increasingly difficult to reconcile with its empirical manifestations, the ideal war spectator came to be seen as someone with an active imagination rather than superior eyesight. One of the central arguments of this book has been that this marked the onset of "total" war since warfare could become all-consuming only once it ceased to be witnessable in its entirety; that is, it could become total only once it had to be *imagined* as such. The unprecedented scope and consequence of military combat over the last two centuries has thus been as much a product of fantasies about war as the mobilization of populations, resources, and technological advances.

As a construct or an ideal, as well as a description of the vanishing border between the military and civilian domains, war's "totality" has had contradictory ramifications. In the century after Waterloo, fighting was increasingly accorded an auratic quality. If the battlefield was regarded as the ultimate exhibition of historical agency and human destiny, it was also felt that viewing it firsthand would reveal something fundamental about the nature of human perception, a nightmare captured in Ernst Jünger's vision of a social realm, in which a photograph of someone at the instant of death became the archetype of the experience of everyday life. Despite its mystique, the modern military spectacle has been distinguished by its failure to meet the expectations it instills—or tries to instill—in its audiences. War invariably has something "extra" to show and tell, a virtual or specular dimension that escapes the dictates of both its grammar and its logic. While Hobbes argued that a semblance of the intent to aggress was more essential to war than any particular act of violence, Clausewitz maintained that the performance of an intent to fight never remained entirely within the control of the soldiers and politicians who staged it. While it is the defining instantiation of war's consequences, a battle can never serve as a perfect representation of a war's causes and designs. Even in the world wars of the twentieth century,

war's "total" character has never lived up to its billing, the essential signifying act of the war machine proving to be a feint as much as an actual
thrust. Over the past two hundred years, war's audiences have thus
exhibited inconsistent responses to the greatest show of violence on earth.
At times enthralled or overwhelmed, they have also been detached, disinterested, and even bored. The ultimate irony of the modern field of combat is that its uncertain contours and unimaginable speed and complexity
are not the archetype of the fog of war. In the end, the battle may be the
least mysterious thing about war.

The argument that no military campaign entirely controls the simula-
tions of intent it sets in motion has important implications for contemporary efforts to contest the authority of both state and corporate militarism. The belief that a few elites direct a permanent war economy is
another version of what Foucault called the "military dream of society."
An ideal of organization that is never fully realized, this is itself a militaristic fantasy of control designed to heal the irreconcilable rift that Hobbes
described between war and the battles that are fought in its name. As
ruthlessly self-legitimating and self-perpetuating as the military-industrial
complex may seem, it is not an omnipotent force. At the same time, the
fact that no military program is fully in charge of its own signifying practices by no means makes warfare less pernicious. War—even war understood as a complex interplay of virtual and actual forces that aim to pre-
empt any judgment of them by casting themselves as a totalizing field that
permits of no outside—would be an easier performance to assess and
combat if it could prove itself the master of its own fog.

The failure of campaigns to dominate their onlookers may offer an opportunity for resistance, a bulwark against the absolute authority of a
military phenomenology that dictates both what we see and what it means
for us to do so. We certainly should not discount the starkly self-ironized
posture of the modern media consumer and its potential to effect change.
Nonetheless, a heightened degree of self-awareness on the part of war's
audiences may be less a sign of a critical distance from the military enterprise than a confirmation that the onlooker's posture toward and reaction
to the show has always already been shaped by the military's own—
imperfect—systems of self-representation. The conviction that we can
gain insight into the nature of military power by securing a privileged
vantage point at once inside and outside war's phantasmagoric "totality" is
similar to the belief that troubled Napoleon's contemporaries such as

Wordsworth and Coleridge, for whom it was by no means clear that one could follow war without being absorbed by it, no matter how loudly one protested against its human costs. Civilian efforts to win control of warfare by securing a god's-eye view of it are informed by the same unstable gap between the experience of combat and views of what it must be like that informs military thinking. To assume the mantle of the modern witness to military strife is thus to place in jeopardy not only one's autonomy vis-à-vis the war machine but also one's very claim to exercise a power of judgment that is anything but an act of war in its own right.

For future attempts to transform the representational and material dynamics of the military, it will not be enough to understand "watching war" as something that bystanders do, whether out of fear or for entertainment, or that combatants do out of necessity. Becoming an observer of military conflicts always involves a decision about whether war should be conceptualized by analogy with peacetime social and political processes or whether sociopolitical dynamics should be seen as products of a universal military praxis. To call into question the integrity of observation—however it is conceived—is insufficient. The authority of total war will truly be threatened only when the scope of the imagination that underwrites its absolutist claims becomes an object of critique. It is in this vein that this book has tried to lay the groundwork for a new conception of state violence no longer informed by fantasies about the power we think we acquire as onlookers to battles, a power that no public or military has ever fully possessed.

Notes

Introduction

1. Jack Nicholson, "Audio Commentary," *The Passenger*, directed by Michelangelo Antonioni (1975; Culver City, CA: Sony Classics Release, 2006), DVD.

2. Ibid.

3. Edmund Burke, *The Correspondence of Edmund Burke*, 10 vols., ed. T. L. Copeland et al. (Cambridge: Cambridge University Press, 1958–78), 6:10.

4. "From this moment until that in which our enemies shall have been driven from the territory of the Republic, all Frenchmen are permanently requisitioned for service in the armies." Quoted in David Bell, *The First Total War: Napoleon's Europe and the Birth of Warfare as We Know It* (New York: Houghton Mifflin, 2007), 148.

5. Carl von Clausewitz, *On War*, ed. and trans. Michael Howard and Peter Paret (Princeton, NJ: Princeton University Press, 1989), 592.

6. Raymond Williams, *Keywords: A Vocabulary of Culture and Society* (New York: Oxford University Press, 1983), 193–94.

7. Georg Lukács, *The Historical Novel*, trans. Hannah Mitchell and Stanley Mitchell (Lincoln: University of Nebraska Press, 1983), 23–24. Lukács adds: "The inner life of a nation is linked with the modern mass army in a way it could not have been with the absolutist armies of the earlier period" (ibid., 24).

8. For discussions of the broad daily newspaper readership across Europe at the end of the eighteenth century, see the collection of essays in Hannah Barker and Simon Burrows's *Press, Politics, and the Public Sphere in Europe and North America, 1760–1820* (New York: Cambridge University Press, 2002). Jerome Christensen has written that "modern wartime, which is not an event but a condition of eventfulness—that is, the simulation of dailiness within an imposed totality—is inconceivable without journalism." *Romanticism at the End of History*

(Baltimore: Johns Hopkins University Press, 2000), 4. Stuart Semmel echoes the importance of newspapers for the new war experience: "For those not fighting, the war had evidenced itself (to an extent not possible in earlier ages) in the intangible world of print reportage." "Reading the Tangible Past: British Tourism, Collecting, and Memory After Waterloo," *Representations* 69 (Winter 2000): 10. In a similar vein, Norbert Bolz has pithily averred that "the history of mass media is the *historia in nuce* of modern war." *Theorie der neuen Medien* (Munich: Raben, 1990), 82; my translation.

9. For a superb study of how British culture of the late eighteenth and early nineteenth centuries was shaped by efforts to engage with wars that were always fought elsewhere, see Mary A. Favret, *War at a Distance: Romanticism and the Making of Modern Wartime* (Princeton, NJ: Princeton University Press, 2010).

10. As Christensen has argued: "Wartime becomes modern as it becomes spectacle; and because modern war is spectacle it is always to some extent a cold war, conducted by means of strategic representations of remote conflict and waged at home on behalf of some citizens against others." *Romanticism at the End of History*, 4.

11. Favret follows Christensen in arguing that the everyday quality of war emerged in the Napoleonic era. See "Everyday War," *ELH* 72 (2005): 605–33.

12. Baudrillard's understanding of dissimulation and its implications for modern warfare was popularized by Barry Levinson's 1997 film *Wag the Dog*, in which a Hollywood producer is hired by the White House to divert attention from a sex scandal by staging a fake war with Albania.

13. On the "military-entertainment complex," see W. J. T. Mitchell, "The War of Images," *University of Chicago Magazine* (December 2001): 21–23.

14. Many war correspondents assume an ironic attitude toward their alleged lack of impartiality and report on their own biases. Embedded reporters in particular often self-consciously celebrate the degree to which they have become enamored of their hosts, eagerly detailing their disenchantment when the romance turns sour. Of course, the very notion of operating independently on a battlefield is arguably something of a fantasy since the men and women of the press corps invariably rely on the military to protect them. For a discussion of these dynamics see "Five Years On: Media's Role in Iraq," *Christian Science Monitor* (March 19, 2008), editorial section: 8.

15. The remarks of Associated Press writer John Rice describing the American bombardment of Baghdad typify this feature of contemporary reporting: "What was strange as allied planes poured explosives onto Baghdad was how appallingly beautiful it was. Air raid sirens would scream and then red and white anti-aircraft fire streaked into the black night sky from all directions over a darkened city in January and February 1991. It was an awesome fireworks

display that the muddy nighttime television pictures never quite managed to capture." "Fear and Awe as Bombs Fell on Baghdad," Associated Press, International News Section, March 18, 2003.

16. James Dao, "First Person Combat: In a Minefield," *New York Times*, June 7, 2011, http://atwar.blogs.nytimes.com/2011/06/07/first-person-combat-in-a-minefield/.

17. Paul Virilio, *War and Cinema: The Logistics of Perception*, trans. Patrick Camiller (New York: Verso, 1989), 7. Virilio adds: "From Machiavelli to Vauban, from von Moltke to Churchill, at every decisive episode in the history of war, military theorists have underlined this truth: 'The force of arms is not brute force but spiritual force' (Sun Tzu)" (ibid., 5). Virilio also argues that weapons do not just maim or kill but structure and augment our relationship to the sensory realm as well: "Weapons are tools not just of destruction but also of perception—that is to say, stimulants that make themselves felt through chemical, neurological processes in the sense organs and the central nervous system, affecting human reactions and even the perceptual identification and differentiation of objects" (ibid., 5–6).

18. Guy Debord, *Society of the Spectacle*, trans. Ken Knabb (Detroit: Black and Red, 1983), 7.

19. Ibid. On the unifying and dividing dimensions of spectacle see Samuel Weber, "War, Terrorism, and Spectacle, or: On Towers and Caves," *Grey Room* 7 (Spring 2002): 14–23.

20. Historian David Bell has recently made a case for the Napoleonic era as the birthplace of total war, arguing that the period was defined by "concerted political attempts to harness entire societies—every human being, every resource—to a single, military purpose," efforts, Bell suggests, that properly constituted the beginning of what theorists after 1918 will term "total war." *First Total War*, 9.

21. Quoted in Friedrich Kittler, "Media and Drugs in Pynchon's Second World War," in *Reading Matters: Narrative in the New Media Ecology*, ed. Joseph Tabbi and Michael Wutz (Ithaca, NY: Cornell University Press, 1997), 171.

22. Walter Benjamin, "On Some Motifs in Baudelaire," in *Selected Writings*, vol. 4, *1938–1940*, ed. Howard Eiland and Michael W. Jennings (Cambridge, MA: Harvard University Press, 2003), 316.

23. On censorship and control of the press in Napoleonic France see Michael Marrinan, "Literal/Literary/'Lexie': History, Text, and Authority in Napoleonic Painting," *Word and Image* 7(3) (July–September 1991): 178ff.

24. As Christopher Prendergast explains, "The bulletin was something of a discursive institution in Napoleonic France. Not only did it appear in the official press, it was also circulated, in simplified and illustrated form, throughout rural France, posted on the walls of Paris, declaimed by actors in theaters."

Napoleon and History Painting: Antoine-Jean Gros's La Bataille de Eylau (Oxford: Clarendon, 1997), 129. If the Napoleonic war machine perfected and expanded the war bulletin, it was hardly its invention, and, in fact, such bulletins had long been known not only for their gripping verbal narratives but for their arresting images as well: "[T]he Eighty Years' War (1568–1648), the latter part of which coincided with the Thirty Years' War (1618–1648), was the first major European conflict in which printed images played a significant role. Vast numbers of broadsheets and pamphlets circulated, often incorporating graphic images for their persuasive value and emotional impact." Leslie M. Scattone, introduction, in *The Plains of Mars: European War Prints, 1500–1825, from the Collection of the Sarah Campbell Blaffer Foundation,* by James Clifton and Leslie M. Scattone (New Haven, CT: Yale University Press, 2009), 2.

25. "Of the Necessity of a Censorship in the Press," in *Memoirs of Prince Metternich,* ed. Prince Richard Metternich, trans. Mrs. Alexander Napier, 4 vols. (New York: Charles Scribner's Sons, 1881), II: 226–27 (note dated June 23, 1808)—quoted in Marrinan, "Literal/Literary/'Lexie,'" 196n30.

26. Richard Whately, *Historic Doubts Relative to Napoleon Bonaparte,* ed. Ralph S. Pomeroy (Berkeley, CA: Scolar Press, 1985), 13.

27. Clausewitz, *On War,* 102.

28. John Booth, *Battle of Waterloo* (London: printed for J. Booth and T. Egerton, 1815), I: 63. In the popular mythology Goethe was similarly endowed with the "gaze of an eagle" that, Medusa-like, was unbearable. See Rüdiger Safranski, *Goethe und Schiller: Geschichte einer Freundschaft* (Munich: Hanser, 2009), 17.

29. On the "solar myth of the Revolution," see Jean Starobinski, *1789: The Emblems of Reason,* trans. Barbara Bray (Charlottesville: University Press of Virginia, 1982), 44ff.

30. One of the major challenges in analyzing the relations between the aesthetic and the military doctrines of this period is that much of what was written about the Napoleonic cult of personality in the nineteenth and twentieth centuries was wittingly or unwittingly governed by the standards of power and control articulated by Napoleon himself. In the generations following his death, the emperor enjoyed a wealth of attention, both positive and negative, from an extraordinary array of European writers, as if weighing in on his reign was *de rigueur* for any serious intellectual. While few historical personages have been subjected to a comparable degree of scrutiny and critique, Napoleon's fans and his detractors alike remain curiously helpless in the face of Napoleonic mythmaking, as if in the course of debunking the emperor's own propaganda, one must inevitably confirm the fundamental truth of his theories of war and politics. Even firsthand accounts of battles tend to read as if the individuals

were simply "seeing" and "experiencing" what Napoleon had said about them in his official proclamations.

31. *CTRL [SPACE]: Rhetorics of Surveillance from Bentham to Big Brother*, ed. Thomas Y. Levin, Ursula Frohne, and Peter Weibel (Cambridge, MA: MIT Press, 2002), 10.

32. Quoted in Paul Virilio, *City of Panic*, trans. Julie Rose (New York: Berg, 2004), 53.

33. Michel Foucault, *Discipline and Punish: The Birth of the Prison*, trans. Alan Sheridan (New York: Pantheon, 1977), 217.

34. In *Techniques of the Observer* Jonathan Crary offers a different account of how "Foucault's opposition between spectacle and surveillance becomes untenable; [and] his two distinct models here collapse onto one another." *Techniques of the Observer: On Vision and Modernity in the Nineteenth Century* (Cambridge, MA: MIT Press, 1990), 112.

35. Cathy Caruth has described the dynamics of traumatic experience in detail: "The experience of trauma, the fact of latency, would thus seem to consist, not in the forgetting of a reality that can hence never be fully known; but in an inherent latency within the experience itself. The historical power of the trauma is not just that the experience is repeated after its forgetting, but that it is only in and through its inherent forgetting that it is first experienced." "Unclaimed Experience: Trauma and the Possibility of History," *Yale French Studies* 79 (1991): 187.

36. William Wordsworth, "Preface to Lyrical Ballads," *Major British Poets of the Romantic Period*, ed. William Heath (New York: Macmillan, 1973), 400.

37. For some efforts to untangle the complex cultural politics of Wordsworth's preface see Nikki Hessell, "The Opposite of News: Rethinking the 1800 'Lyrical Ballads' and the Mass Media," *Studies in Romanticism* 45(3) (Fall 2006): 331–55; and Thomas Pfau, "'Elementary Feelings' and 'Distorted Language': The Pragmatics of Culture in Wordsworth's Preface to *Lyrical Ballads*," *New Literary History* 24(1) (Winter 1993): 125–46.

38. Quoted in Paul Magnuson, "The Politics of 'Frost at Midnight,'" in *Romantic Poetry: Recent Revisionary Criticism*, ed. Karl Kroeber and Gene W. Ruoff (New Brunswick, NJ: Rutgers University Press, 1993), 193.

39. Samuel Taylor Coleridge, "Fears in Solitude," in *The Collected Works of Samuel Taylor Coleridge*, vol. 16, *Poetical Works* I.1, ed. J. C. C. Mays (Princeton, NJ: Princeton University Press, 2001), 468. The poem appears on pages 468–77; subsequent references are by line number. Although "Fears in Solitude" has rarely been regarded as a major aesthetic achievement, it is frequently referenced in accounts of the development of Coleridge's political thought. Written at a point at which the poet's radicalism had won him sufficient notoriety that he

and Wordsworth were allegedly tailed by government spies, the text has alternately been interpreted as Coleridge's attempted refutation of charges of Jacobinism through a declaration of love for his country, as his effort to continue his critique of the Pitt government in a less conspicuous fashion, or as evidence of the beginnings of his shift toward conservatism. In 1807 Coleridge noted that "when the poem was published he was called a traitor both to his country and to his family." Ben Brice, *Coleridge and Scepticism* (Oxford: Oxford University Press, 2007), 131. Coleridge's decision to reprint the text in *The Friend* has been interpreted as an attempt to reaffirm his patriotism. See *The Friend* II, *The Collected Works of Samuel Taylor Coleridge*, vol. 4, ed. Barbara E. Rooke (Princeton, NJ: Princeton University Press, 1969), 24–25.

If "Fears in Solitude" appears to share some of Wordsworth's anxieties, it has also been read as a response to the preface to *Lyrical Ballads*. Onita Vaz, for example, proposes that the poem demonstrates the ability of the imagination to "dissolve the conceptual boundaries that purportedly divide private lyric utterance and public discourse," potentially rendering obsolete the very opposition that informed Wordsworth's scathing attack on the daily press. Onita Vaz, "Half-Asleep on Thresholds: Fragile Boundaries in Coleridge's 'Fears in Solitude,'" in *Romanticism: Comparative Discourses*, ed. Larry H. Peer and Diane Long Hoeveler (Aldershot, UK: Ashgate, 2006), 55.

40. Coleridge, "Fears in Solitude," l. 93–96.

41. Ibid., l. 104–7.

42. A year after composing the text, Coleridge added a postscript: "The above poem is perhaps not Poetry—but rather a sort of Middle thing between Poetry & Oratory—Sermoni proprior.—Some parts are, I am conscious, too tame even for animated Prose." *Poetical Works* I.1, 469. Hovering uncertainly between verse and declamatory speech and yet at points too bland and docile to be either, the very existence of "Fears in Solitude" prompts Coleridge to express a more basic fear of a language that cannot control its own generic identity. With the 1807 publication of the poem Coleridge noted that some lines in the text are really "*Prose* that in a frolic . . . put on a masquerade Dress of Metre, & like most Masquerades, blundered in the assumed character" (ibid.).

43. Ibid., "Fears in Solitude," l. 69–70.

44. Ibid., l. 58–59.

45. Ibid., l. 109–14.

46. Ibid., l. 115–17. In a superb analysis of Coleridge's poem Mark Jones argues that the "fears" referenced in the title are primarily anxieties about "public-sphere performativity and its unruly dissemination of power" and that the poem is a meditation on the dynamics of self-realizing alarmism and hence a "para-performative text, an exercise in not doing things with words." "Alarmism,

Public-Sphere Performatives, and the Lyric Turn: Or, What Is 'Fears in Solitude' Afraid of?" *boundary 2* 30(3) (2003): 96–97.

47. Vaz makes a similar argument in "Half-Asleep on Thresholds," 61.

48. Coleridge, "Fears in Solitude," l. 118–22.

49. See Coleridge, *The Friend* II, 25.

50. Coleridge, *Poetical Works* 2: 595.

51. Regina Hewitt, *The Possibilities of Society: Wordsworth, Coleridge, and the Sociological Viewpoint of English Romanticism* (Albany: State University of New York Press, 1997), 121.

52. Earlier versions of sections of the discussion of Clausewitz here and in the conclusion appeared in "How to Do Things with Clausewitz," *Global South* 3(1) (April 2009): 18–29, and are used with the permission of Indiana University Press.

53. On the remarkable uniformity of Enlightenment military theory, whose authors "did not differ in the fundamentals of their guiding objective—the search for a general theory of war—which derived from their intellectual environment," see Azar Gat, *The Origins of Military Thought from the Enlightenment to Clausewitz* (Oxford: Clarendon, 1989), 139. Gat observes that even those authors who questioned the notion that there are immutable laws of war were ultimately unable to reject rationalist ideals of order.

54. Clausewitz's major claims are accorded such lapidary authority that someone with only a secondhand knowledge of his work might assume that he was an aphorist. His inheritors have long puzzled over this state of affairs. As the Prussian soldier and military theorist Max Jähn wrote in 1891: "There is something strange about Clausewitz's influence," for even though his "almost mystical" texts are not actually that widely read, his "opinions have spread throughout the entire army and have proven immeasurably fruitful." *Geschichte der Kriegswissenschaften*, quoted in John A. Lynn, *Battle: A History of Combat and Culture* (Boulder, CO: Westview, 2003), 211.

55. Clausewitz, *On War*, 101; translation modified.

56. In both German and English the figurative sense of *Nebel* (fog) "as confusion" or "bewilderment" had been established for centuries and canonized as a "formal" meaning (or "dead metaphor") in dictionaries well before Clausewitz wrote *On War*. In the early nineteenth century *Nebel* was also vernacular for *Rausch* (intoxication).

57. Clausewitz, *On War*, 140.

58. Ibid., 143.

59. Ibid., 119; translation modified.

60. Ibid., 120.

61. Ibid., 121.

62. Ibid., 87. In a slightly different formulation, Clausewitz writes that war is "a true political instrument, a continuation of political intercourse, carried on with other means" (ibid.).

63. Ibid., 75.

64. Clausewitz insists that war is never a fluke or a flash in the pan but always "lasts long enough . . . to remain subject to the action of a superior intelligence" (ibid., 87).

65. Ibid., 75.

66. Ibid., 260.

67. Ibid.

68. Ibid., 77.

69. Ibid., 248.

70. Ibid., 78.

71. Beatrice Heuser argues that Clausewitz rewrites *On War* from a realist perspective. See her *Reading Clausewitz* (London: Pimlico, 2002). For a similar claim see Richard Ned Lebow, *The Tragic Vision: Ethics, Interests, and Orders* (New York: Cambridge University Press, 2003). Against this view one should remember that Clausewitz studied under Kantian popularizers and that his mentor, Gerhard von Scharnhorst, was steeped in Kantian philosophy. In Berlin, where Clausewitz met Hegel, he participated in the *Christlich-Deutsche Tischgesellschaft*, a group whose members included J. G. Fichte, Friedrich Schleiermacher, and Heinrich von Kleist.

72. Clausewitz, *On War*, 86.

73. Ibid., 605; translation modified.

74. Ibid., 87; translation modified.

75. Ibid., 582.

Chapter One

1. Thomas Hobbes, *Leviathan* (New York: Cambridge University Press, 1991), 88–89. An earlier version of the ensuing discussion of Hobbes and Rousseau was published in "Watching War," *PMLA* 124(5) (October 2009): 1648–61, and appears here by permission of the Modern Language Association of America.

2. Paul Virilio, *War and Cinema: The Logistics of Perception*, trans. Patrick Camiller (New York: Verso, 1989), 26.

3. See Jean Baudrillard, *Simulation and Simulacra*, trans. Sheila Faria Glaser (Ann Arbor: Michigan University Press, 1994), 37–38.

4. Jean Baudrillard, *The Gulf War Did Not Take Place*, trans. Paul Patton (Bloomington: Indiana University Press, 1995), 31–32.

5. Ibid., 32.

6. This point has largely been missed by contemporary media studies, which tends to underestimate the complexity of the military-representational complex.

7. In this respect modern war is, properly speaking, "uncanny." Sigmund Freud famously maintained that "an uncanny effect is often and easily produced when the distinction between imagination and reality is effaced, as when something that we have hitherto regarded as imaginary appears before us in reality, or when a symbol takes over the full functions of the thing it symbolizes, and so on." "The Uncanny," in *Standard Edition of the Complete Psychological Works of Sigmund Freud*, ed. and trans. James Strachey, vol. 17 (London: Hogarth, 1953), 244.

8. Norman Bryson, *Word and Image: French Painting of the Ancien Régime* (New York: Cambridge University Press, 1981), 36.

9. Ibid., 35.

10. Ibid., 36.

11. Ibid.

12. Ibid., 38.

13. Ibid., 37; emphasis added.

14. Ibid., 36.

15. Ibid. It is hardly a new idea to suggest that the historicity of war is distinguished by the fact that the story of a war is told as it occurs rather than afterward. At the opening of the *History of the Peloponnesian War* Thucydides announces that "Thucydides the Athenian wrote the history of the war fought between Athens and Sparta, beginning the account at the very outbreak of the war, in the belief that it was going to be a great war and more worth writing about than any of those which had taken place in the past." *History of the Peloponnesian War*, trans. Rex Warner (New York: Penguin, 1972), 35. In Thucydides's terms, war and its documentation appear concomitantly in an investigation that is overtly self-reflexive because, from the start of conflict, the significance of the incidents at hand is never in question, and, in fact, by their very nature these incidents call out to be documented. For Thucydides a war becomes historical at the point it begins; it takes place in part by testifying to its own significance. War is center stage in historical analyses because of its ostensible status as self-evidently meaningful. It is an event whose significance literally cannot be overlooked and that need not wait for posterity to be appreciated. In war, Thucydides thus found nothing less than what G. W. F. Hegel would describe millennia later as the self-interpretive process of historical praxis in which the *res gestae* and the *historia rerum gestarum* are produced synchronously; battles are the archetype of historical occurrences that are complemented by expositions of their own significance that appear simultaneously with them. See G. W. F. Hegel, *The Philosophy of History*, trans. J. Sibree (New York: Dover, 1956), 60.

16. Among other things this suggests that the Western historiographical tradition has no schema for an event of peace—whatever peace is, it does not "happen." This may be why wars waged in the name of peace are usually the bloodiest wars of all.

17. One consequence is that even spirited critiques of militarism tend unwittingly to reaffirm militaristic paradigms of history. In a late interview Michel Foucault declared that "the history which bears and determines us has the form of a war rather than that of a language: relations of power, not relations of meaning." *Power/Knowledge: Selected Interviews and Other Writings*, ed. Colin Gordon (New York: Pantheon, 1980), 114. It is doubtful whether the form of war is ever conceivable in the absence of language and whether relations of power ever exist to the exclusion of relations of meaning, but what is striking in this quotation is that Foucault's generalization of warfare as the form of historicity itself accords war absolute primacy as the arbiter of cultural meaning.

18. Bryson, *Word and Image*, 36.

19. Jean-Jacques Rousseau, *Emile: Or, on Education*, trans. Alan Bloom (New York: HarperCollins, 1979), 237.

20. Ibid.

21. Ibid., 239.

22. Ibid., 238.

23. Ibid.

24. Ibid., 239.

25. Ibid.

26. Ibid., 239–40.

27. Ibid., 240.

28. Central to this myth of the one-day transformation of the world was Austerlitz, which, as John A. Lynn has argued, was not Napoleon's first victory but "the clash that more than any other gave tangible reality to the ideal of decisive battle, a concept that would haunt the nineteenth and twentieth centuries." *Battle: A History of Combat and Culture from Ancient Greece to Modern America* (Boulder, CO: Westview, 2003), 180.

29. J. Christopher Herold, ed. and trans., *The Mind of Napoleon: A Selection from His Written and Spoken Words* (New York: Columbia University Press, 1961), 203.

30. Conversation, Saint Helena, 1815, quoted in ibid., 222–23. Later Napoleon would write: "There is a moment in every battle at which the least maneuver is decisive and gives superiority, as one drop of water causes overflow" (ibid., 223).

31. On tactical innovations in fighting during this period see Robert B. Holtman, *The Napoleonic Revolution* (Philadelphia: Lippincott, 1967); John Gooch, *Armies in Europe* (London: Routledge and Kegan Paul, 1980); and

Gunther E. Rothenberg, *The Art of Warfare in the Age of Napoleon* (Bloomington: Indiana University Press, 1978).

32. Carl von Clausewitz, *On War*, ed. and trans. Michael Howard and Peter Paret (Princeton, NJ: Princeton University Press, 1989), 259.

33. Ibid.; emphasis in original.

34. Ibid., 258.

35. Georg Lukács, *The Historical Novel*, trans. Hannah Mitchell and Stanley Mitchell (Lincoln: University of Nebraska Press, 1983), 19.

36. Victor Hugo, *Les Misérables*, trans. Norman Denny (New York: Penguin, 1982), 287.

37. Ibid., 291.

38. Virilio, *War and Cinema*, 20.

39. Hugo, *Les Misérables*, 291.

40. Ibid., 290–91.

41. Ibid., 313.

42. Ibid., 285–86.

43. Ibid., 302.

44. Ibid., 302–3.

45. Ibid., 313.

46. Ibid., 320.

47. This encounter acquires major importance for the plot when years later Thénardier's family finds itself by chance living next to the baron's son.

48. As Stuart Semmel characterizes it, "If the revolutionary wars had tolled the death knell of the eighteenth-century aristocratic Grand Tour, the end of the Napoleonic wars ushered in the first hints of modern mass tourism. The months and years following Waterloo saw instant historical tourism of a rare type, comparable with the rash of Westerners unleashed on Berlin in 1989." "Reading the Tangible Past: British Tourism, Collecting, and Memory After Waterloo," *Representations* 69 (Winter 2000): 10. On battlefield tours see also Philip Shaw, *Waterloo and the Romantic Imagination* (New York: Palgrave Macmillan, 2002), esp. 67–71.

49. John Scott, *Paris Revisited in 1815, by Way of Brussels: Including a Walk Over the Field of Battle at Waterloo* (London: Longman, 1816), 201.

50. See Shaw, *Waterloo and the Romantic Imagination*, 70–71. Shaw argues that battlefield tourism is designed to protect the visitors from the shock of war's violence.

51. Stuart Semmel explains: "Within weeks of the battle of Waterloo, John Scott found battlefield locals selling weapons, bullets, buttons, 'letters taken from the pockets of the dead,' to 'every fresh arrival of visitors.'" "Reading," 24.

52. Hugo, *Les Misérables*, 297. Contemporary scholars are hopeful that this "degradation" of the sites of crucial events can be reversed with the aid of

computer technology. New digital maps are facilitating re-creations of famous battlefields that correct for the changes in landscape topography, vegetation, and construction that have since altered them, in theory making it possible to simulate the vantage point that a given general enjoyed at the moment a key decision in a battle was made. See Patricia Cohen, "Digital Maps Are Giving Scholars the Historical Lay of the Land," *New York Times*, July 26, 2011, www .nytimes.com/2011/07/27/arts/geographic-information-systems-help-scholars -see-history.html?_r=1&hp.

53. Shaw, *Waterloo and the Romantic Imagination*, 18. Shaw argues that "it is in the work of the Romantic poets that ideas of nationhood, authority and the relations between violence and identity are most severely tested. . . . [T]he Waterloo writings of Scott, Southey, Coleridge, Wordsworth and Byron speak volubly of the impossibility of private and public imaginings" (ibid., x).

54. See Alessandro Barbero, *The Battle: A New History of Waterloo*, trans. John Cullen (New York: Walker, 2005), 313.

55. On the fascination with visiting battle sites and standing at the observation points Napoleon himself had used, see Shaw's *Waterloo and the Romantic Imagination*, especially chapter 2: "Exhibiting War: Battle Tours and Panoramas."

56. Hugo, *Les Misérables*, 317.

57. Simon Bainbridge, *Napoleon and English Romanticism* (New York: Cambridge University Press, 1995), 95.

58. Ibid., 94.

59. Chateaubriand, *The Memoirs of Chateaubriand*, trans. Robert Baldick (New York: Knopf, 1961), 277.

60. Ibid., 277–78.

61. Immanuel Kant, *Critique of Judgment*, trans. Werner S. Pluhar (Indianapolis: Hackett, 1987), 108.

62. Chateaubriand, *Memoirs*, 278.

63. Kant, *Critique of Judgment*, 120; emphasis in original.

64. Ibid. Kant is drawing on Edmund Burke, who in his discussion of the sublime argues that "terror is a passion which always produces delight when it does not press too close." Edmund Burke, *A Philosophical Enquiry Into the Origin of Our Ideas of the Sublime and Beautiful*, ed. James T. Boulton (Notre Dame, IN: University of Notre Dame Press, 1986), 46.

Chapter Two

1. On the nature and experience of the Napoleonic field of combat see John Keegan, *The Face of Battle: A Study of Agincourt, Waterloo, and the Somme* (New York: Penguin, 1976), especially chapter 1. See also the collection of war narratives edited by Keegan titled *The Book of War* (New York: Penguin, 1999).

2. Victor Hugo, *Les Misérables*, trans. Norman Denny (New York: Penguin, 1982), 316.

3. Alessandro Barbero, *The Battle: A New History of Waterloo*, trans. John Cullen (New York: Walker, 2005), 311. In commenting on Waterloo, contemporary historians such as Barbero often simply repeat what novelists such as Hugo wrote a century before: "Of all set battles, it was fought on the narrowest front in relation to the number of troops engaged." *Les Misérables*, 316.

4. See Keegan, *Face of Battle*, 140; the collection of eyewitness accounts in Antony Brett-James, ed. and trans., *The Hundred Days: Napoleon's Last Campaign from Eyewitness Accounts* (New York: St. Martin's, 1964); and Rory Muir, *Tactics and the Experience of Battle in the Age of Napoleon* (New Haven, CT: Yale University Press, 1998), esp. 24–25. Muir writes that "there is no doubt that when battalions of infantry became locked in an indecisive firefight they would soon surround themselves with a dense cloud of smoke through which they could scarcely see their target, and which greatly contributed to the stunned daze into which they often sank." *Tactics*, 25.

5. *The Mind of Napoleon: A Selection from His Written and Spoken Words*, ed. and trans. J. Christopher Herold (New York: Columbia University Press, 1961), 204.

6. Michael Marrinan, "Literal/Literary/'Lexie': History, Text, and Authority in Napoleonic Painting," *Word & Image* 7(3) (July–September 1991): 183–84.

7. The best-known entry in the contest was Baron Antoine-Jean Gros's now famous *Napoleon Visiting the Battlefield of Eylau*, first exhibited at the Paris Salon of 1808. On French efforts to spin the Battle of Eylau see Christopher Prendergast, *Napoleon and History Painting: Antoine-Jean Gros's* La Bataille de Eylau (Oxford: Clarendon, 1997); and Marrinan, "Literal," 177. See also Robert Holtman, *Napoleonic Propaganda* (Baton Rouge: Louisiana State University Press, 1050), 92–96.

8. Walter Scott, *Paul's Letters to His Kinsfolk* (Philadelphia: republished by Moses Thomas from the Edinburgh edition, 1816), 117–18. For another analysis of this passage see Stuart Semmel, "Reading the Tangible Past: British Tourism, Collecting, and Memory After Waterloo," *Representations* 69 (Winter 2000): 14.

9. The rise of the Napoleonic war imaginary sees the start of a long tradition of both casual and concerted efforts to make the battles of the past "go away" by simply denying that they ever took place. Throughout the nineteenth and early twentieth centuries, for example, attempts to use classical texts to locate the precise site of Caesar's defeat of the Gauls, the Battle of Alésia, prompted a nationalist controversy in France, which centered on the question of whether this crushing loss actually occurred. To this day, characters in *Asterix* comics joke, "Alésia? Where's that?"

10. William Godwin, *Enquiry Concerning Political Justice and Its Influence on Modern Morals and Happiness*, ed. Isaac Kramnick (London: Penguin Classics, 1985), 510.

11. See Gillian Russell, *The Theatres of War: Performance, Politics, and Society, 1793–1815* (Oxford: Clarendon, 1995), 179.

12. Ibid., 13–14, 180.

13. Paul Fussell, *The Great War and Modern Memory* (New York: Oxford University Press, 1977), 191. Fussell complements his point about conscription and the theatricality of warfare with an argument about the way in which soldiers actually experience the violence in which they participate, claiming that "it is . . . the very hazard of military situations that turns them theatrical. And it is their utter unthinkableness: it is impossible for a participant to believe that he is taking part in such murderous proceedings in his own character. The whole thing is too grossly farcical, perverse, cruel, and absurd to be credited as a form of 'real life' " (ibid., 192).

14. Carl von Clausewitz, *On War*, ed. and trans. Michael Howard and Peter Paret (Princeton, NJ: Princeton University Press, 1989), 113; translation modified.

15. The formative organizational force of warfare is nicely captured in the oft-quoted fragment of Heraclitus: "War is the father and king of all, and some he shows as gods, others as humans; some he makes slaves, others free." *A Presocratics Reader*, ed. Patricia Curd, trans. Richard D. McKirahan (Indianapolis: Hackett, 1996), 37.

16. Clausewitz, *On War*, 113.

17. Ibid.

18. Fussell, *Great War and Modern Memory*, 191–92.

19. Focusing on the performative dimensions of the battlefield provides a new way to think about the immense popularity of battle reenactments in the nineteenth and twentieth centuries. In an uncanny fashion the forces of simulation and dissimulation inherent in combat seem to give participants in such restagings of past clashes an odd hope that if the battle could just be replayed one more time, the outcome might be different since after all it was "only" play the first time.

20. An earlier version of the ensuing discussion of Stendhal was published in "Watching War," *PMLA* 124(5) (October 2009): 1648–61, and appears here by permission of the Modern Language Association of America.

21. For a spirited analysis of the opening of Stendhal's novel see Nicola Chiaromonte, *The Paradox of History* (Philadelphia: University of Pennsylvania Press, 1985), 1–16. For a comparison of Stendhal's Waterloo with Hugo's see Gottfried Schwarz, *Krieg und Roman: Untersuchungen zu Stendhal, Hugo, Tolstoj, Zola und Simon* (Frankfurt am Main: Lang, 1992), 29–45. The tradition of picaresque war

narratives—fictional and nonfictional—long predates Stendhal. It is notable that the contemporary historians who have encouraged us to revisit famous battles from the perspective of the common soldier rather than the commanding general have largely neglected these examples of what a nontraditional war story might be, although they are prominent in the Western literary canon from Shakespeare through the Baroque. On the experience of war in Shakespeare see Nick de Somogyi, *Shakespeare's Theatre of War* (Brookfield, VT: Ashgate, 1998).

22. Stendhal, *Charterhouse of Parma*, trans. Richard Howard (New York: Modern Library, 2000), 43.

23. Ibid.; translation modified. I am grateful to Hugh Hochman for his comments on this passage.

24. Ibid., 44.

25. Ibid.; translation modified.

26. Ibid., 60.

27. Ibid., 3.

28. Ibid., 482.

29. Maurice Samuels, *The Spectacular Past: Popular History and the Novel in Nineteenth-Century France* (Ithaca, NY: Cornell University Press, 2004), 263.

30. Ibid., 265. On Stendhal's novel as a critique of nineteenth-century engagements with a meaningful past see also Katherine Golsan, "History's Waterloo: Prediction in *La chartreuse de Parme*," *Nineteenth-Century French Studies* 24 (Spring–Summer 1996): 332–46.

31. Stendhal, *Charterhouse*, 86.

32. Ibid., 73.

33. Walter Benjamin argued that one of the ironies of the modern media is that the very forces that invite audiences to let their imaginations have free rein also work against the imagination: "The principles of journalistic information (newness, brevity, clarity, and, above all, lack of connection between the individual news items) contribute as much to this as the layout of the pages and the style of writing. (Karl Kraus never tired of demonstrating the extent to which the linguistic habitus of newspapers paralyzes the imagination of their readers.)" "On Some Motifs in Baudelaire," in *Selected Writings*, vol. 4, *1938–1940*, ed. Howard Eiland and Michael W. Jennings (Cambridge, MA: Harvard University Press, 2003), 316.

34. The description Theodor W. Adorno offered of the Second World War can also be read as a characterization of Europe at the start of the nineteenth century:

The total obliteration of the war by information, propaganda, commentaries, with camera men in the first tanks and war reporters dying heroic deaths, the mish-mash of enlightened manipulation of public opinion and oblivious activity: all this is another expression for the withering of experience, the vacuum between men and their fate, in which their real fate lies. It is as if the reified, hardened plaster-cast of events takes the place of events themselves. (*Minima Moralia: Reflections from Damaged Life*, trans. E. F. N. Jephcott [New York: Verso, 1989], 55)

35. Leo Tolstoy, *War and Peace*, trans. Richard Pevear and Larissa Volokhonsky (New York: Knopf, 2007), 754.

36. Ibid., 784, 1008.

37. Ibid., 759.

38. Ibid., 771.

39. Ibid., 791.

40. On these questions see Thomas P. Saine, *Black Bread—White Bread: German Intellectuals and the French Revolution* (Columbia, SC: Camden House, 1988), 204–7.

41. Patricia Anne Simpson observes that some critics "have emphasized the contextual motivations for Goethe's inscription of this experience [decades after the fact], including the worsening political circumstances in Germany and the possibility of a revolution that prompted a retrospective look at the French Revolution and its repercussions." *The Erotics of War in German Romanticism* (Lewisburg, PA: Bucknell University Press, 2006), 192.

42. J. W. von Goethe, *Poetry and Truth, Part Four: Campaign in France 1792, Siege of Mainz*, trans. Thomas P. Saine (New York: Suhrkamp, 1987), 643. The *Deutsches Wörterbuch* of Jacob Grimm and Wilhelm Grimm lists Goethe's *Campaign in France* as one of the earliest sources for the word *Kriegstheater* (Leipzig: von S. Hirzel, 1854–). *Campaign in France* continues a meditation on the relationship between war and drama that Goethe began decades earlier in *Wilhelm Meister's Theatrical Calling*.

43. Jonathan Crary has argued that in the first part of the nineteenth century the individual observer is accorded new authority as vision becomes a physiological event that takes place within the body. One of Crary's aims is to show that changing understandings of the subjectivity of visual processing require us to move beyond the familiar clichés about the Romantic privileging of the individual mind and that "visual experience in the nineteenth century, despite all the attempts to authenticate and naturalize it, no longer has anything like the apodictic claims of the camera obscura to establish its truth." *Techniques of the Observer: On Vision and Modernity in the Nineteenth Century* (Cambridge, MA: MIT Press, 1990), 14. At the same time, Crary wants to demonstrate that the autonomy of subjective vision also allows for new forms of social control.

44. The Valmy cannonade took place on September 20. On September 21 and 22 the monarchy was officially abolished, and the First French Republic was declared. For a discussion of the beginning of the French revolutionary wars see Gunther E. Rothenberg, *The Art of Warfare in the Age of Napoleon* (Bloomington: Indiana University Press, 1978), 31–36.

45. Goethe, *Campaign in France*, 651–52.

46. Quoted in Friedrich A. Kittler, *Gramophone, Film, Typewriter*, trans. Geoffrey Winthrop-Young and Michael Wutz (Stanford, CA: Stanford University Press, 1999), 130.

47. Ibid., 129–30.

48. Goethe, *Campaign in France*, 634.

49. Ibid., 655.

50. Ibid., 676.

51. Tolstoy, *War and Peace*, 291.

52. Quoted in James Clifton, "Mediated War," in *The Plains of Mars: European War Prints, 1500–1825, from the Collection of the Sarah Campbell Blaffer Foundation*, ed. James Clifton and Leslie M. Scattone (New Haven, CT: Yale University Press, 2009), 46.

53. Ibid.

54. James Clifton argues: "The tendency of monumental battle paintings to engulf the viewer was increased exponentially with the advent of panoramas— often of battle scenes—in the late eighteenth century and their proliferation in the early years of the nineteenth century" (ibid., 45–46).

55. Marrinan sees history paintings and later the panorama as "attempts to develop types of representation where the process of narration unfolds in concert with a spectator who can move," a motion that will ultimately be taken over by the movie camera, which will move for the spectator. Marrinan, "Literal," 193–94.

56. Bernard Comment, *The Panorama* (London: Reaktion, 1999), 8.

57. In his remarks on the panorama Walter Benjamin dwells on the lack of windows: "The interest of the panorama is in seeing the true city—the city indoors. What stands within the windowless house is the true." *The Arcades Project*, trans. Howard Eiland and Kevin McLaughlin (Cambridge, MA: Harvard University Press, 1999), 532.

58. Jeff Wall, "Restoration: Interview with Martin Schwander," in *Jeff Wall*, ed. Thierry de Duve, Arielle Pelenc, and Boris Groys (London: Phaidon, 2002), 135.

59. For a discussion of the creation of the image see Richard Vine, "Wall's Wager," *Art in America* (April 1996): 89.

60. *Contacts*, vol. 2, *The Renewal of Contemporary Photography: The World's Greatest Photographers Reveal the Secrets Behind Their Images* (France: Arte Video; Chicago: Facets Video, 2000), DVD.

61. Wall, "Restoration," 129.

62. Wall was trained as an art historian, and his writings about contemporary artists have been influential. His willingness to discourse at length about his own artworks can at times give the impression that he is engaged in the same gesture of control that the panorama itself employed as he tells his audience exactly how they should look at what he is showing them. Some of the scholarship about Wall's work has suffered from a tendency to repeat his interpretations of his photographs as though they were self-evidently definitive.

63. Wall, "Restoration," 129.

64. Ibid., 131.

Chapter Three

1. On technological representation and war since the nineteenth century see Caroline Brothers, *War and Photography: A Cultural History* (New York: Routledge, 1997); Manuel Köppen, *Das Entsetzen des Beobachters: Krieg und Medien im 19. und 20. Jahrhundert* (Heidelberg: Universitätsverlag Winter, 2005); Gerhard Paul, *Bilder des Krieges/Krieg der Bilder: Die Visualisierung des modernen Krieges* (Munich: Schöningh, 2004); and John Taylor, *Body Horror: Photojournalism, Catastrophe, and War* (New York: NYU Press, 1998).

2. Peter Maslowski, *Armed with Cameras: The American Military Photographers of World War II* (New York: Macmillan, 1993), 4. Maslowski partly bases this argument on comments made as the new technology was first emerging, as when a *New York Times* reporter wrote in September 1862: "We recognize the battlefield as a reality, but it stands as a remote one" (ibid., 3).

3. Joel Snyder, "Photographers and Photographs of the Civil War," in *The Documentary Photo as a Work of Art* (Chicago: David and Alfred Smart Gallery, University of Chicago, 1976), 20.

4. Snyder cautions against assuming that technological limitations explain why there were almost no action photos in the American Civil War. On the limitations of the wet-plate process and the constraints it imposed on attempts to take pictures of battles as they happened, see Robert Taft, *Photography and the American Scene: A Social History, 1839–1889* (New York: Peter Smith, 1964); and Doug Munson, "The Practice of Wet-Plate Photography," in *The Documentary Photograph as a Work of Art: American Photographs 1860–1876*, ed. Joel Snyder and Doug Munson (Chicago: David and Alfred Smart Gallery, University of Chicago, 1976), 33–38.

5. See, for example, Susan D. Moeller, *Shooting War: Photography and the American Experience of Combat* (New York: Basic Books, 1989), 18.

6. Jay Ruby writes that "beginning with the advent of the 'illustrated press' in the mid-nineteenth century (e.g., *London Illustrated Press* and *Harper's Weekly*),

the pictorial representation of death, particularly during wartime, became a common feature of reportage." *Secure the Shadow: Death and Photography in America* (Cambridge, MA: MIT Press, 1995), 13. Although it was not until the late nineteenth century that newspapers could print reproductions of photos rather than engravings of them, many photographs were exhibited in galleries, and large numbers were reproduced and distributed in individual copies, so by the time of the American Civil War, such images were in widespread circulation.

7. On the restrictions on battlefield photography in the First World War see John Keegan, introduction, in Phillip Knightley, *The Eye of War: Words and Photographs from the Front Line* (Washington, DC: Smithsonian Books, 2003), 7; and Ruby, *Secure the Shadow*, 15.

8. Associated Press, "Iraq Prisoner Abuse 'Un-American,' Says Rumsfeld," *Washington Times*, May 7, 2004, www.washingtontimes.com/news/2004/may/7/20040507-115901-6736r/. It is crucial to remember that the photos that blind-sided Rumsfeld and the Pentagon were not Snyder's close-ups of the "center of the action" but carefully crafted scenes, arranged like studio portraits or the stylized setups that professional art photographers might orchestrate. If Rumsfeld called the resulting images "unbelievable," it makes no sense to ask whether what disturbed him more was that the guards were torturing prisoners or that they were photographing themselves doing so because, in this grisly performance art, there was no clear difference between the act of torture and the act of recording it with a camera. It could easily be argued that the soldiers committed these acts only because they were being photographed.

9. Louis Roug, "Extreme Cinema Vérité," *Los Angeles Times*, March 14, 2005, http://articles.latimes.com/2005/mar/14/world/fg-video514.

10. Maslowski, *Armed with Cameras*, 5–6.

11. During the First World War, news editors apparently hoped that individual soldiers would flood the press with illegal images from pocket cameras, but this did not transpire. See Duncan Anderson, *Glass Warriors: The Camera at War* (London: HarperCollins, 2005), 91.

12. *National Geographic* (September 1944), 25.

13. See Jorge Lewinski, *The Camera at War: A History of War Photography from 1848 to the Present Day* (New York: Simon and Schuster, 1978), 95ff. During the Second World War the Office of War Information reviewed the photos printed in newspapers and magazines and the film footage aired in the newsreels shown before movies in local cinemas. All the major news organizations voluntarily adopted the government's official code of wartime practices for the press.

14. John Steinbeck, *Once There Was a War* (New York: Viking, 1958), 155–56.

15. Nicholas Mirzoeff, *Watching Babylon: The War in Iraq and Global Visual Culture* (New York: Routledge, 2005), 77.

16. Ibid.

17. As it became more common in the later years of the Second World War for the press to publish pictures of dead U.S. servicemen, the images tended to be similar to the New Guinea photo in that they generally did not show gross mutilations, the wounded bleeding to death, or obviously burned bodies. See Maslowski, *Armed with Cameras*, 82ff.

18. See Allyson Booth, *Postcards from the Trenches: Negotiating the Space Between Modernism and the First World War* (New York: Oxford University Press, 1996), 21.

19. *Life* 42(12) (September 20, 1943): 34. For a discussion of this image see Barbie Zelizer, *Remembering to Forget: Holocaust Memory Through the Camera's Eye* (Chicago: Chicago University Press, 1998), 36.

20. Susan Sontag, *On Photography* (New York: Farrar, Straus and Giroux, 1973), 70. One could ask more questions about the psychological assumptions informing the decision to use this image in an effort to galvanize the American public. Why, for example, was there no concern that the photograph might demoralize its audience?

21. Michael Marrinan, "Literal/Literary/'Lexie': History, Text, and Authority in Napoleonic Painting," *Word & Image* 7(3) (July–September 1991): 187. Like the photo of dead soldiers that appeared in *Life*, the war images of the Napoleonic era had an uneasy relationship to the verbal texts that were shown alongside them and purported to explain them. Many battle paintings of the period were exhibited with quotations from official government propaganda bulletins, the dogmatic claims of which the paintings were presumed to illustrate.

22. Ibid., 191. See also 186–87.

23. In some paintings of the period, it is not that art is used to glorify war so much as the existence of war is celebrated as a tribute to art. See Christopher Prendergast, *Napoleon and History Painting: Antoine-Jean Gros's* La Bataille d'Eylau (Oxford: Clarendon, 1997), 80.

24. Mark E. Neely Jr. explains: "Photography was more a business than an art. Recordkeeping was poor; these men were primarily making money, not history. Few photographers, if any, were directly tied to news organizations. Most were what we might call freelancers, trying to capture images to sell to ordinary citizens or to the soldiers themselves for money to put food on the table." Preface to *Landscapes of the Civil War: Newly Discovered Photographs from the Medford Historical Society*, ed. Constance Sullivan (New York: Knopf, 1995), 12.

25. On Civil War portraiture see William F. Stapp, introduction to *Landscapes of the Civil War*, 18.

26. Alan Trachtenberg, *Reading American Photographs: Images as History, Mathew Brady to Walker Evans* (New York: Hill and Wang, 1990), 74–75.

27. Steven Conn, "Narrative Trauma and Civil War History Painting, or Why Are These Pictures So Terrible?" *History and Theory* 41(4) (December 2002): 33, 21. Conn concludes that the Civil War coincided with a "revolutionary moment in American visual culture. Photography and mass-produced graphic illustrations in newspapers and magazines created thousands of images of the war. The speed with which these images could be created, and the possibility of their reproduction ad infinitum, proved tough competition for artists who still worked with paint on canvas" (ibid., 21).

28. Ibid., 35.

29. See Neely, preface, 9–14. Whatever one's emphasis, it is important that we not be too quick to identify technological change as the sole cause of shifts in the way in which the public views images of warfare remotely. Decades after the invention of the process to mass-produce photos economically for newspapers, many editors continued to rely on traditional engravings because dramatic narrative illustrations constructed on the model of traditional history paintings were still extremely popular. In other words, it is wrong to assume that the public embraces the products of novel media simply for the sake of their novelty.

30. "When it came to battles, photography robbed armed conflict of the operatic glamour often given it by traditional painting." H. H. Arnason, Marla F. Prather, and Daniel Wheeler, *History of Modern Art* (New York: Abrams, 1998), 41.

31. Trachtenberg, *Reading American Photographs*, 75.

32. On the complex relationship between Gardner's images and their accompanying texts see Anthony W. Lee and Elizabeth Young, *On Alexander Gardner's* Photographic Sketch Book of the Civil War (Berkeley: University of California Press, 2007).

33. Alexander Gardner, *Gardner's Photographic Sketchbook of the War 1861–1865* (New York: Delano Greenidge Editions, 2001), 80.

34. Ibid., preface (no page number).

35. Ibid., 90.

36. Ibid.

37. For a thorough discussion of how this scene was manufactured see William Frassanito, *Gettysburg: A Journey in Time* (New York: Scribner's Sons, 1975), 186–92. Frassanito claims that Gardner and his associates photographed

this body six times in two different locations over the course of an hour before getting the "perfect" shot.

38. The revelation that Gardner moved his corpses to suit his tastes is part of an established history of casting doubt on the circumstances surrounding photographic depictions of the recently deceased. Another well-known example involves the escapades of Arthur Fellig, aka Weegee, who worked on the Lower East Side of New York City in the 1930s and 1940s. While Fellig claimed to monitor police radios and arrive at murder scenes just after they had occurred, scholars have questioned how "fresh" his views to a kill actually were.

39. Gardner, *Gardner's Photographic Sketchbook*, 90.

40. Frassanito, *Gettysburg*, 192.

41. Although the verb "shoot" was not used to describe taking a picture with a camera until the final decade of the nineteenth century, it is clear that Gardner is reflecting on the link between taking pictures and taking shots at one's enemy.

42. See Stapp, introduction, 18.

43. Reports from Sevastopol reached the public in London more quickly than reports from the Falkland Islands did in 1982. See Paul Reynolds, "Israel Seeks Airwave Supremacy," BBC News, January 12, 2009, http://news.bbc.co .uk/2/hi/middle_east/7823887.stm.

44. See Ulrich Keller, *The Ultimate Spectacle: A Visual History of the Crimean War* (New York: Routledge, 2001), 119–71; and Susan Sontag, *Regarding the Pain of Others* (New York: Farrar, Straus and Giroux, 2002), 53–54.

45. After studying the photos, consulting with a variety of experts, and taking a trip to the site where the pictures were made, Errol Morris concluded the following:

> And so, it turns out that Keller, [Mark] Haworth-Booth [former curator of photography at the Victoria and Albert Museum in London] and Sontag are right. It is OFF [photo with no cannonballs on the road] before ON [photo with cannonballs on the road]. I tried hard to prove that Keller and Sontag were wrong—to prove that ON came before OFF. I failed. I can't deny it. But I did prove that they were right for the wrong reasons. It is not their assessment of Fenton's character or lack of character that establishes the order of the pictures. Nor is it sun angle and shadow. Rather it is the motion of ancillary rocks—rocks that had been kicked, nudged, displaced between the taking of one picture and the other. Rocks that no one cared about. "Those little guys that got kicked aside," as [my friend] Dennis [Purcell] called them. Their displacement was recorded on those wet collodion plates not because someone wanted to record it. It happened inadvertently. Ancillary rocks, ancillary evidence—essential information. (*Believing Is Seeing (Observations on the Mysteries of Photography)* [New York: Penguin, 2011], 69)

46. Sontag, *Regarding the Pain of Others*, 50. It is telling that Sontag seems to distinguish sharply between the artifice of arranging people or bodies and the artifice of arranging inanimate objects. Throughout her writings on photography she is markedly inconsistent when it comes to the question of whether all photos are in some respect "posed." In some instances she is acutely attuned to the staged elements of pictures that others have celebrated as "un-tampered evidence." At other junctures she lapses into a naïve faith in the evidentiary powers of the photographic medium.

47. Richard Pare, *Roger Fenton* (New York: Aperture Foundation, 1987), cited by Morris, *Believing Is Seeing*, 17–18.

48. In discussions of Fenton's photograph it is usually mentioned in passing that the biblical quote employed as its title is a reference to the line from Tennyson's poem about the annihilation of the Light Brigade, the British cavalry unit that rode "into the valley of death." As maps made during the Crimean War clearly show, however, *Valley of the Shadow of Death*, the title of Fenton's photograph, was the British soldiers' nickname for a spot that was bombarded from three major Russian artillery batteries, whereas the "Valley of Death" that Tennyson would make famous was farther to the east. It is possible that Fenton assumed that many reading his title would conflate the two locales. See Morris, *Believing Is Seeing*, 21.

49. See Theodore Barber, "Phantasmagorical Wonders: The Magic Lantern Ghost Show in Nineteenth-Century America," *Film History* 3(2) (1989): 73–86.

50. On the "about-to-die image" see Barbie Zelizer, "The Voice of the Visual in Memory," in *Framing Public Memory*, ed. Kendall R. Phillips (Tuscaloosa: University of Alabama Press, 2004), 157–86.

51. In support of the notion that photography can capture something that motion pictures cannot, it should be noted that the Vietnamese general executed his victim in front of both an Associated Press photographer and an NBC cameraman, but the resulting video of the event is almost entirely unknown.

Looking beyond war, the most famous instant-of-death photograph is probably the picture of Jack Ruby shooting Lee Harvey Oswald shortly after the assassination of John F. Kennedy.

52. Ulrich Baer, *Spectral Evidence: The Photography of Trauma* (Cambridge, MA: MIT Press, 2002), 7.

53. See Lewinski, *Camera at War*, esp. 88–89; and Phillip Knightley, *The First Casualty: From the Crimea to Vietnam: The War Correspondent as Hero, Propagandist, and Myth Maker* (New York: Harcourt Brace Jovanovich, 1976), 209–12. Knightley concludes that the existing evidence makes it impossible to decide how Capa's photo was made, but new evidence and new charges of inauthenticity emerge each decade. For the most recent manifestation of the controversy see: Giles Tremlett, "Wrong Place, Wrong Man? Fresh Doubts on Capa's Famed War

Photo," *Observer* (*Guardian*), June 14, 2009, www.guardian.co.uk/world/2009
/jun/14/robert-capa-spain-photography; and Larry Richter, "New Doubts
Raised Over Famous War Photo," *New York Times*, August 17, 2009, www
.nytimes.com/2009/08/18/arts/design/18capa.html?_r=1&hp.

54. Quoted in Lewinski, *Camera at War*, 89.

55. Sontag, *Regarding the Pain of Others*, 59–60.

56. Recent incidents involving U.S. forces in Afghanistan suggest that killing for the sake of a picture is not nearly as rare as one might hope. See Matth-
ias Gebauer and Hasnain Kazim, "US Army Apologizes for Horrific Photos
from Afghanistan," *Spiegel Online International*, March 21, 2011, www.spiegel
.de/international/world/0,1518,752310,00.html.

57. Quoted in Anderson, *Glass Warriors*, photo section between 134 and 135.

58. Eddie Adams, "Eulogy," *Time*, July 27, 1998, 19.

59. Ibid.

60. Ernst Jünger, *On Pain*, trans. David C. Durst (New York: Telos,
2008), 39.

61. Ibid., 39, 40.

62. Ibid., 39. Invoking Karl-Heinz Bohrer's account of shock and terror as
a perceptual mode in his *Die Ästhetik des Schreckens*, Brigitte Werneburg and
Christopher Phillips stress that Jünger "links the technology of warfare with
the techniques of perception. Modern technological warfare engenders a specifically modern form of perception, which centers on the experience of terror
and shock." "Ernst Jünger and the Transformed World," *October* 62 (Autumn
1992): 50.

63. In addition to *The Dangerous Moment* Jünger edited two books of photos from the First World War; he also produced *The Transformed World* (1933),
an account of the crisis of the modern world largely organized around documentary photos.

64. Jünger's "aestheticization of violence" is more complicated than is often
thought to be the case. In one of the most famous passages from his wartime
memoirs he offers an account of an evening bombing raid he experienced in
German-occupied Paris in 1944: "During the second wave, at sunset, I held in my
hand a glass of burgundy with strawberries floating in it. The city with its red
towers and domes lay stretched out in breathtaking beauty like a chalice that is
overflown for deadly pollination. Everything was *Schauspiel* [pageant, spectacle,
drama], pure power, affirmed and exalted by pain." *German Writings Before and
After 1945*, ed. Jürgen Peters (New York: Continuum, 2002), 33. This passage is
routinely invoked as evidence of Jünger's militaristic—if not fascistic—conflation
of pleasure, pain, and the manifestation of power in which the most banal amen-
ities of the faux-aristocratic lifestyle—here burgundy and strawberries—go

hand in hand with the destruction of a city. However, what Jünger calls "beauty" is actually the instability of the representational schemas that war sets in play, which means that, despite what he explicitly says, Jünger is writing in the idiom of the sublime as much as of the beautiful. The key question in diagnosing the ideological tenor of his text is whether he believes that it is possible to control the interplay of these signifying dynamics or whether the experience of being a war spectator is distinguished by the recognition that one is constantly forced to sacrifice one's linguistic powers, a sacrifice through which one wins no corresponding intellectual or moral authority.

65. Ernst Jünger, "On Danger," trans. Donald Reneau, *New German Critique* 59 (Spring–Summer 1993): 30.

66. Versions of the insight that the subject of war and the subject of perception are identical constructs recur throughout the twentieth century. Paul Virilio attributes this claim to Maurice Merleau-Ponty: "The problem of knowing who is the subject of the state and war will be of exactly the same kind as the problem of knowing who is the subject of perception." Cited in Paul Virilio, *War and Cinema: The Logistics of Perception*, trans. Patrick Camiller (New York: Verso, 1989), 2.

67. Walter Benjamin, "On Some Motifs in Baudelaire," in *Selected Writings*, vol. 4, *1938–1940*, ed. Howard Eiland and Michael W. Jennings (Cambridge, MA: Harvard University Press, 2003), 317. In a slightly earlier text Benjamin clarified his reliance on Proust's vocabulary: "Concerning the *mémoire involontaire*: not only do its images not come up when we try to call them up; rather, they are images which we have never seen before we remember them . . . Yet these images, developed in the darkroom of the lived moment, are the most important we will ever see." "A Short Speech on Proust" (delivered on his fortieth birthday, 1932), quoted in Miriam Hansen, "Benjamin, Cinema, and Experience: 'The Blue Flower in the Land of Technology,'" *New German Critique* 40 (Winter 1987): 179. In "The Storyteller" (1936) Benjamin makes it clear that he, like Freud and Jünger, was guided in his reflections on these problems by the ails of shell-shocked veterans returning home from the Great War: "Beginning with the First World War, a process became apparent which continues to this day. Wasn't it noticeable at the end of the war that men who returned from the battlefield had grown silent—not richer but poorer in communicable experience?" "The Storyteller," in *Selected Writings*, vol. 3, *1935–1938*, ed. Howard Eiland and Michael W. Jennings (Cambridge, MA: Harvard University Press, 2002), 143–44.

68. Benjamin writes: "Thus, technology has subjected the human sensorium to a complex kind of training. There came a day when a new and urgent need for stimuli was met by film. In a film, perception conditioned by shock [*chockförmige*

Wahrnehmung] was established as a formal principle." "On Some Motifs," 328. Benjamin is particularly interested in the ways in which repeated exposure to shock trains consciousness to parry its blows: "Perhaps the special achievement of shock defense is the way it assigns an incident a precise point in time in consciousness, at the cost of the integrity of the incident's contents" (ibid., 319). For Benjamin, Baudelaire's poetry is a sustained exploration of shock defense.

69. Ibid., 328. A number of scholars have explored the implications of Benjamin's theory of shock for other representational media. See, for example, Avital Ronell's "TraumaTV: Twelve Steps Beyond the Pleasure Principle," *Finitude's Score: Essays for the End of the Millennium* (Lincoln: University of Nebraska Press, 1994), 305–28. Drawing on Sontag and Debord, Marc Redfield has developed a notion of "virtual trauma" in order to help understand the television coverage of 9/11 and the violence inherent in media technology in general. See *The Rhetoric of Terror: Reflections on 9/11 and the War on Terror* (New York: Fordham University Press, 2009), esp. 3–4, 29.

70. Eduardo Cadava, "'Lapsus Imaginis': The Image in Ruins," *October* 96 (Spring 2001): 48.

71. Quoted in *Napoleon on the Art of War*, ed. and trans. Jay Luvaas (New York: Simon and Schuster, 1999), 132. The epigraph to Cartier-Bresson's book *Images à la sauvette* (published in English as *The Decisive Moment*) was a quotation from the seventeenth-century Cardinal de Retz: "There is nothing in this world that does not have a decisive moment." *The Decisive Moment: Photography by Henri Cartier-Bresson* (New York: Simon and Schuster, 1952), no page number.

72. Cartier-Bresson, *Decisive Moment*, no page number.

73. Quoted in Adam Bernstein, "The Acknowledged Master of the Moment," *Washington Post*, August 5, 2004.

74. Quoted in ibid.

75. The size, detail, and panoramic quality of these photographs invite comparisons with the work of Andreas Gursky, but whereas Gursky's shots often seem to be taken from the perspective of a surveillance camera, the subjective gaze of Delahaye's images is harder to pin down.

76. Peter Lennon, "The Big Picture," *Guardian*, January 31, 2004, www .guardian.co.uk/artanddesign/2004/jan/31/photography. The suggestion that Delahaye needed to change his vocation points toward the much-discussed crisis in contemporary photojournalism, precipitated by the fact that few news outlets are still willing to pay for elaborate photo essays from the field. It is frequently said that many photographers who would not otherwise have looked to exhibiting in galleries or publishing books of their work have had to try to become part of the art world in order to make a living.

77. Michael Fried has argued that what one sees in Delahaye's work is "not Cartier-Bresson's 'decisive moment' so much as one that allows a maximum of

slow, exploratory penetration by the viewer." "On Luc Delahaye," *Artforum* (March 2006): 66.

78. "Les 'tableaux d'histoire' contemplatifs de Luc Delahaye," interview with Luc Delahaye by Michael Guerrin, *Le Monde*, March 3, 2003, 17; quoted in Michael Fried, *Why Photography Matters as Art as Never Before* (New Haven, CT: Yale University Press, 2008), 187; translation modified.

79. Jörg Colberg, "A Conversation with Luc Delahaye," *American Photo*, June 12, 2007, http://jmcolberg.com/weblog/2007/06/a_conversation_with_luc _delahaye.html.

80. "Les 'tableaux d'histoire' contemplatifs de Luc Delahaye," interview with Luc Delahaye by Michael Guerrin.

81. Colberg, "Conversation with Luc Delahaye."

82. Bill Sullivan, "The Real Thing: Photographer Luc Delahaye," *Artnet*, April 10, 2003, www.artnet.com/magazine/features/sullivan/sullivan4-10-03. asp.

83. In another interview Delahaye related: "I find the stillness in speed, as I find the silence in the noise." *Paroles d'artistes / Acquisitions du Musée national d'art moderne-Cci, Centre Pompidou*, vol. 1 (Paris: Éditions du Centre Pompidou, 2006), DVD.

84. Foreword to *Decisive Moment*, final page (no page numbers).

85. Lennon, "Big Picture."

86. Colberg, "Conversation with Luc Delahaye." Delahaye was somewhat less than forthcoming in his response: "No, I don't feel the need to do what has already been done" (ibid.).

87. Sontag, *On Photography*, 168.

88. Ibid., 110.

89. Ibid., 20.

90. Alessandra Stanley, "Bob Hope's Spirit, but No Cheesecake," *New York Times*, June 12, 2009.

91. Even with these clarifications one could still argue that Sontag's argument simplifies the considerable mediation involved in any engagement with photographic or cinematic documents as historical evidence. Discussing records of the atrocities of the Third Reich, she writes: "At the time of the first photographs of the Nazi camps, there was nothing banal about these images. After thirty years, a saturation point may have been reached. In these last decades, 'concerned' photography has done at least as much to deaden conscience as to arouse it." *On Photography*, 21. In fact, scholars have argued that in the first instance the shocking nature of photographs of concentration camps necessitated supplementary proof in order to discount viewers' suspicions that what they were viewing was simply not real: "But if the documentary evidence from the liberated camps validated the eyewitness accounts, the images

themselves were so unbelievable they in turn required eyewitness corroboration. The footage could scarcely be credited as real. The Army conducted excursions through the camps . . . and arranged for government, press, and Hollywood officials to visit the actual locations." Thomas Doherty, *Projections of War: Hollywood, American Culture, and World War II*, rev. ed. (New York: Columbia University Press, 1999), 249.

92. Sontag, *On Photography*, 20–21.

93. Ibid., 168.

94. Ibid., 23. Judith Butler has strongly critiqued this argument:

> In my view, it won't do to say, as Sontag repeatedly does throughout her writings on photography, that the photograph cannot by itself provide an interpretation, that we need captions and written analysis to supplement the discrete and punctual image, which can only affect us and never offer a full understanding of what we see. . . . [I]t seems important to consider that the photograph, in framing reality, is already interpreting what will count within the frame; this act of delimitation is surely interpretive, as are the effects of angle, focus, and light. ("Photography, War, Outrage," *PMLA* 120[3] [May 2005]: 823)

For a response to Butler's critique more sympathetic to Sontag see Manisha Basu, "The Hamartia of Light and Shadow: Susan Sontag in the Digital Age," *Postmodern Culture* 16(3) (2006).

95. At other points Sontag seems to grant that the "reality" of the situation is more complex than this notorious passage would suggest: "The photograph gives mixed signals. Stop this, it urges. But it also exclaims, What a spectacle!" *On Photography*, 76–77.

96. Sontag does go out of her way to distance herself from the claim that there is no clear distinction between the media's presentation of war and war, a view she associates with Guy Debord and Jean Baudrillard and dismisses as a folly that only privileged Westerners have the luxury of enjoying.

97. Theodora Vischer and Heidi Naef, introductory notes, in *Jeff Wall: Catalogue Raisonné 1978–2004* (Basel: Schaulager, 2005), 338. In an interview Wall described the process of creating the image piece by piece, shooting one or two actor-soldiers at a time. *Contacts*, vol. 2, *The Renewal of Contemporary Photography: The World's Greatest Photographers Reveal the Secrets Behind Their Images* (France: Arte Video, 2000), DVD. Richard Vine emphasizes the precision that went into the crafting of Wall's picture:

> What looks like a roadside gully filled with costumed actors is in fact an elaborate studio setup. Every stone, twig, mound of dirt and piece of scrap

metal was gathered into a warehouse-sized interior reminiscent of a classic Hollywood soundstage. In this way, lighting could be perfectly controlled for the final composite that was computer-assembled from four weeks' worth of individual and small-group shots. In short, though its subject is ostensibly chaos, *Dead Troops* is itself an obsessively planned and orchestrated performance. ("Wall's Wager," *Art in America* [April 1996]: 93)

98. Sontag, *Regarding the Pain of Others*, 123.

99. Marsha Lederman, "The Master of 'Blatant Artifice' Speaks," *Toronto Globe and Mail*, May 24, 2008.

100. *Jeff Wall: Selected Essays and Interviews* (New York: MOMA, 2007), 260.

101. *Contacts: The Renewal of Contemporary Photography.*

102. Louis Kaplan has observed that "Sontag's review of *Dead Troops Talk* avoids the mention of any such prankster antics on the part of the dead troops and offers a more somber reading that is devoid of Bataille's anguished gaiety." "Unknowing Susan Sontag's *Regarding*: Recutting with Georges Bataille," *Postmodern Culture* 19(2) (January 2009).

103. Sontag, *Regarding the Pain of Others*, 125–26.

104. Jean Baudrillard ridiculed Sontag for exploiting the war for her own purposes in her performance for the media. See Jean Baudrillard, "No Reprieve for Sarajevo," trans. Patrice Riemens, *CTheory*, September 28, 1994, www .ctheory.net/articles.aspx?id=60; originally published in *Liberation*, January 8, 1994.

105. In this respect, despite the fact that Sontag explicitly notes that "no one is looking out of the picture," the implicit logic of her analysis of Wall is at odds with Michael Fried's argument that this photo "is consistent with the crucial principle of the Diderotian *tableau*—the use of absorptive motifs and structures to establish the ontological illusion that the beholder does not exist." *Why Photography Matters*, 34.

Chapter Four

1. Norman Bryson has suggested that "in the descriptions of battle one sees a marked tendency towards a signification that is highly abstract: the model here is the war-room, with its maps and pointers, markers and counters. Although only a simulacrum of the battlefield, the war-room is also its real theater: in the conversion from the mud and chaos of the field to the hygienic spread of the diagram, nothing essential is lost. On the contrary, the essence of the battle is revealed in the schema." *Word and Image: French*

Painting of the Ancien Régime (New York: Cambridge University Press, 1981), 36.

2. John Keegan has argued that, by 1914, a general took it as a matter of course that his battlefield would inevitably be beset by a "cloud of unknowing"; hence his main work "had now to be done in his office, before the battle began." *The Face of Battle: A Study of Agincourt, Waterloo, and the Somme* (New York: Penguin, 1976), 265. Major General J. F. C. Fuller, a British officer and military theorist who is best known for the visions of a completely mechanized army that he developed between the First and Second World Wars, described the rise of the modern war room in starkly negative terms. He wrote of "the amazing unconscious change which rose out of the Franco-Prussian War, and which in a few years obliterated true generalship, dehumanizing and despiritualizing the general until he was turned into an office soldier." *Generalship: Its Diseases and Their Cure* (Harrisburg, PA: Military Service Publishing, 1936), 51.

3. Stephen Kern, *The Culture of Time and Space: 1880–1918* (Cambridge, MA: Harvard University Press, 1983), 295.

4. Vincent Sherry, *The Great War and the Language of Modernism* (New York: Oxford University Press, 2003), 6; and Samuel Hynes, *A War Imagined: The First World War and English Culture* (New York: Collier, 1990), xi. Simultaneously a site of creation and destruction, Europe between 1914 and 1918 has been regarded as the birthplace of artistic, political, and technological trends that bore the most succulent and bitter of fruits. One of the best-known arguments for the cultural significance of the First World War in Britain is Paul Fussell's *The Great War and Modern Memory* (New York: Oxford University Press, 1975). For one of the strongest claims for the impact of the Great War on subsequent avant-garde art movements see Modris Eksteins, *Rites of Spring: The Great War and the Birth of the Modern Age* (New York: Anchor, 1989).

5. Jay Winter and Blaine Baggett write that "the recognition that something terrible, something overwhelming, something irreversible had happened in the Great War explains its enduring significance for those born after the Armistice. For this war was not only the most important and far-reaching political and military event of the century; it was also the most important imaginative event." *The Great War and the Shaping of the 20th Century* (New York: Penguin, 1996), 361.

6. Erich Ludendorff, *Ludendorff's Own Story* (New York: Harper and Brothers, 1920), 2. The original German text was *Meine Kriegserinnerungen 1914–1918* (Berlin: Mittler und Sohn, 1919).

7. During the First World War, German discussions about the possibility of fostering a genuine "people's war" were partly shaped by the ideological debates

surrounding the famous *levée en masse* of August 1793, with which the fledgling First Republic of France attempted to put the entire population at the service of the army. See Michael Geyer, "People's War: The German Debate About a *Levée en masse* in October 1918," in *The People in Arms: Military Myth and National Mobilization Since the French Revolution*, ed. Daniel Moran and Arthur Waldron (New York: Cambridge University Press, 2003).

8. For a discussion of the impact that visions of a "greater" Great War had on interwar modernism in Europe see Paul K. Saint-Amour, "Airwar Prophecy and Interwar Modernism," *Comparative Literature Studies* 42(2) (2005): 130–61.

9. Arguing that the Napoleonic era saw the advent of total war, David Bell is nonetheless cautious about the term:

> The concept of "total war" deserves some explanation. It has enormous resonance, and many historians have used it to describe the wars of 1792–1815. But it is also one of those concepts that seems to get blurred the closer you come to it. It is often defined as a war involving the complete mobilization of a society's resources to achieve the absolute destruction of an enemy, with all distinction erased between combatants and noncombatants. This formulation seems, at first, clear enough. But can any real war live up to this ideal standard? (Even a massive thermonuclear exchange would not involve the mobilization of all of a society's resources!) And if not, what determines which wars come sufficiently close to the ideal to qualify? The ambiguities are such that one leading scholar, Roger Chickering, has come close to concluding that the concept should simply be scrapped. (*The First Total War: Napoleon's Europe and the Birth of Warfare as We Know It* [New York: Houghton Mifflin, 2007], 7–8)

For his part, Chickering criticizes modern scholars for relying almost exclusively on a romantic bildungsroman in which the maturation process of "total war" begins with the French Revolution and the Napoleonic era and culminates in Hiroshima as its key features—the size of armies, the mobilization of entire economies for the war effort, improvements in killing technologies—gradually become manifest. See Chickering's "Total War: The Use and Abuse of a Concept," in *Anticipating Total War: The German and American Experiences, 1871–1914*, ed. Manfred F. Boemeke, Roger Chickering, and Stig Förster (New York: Cambridge University Press, 1999), 13–15.

10. Cited in Mark E. Neely Jr., "Was the Civil War a Total War?" in *On the Road to Total War: The American Civil War and the German Wars of Unification, 1861–1871*, ed. Stig Förster and Jörg Nagler (Cambridge: Cambridge University Press, 1997), 33. Douhet also wrote about "la guerra integrale," echoing

Georges Clemenceau's 1917 call for France to fight "la guerre intégrale." On Douhet as a war theorist see Ira Katznelson, *Desolation and Enlightenment: Political Knowledge After Total War, Totalitarianism, and the Holocaust* (New York: Columbia University Press, 2003), esp. 18ff. See also Chickering, "Total War," 16–17. Chickering notes that different proponents of an "integrated war" envisioned very different things; some hoped for total civilian control of the military, whereas others were aiming for a military dictatorship.

11. Carl von Clausewitz, *On War*, ed. and trans. Michael Howard and Peter Paret (Princeton, NJ: Princeton University Press, 1989), 78.

12. Ibid.

13. Ernst Jünger, "Total Mobilization," in *The Heidegger Controversy: A Critical Reader*, ed. Richard Wolin (Cambridge, MA: MIT Press, 1993), 126. Today the term *total war* is often associated with Joseph Goebbels's call for just such a "total mobilization" in his February 1943 speech following the German defeat at Stalingrad: "Wollt ihr den totalen Krieg?"

14. Jünger, "Total Mobilization," 128, 126.

15. Allyson Booth, *Postcards from the Trenches: Negotiating the Space Between Modernism and the First World War* (New York: Oxford University Press, 1996), 89.

16. Ibid., 94. Jünger was also attuned to the metaphorical potential of the word *line*, as when he wrote in his 1931 essay "On Danger" that "the world war appears as the great red balance line under the bourgeois era." "On Danger," trans. Donald Reneau, *New German Critique* 59 (Spring–Summer 1993): 29.

17. Booth, *Postcards*, 92–93.

18. Ernst Jünger, *Storm of Steel* (first ed. 1920), trans. Michael Hofmann (New York: Penguin, 2004), 33. As is well known, Jünger revised this text no less than eleven times. I cite from the first edition.

19. Quoted in Duncan Anderson, *Glass Warriors: The Camera at War* (London: HarperCollins, 2005), 91.

20. Jünger, *Storm of Steel*, 26.

21. Ibid.

22. Paul Fussell, *The Great War and Modern Memory* (New York: Oxford University Press, 1977), 30.

23. Sigmund Freud, "Thoughts for the Times on War and Death," in *The Standard Edition of the Complete Psychological Works of Sigmund Freud*, ed. James Strachey (London: Hogarth, 1957–1974), vol. 14: 287. Acknowledging that collective enmity is something of a mystery, Freud speculates that when people are considered as a group, "all individual moral acquisitions are obliterated, and only the most primitive, the oldest, the crudest mental attitudes are left" (ibid., 288).

24. Ibid., 289.

25. Freud claims that our cultural attitudes toward death are different strategies for putting aside thoughts about the Grim Reaper's plans for us. At the same time, he proposes that life without any prospect of death has no interest. With nothing at stake, our experience becomes impoverished, even empty. To address this *ennui*, people engage with the phenomenon of human finitude through a variety of different media, foremost among which, Freud notes, are novels and the theater. Reading *Madame Bovary* or watching *Hedda Gabler* offers us an intimate engagement with mortality as we perish with the heroine, then rise from the ashes to watch and perish again with another heroine the following night. In the process, says Freud, life becomes interesting once more. As Samuel Weber has argued, Freud seems to be describing death as a spectator sport. Samuel Weber, *Targets of Opportunity: On the Militarization of Thinking* (New York: Fordham University Press, 2005), 57.

26. Paul Virilio, *War and Cinema: The Logistics of Perception*, trans. Patrick Camiller (New York: Verso, 1989), 5.

27. On the legal theory of accidents and torts and its importance for literary modernism, see Ravit Reichman, *The Affective Life of Law: Legal Modernism and the Literary Imagination* (Stanford, CA: Stanford University Press, 2009), esp. 18–21.

28. Freud, "Thoughts for the Times on War and Death," vol. 14, 291.

29. Perhaps the best-known text of this discourse is F. T. Marinetti's 1909 "Founding and Manifesto of Futurism," which celebrates the connection between the increasing velocity of automobiles and the rise of car accidents.

30. Whereas in Freud speed is an expression of the impossibility of keeping war's material and signifying forces in lock step, for a writer such as Marinetti, speed is treated as something that augments rather than eludes or confounds experience. This may be why Marinetti, in contrast to Freud, glorifies war.

31. Anton Kaes offers the familiar picture of Jünger's central role in this discourse:

> The most obvious casualty in World War I was the concept of the autonomous subject—itself, as Jünger insists, a creation of the liberal age whose value system and ideology were simply swept away by the dynamics of the machine age. In his treatise of 1932, *Der Arbeiter*, Jünger develops a right-wing utopian image of a radically technological civilization in which a new breed of men, the workers (as worker-soldiers), exist in a constant state of mobilization. Jünger sees modern industrial labor in military terms; Fordism for him is the militarization of the workplace, which he welcomes. The new type of man (*Typus*, as Jünger calls him) who supersedes the bourgeois individual of the nineteenth century could already be seen in the millions of

World War I soldiers, all looking alike under their steel helmets. ("The Cold Gaze: Notes on Mobilization and Modernity," *New German Critique* 59 [Spring–Summer 1993]: 111)

32. Earlier versions of sections of this discussion of *A Fable* appeared in "Great War, Total War, Cold War," *Modernism/Modernity* 16(2) (2009): 211–28. I thank the Johns Hopkins University Press for permission to use this material.

33. "Introduction: Faulkner and War and Peace," in *Faulkner and War*, ed. Noel Polk and Ann J. Abadie (Jackson: University Press of Mississippi, 2004), viii. For a discussion of *A Fable* and its relationship to the theme of war in Faulkner's œuvre in general see Thomas Nordanberg, *Cataclysm as Catalyst: The Theme of War in William Faulkner's Fiction* (Atlantic Highlands, NJ: Humanities Press, 1983).

34. Despite his repeated claims to the contrary, Faulkner himself had no direct experience with the First World War beyond six months of training with the Royal Air Force in Canada in 1918. On the disputes about his service or lack thereof see James G. Watson, "William Faulkner and the Theater of War," in *Faulkner and War*, 20–35.

35. The term *Cold War* is usually credited to George Orwell, who wrote in October 19, 1945, of "the kind of beliefs, and the social structure that would probably prevail in a state which was at once unconquerable and in a permanent state of 'cold war' with its neighbors" (*Tribune*, London). As early as 1947, journalists were using the phrase to characterize U.S.-Soviet relations. While it was not until 1953 that John Foster Dulles, Eisenhower's secretary of state, spoke of a U.S. policy of "massive retaliation" in the event of a Soviet strike, the idea that nuclear weapons would primarily be part of a policy of deterrence via mutually assured destruction was under discussion in the early 1940s, before the first atomic bomb was built.

36. The interdependence of economic and military interests in the contemporary United States is a vestige of such doctrines. Shortly before the close of the Second World War, Charles E. Wilson (later Eisenhower's secretary of defense) used his stature as president of General Motors to call on American businesses to avoid a return to a peacetime production program, arguing that it was necessary to maintain, in what would become a well-known formulation, a "permanent war economy." Today military spending is frequently acknowledged to be a source of enormous profit, zealously protected and nurtured by captains of industry and the politicians they support. The cooperation between governments and multinational corporations characteristic of the "military Keynesianism" of our era ensures that business interests are furthered irrespective of whether wars take the form of clashes between countries or conflicts

between nation-states and extrastate entities or "networks." For some recent characterizations of these dynamics see Carl Boggs, *Imperial Delusions: American Militarism and Endless War* (New York: Rowman and Littlefield, 2005); David Harvey, *The New Imperialism* (New York: Oxford University Press, 2003); and Michael Hardt and Antonio Negri, *Multitude: War and Democracy in the Age of Empire* (New York: Penguin, 2004).

37. Decades after the fall of the Berlin Wall, this Cold War logic is far from extinct. Presenting its conclusion that it should have been possible to anticipate the 2001 attacks on the World Trade Center and the Pentagon, the 9/11 Commission declared that "it is . . . crucial to find a way of routinizing, even bureaucratizing, the exercise of the imagination." *Final Report of the National Commission on Terrorist Attacks Upon the United States*, 2004, 344; http://govinfo.library.unt.edu/911/report/index.htm. This edict amounted to a formal sanction of the assumption that even in a time of ostensible peace, a society must protect itself against aggression by envisioning all of the attacks that could conceivably befall it.

38. William Faulkner, *A Fable* (New York: Vintage, 1978), 25.

39. Ibid., 24.

40. See Polk, "Introduction: Faulkner and War and Peace," vii.

41. Faulkner, *Fable*, 62.

42. Ibid., 65.

43. See Stanley Weintraub, *Silent Night: The Story of the World War I Christmas Truce* (New York: Free Press, 2001), and Malcolm Brown and Shirley Seaton, *Christmas Truce* (New York: Hippocrene Books, 1984).

44. See Ian Westwell, *World War I: Day by Day* (Osceola, WI: MBI, 2000), 129.

45. The possibility that the regiment's mutiny may be symptomatic of a more profound disruption of wartime praxis is reinforced by the book's depiction of crowds. In an early scene townspeople gather to view the captive mutineers prior to their execution. Given Jünger's remarks about soldiers and workers, we might expect a novel about the First World War to dwell on the degree to which individual action has been superseded by a new form of collective agency in which particular combatants or civilians no longer enjoy privileged status as heroes or victims. Yet far from offering a reflection on mass formations or mass experience, *A Fable* seems to move in the opposite direction. In this scene and on each subsequent occasion that a crowd is on the verge of acquiring decisive energy or purpose, the group's momentum stagnates and instead serves as a backdrop for the distinctive volition of a single character. For a discussion of the masses in *A Fable*, see Lothar Hönnighausen, "Imagining the Abstract: Faulkner's Treatment of War and Values in *A Fable*," in *Faulkner and War*, 120–37.

46. Faulkner, *Fable*, 19.

47. This is the ironic obverse of the situation in which an exchange of nuclear weapons would retrospectively prove to have been an impossible operation once one unsuccessfully tried to repeat it—unsuccessfully, that is, since there would be no one around to do so.

48. On the innovations in collective mourning of the First World War, see Stéphane Audoin-Rouzeau and Annette Becker, *14–18: Understanding the Great War*, trans. Catherine Temerson (New York: Farrar, Straus, and Giroux, 2002), 182–202; and K. S. Inglis, "Entombing Unknown Soldiers: From London and Paris to Baghdad," *History and Memory: Studies in Representation of the Past* 5(2) (Fall–Winter 1993): 7–31.

49. See Neil Hanson, *Unknown Soldiers: The Story of the Missing of the First World War* (New York: Knopf, 2006).

50. See *Selected Letters of William Faulkner*, ed. Joseph Blotner (New York: Random House, 1977), 361.

51. *Faulkner in the University: Class Conferences at the University of Virginia 1957–1958* (Charlottesville: University of Virginia Press, 1959), 27.

52. George L. Mosse, *Fallen Soldiers: Reshaping the Memory of the World Wars* (New York: Oxford University Press, 1990), 84.

53. Ibid., 75–76.

54. Hannah Arendt argued that *A Fable* "surpasses almost all of World War I literature in perceptiveness and clarity because its hero is the Unknown Soldier," adding:

> The monuments to the "Unknown Soldier" after World War I bear testimony to the then still existing need for glorification, for finding a "who," an identifiable somebody whom four years of mass slaughter should have revealed. The frustration of this wish and the unwillingness to resign oneself to the brutal fact that the agent of the war was actually nobody inspired the erection of the monuments to the "unknown," to all those whom the war had failed to make known and had robbed thereby, not of their achievement, but of their human dignity. (*The Human Condition* [Chicago: University of Chicago Press, 1998], 181)

55. In "Mourning and Melancholia" (1915), perhaps his most famous wartime essay, Freud stresses that "mourning is regularly the reaction to the loss of a loved person, or to the loss of some abstraction which has taken the place of one, such as one's country, liberty, and ideal, and so on." "Mourning and Melancholia," in *Standard Edition*, vol. 19, 243.

56. It is often noted that Freud takes more than one position on the nature of successful mourning. Compare ibid., 239–58, and *The Ego and the Id*, vol. 19 of *Standard Edition*, 12–66. For an attempt to think through the implications

of Freud's doctrines see Jacques Derrida, *The Work of Mourning*, ed. Pascale-Anne Brault and Michael Naas (Chicago: University of Chicago Press, 2001).

57. Faulkner, *Fable*, 298.

58. Ibid., 299.

59. Stig Förster, introduction to *Great War, Total War: Combat and Mobilization on the Western Front, 1914–1918*, ed. Roger Chickering and Stig Förster (New York: Cambridge University Press, 2000), 6.

60. "Machine Fighting Is Edison's Idea," *New York Times*, October 16, 1915. On the trenches of the Western front as a parody of the industrial world of work see Fussell, *Great War and Modern Memory*.

61. Klaus Theweleit, *Male Fantasies*, vol. 2, trans. Stephen Conway (Minneapolis: University of Minnesota Press, 1989), 162. Observing that "for Theweleit this reconfiguration of body and psyche as weapon is fundamental to fascism," Hal Foster stresses the fascist's ambivalence about his body armor: he both wants it and wants to be rid of it. Hal Foster, "Armor Fou," *October* 56 (Spring 1991): 85.

62. As he took stock of the horrors of the Second World War in 1944, Theodor W. Adorno looked back to the First World War and identified the disjunction between the fragile corporeal condition of the soldiers and the network of killing machines surrounding them as central to the confusion that plagued their efforts to relate what they endured, arguing that "the body's incongruity with mechanical warfare made real experience impossible. No one could have recounted it." *Minima Moralia: Reflections from Damaged Life*, trans. E. F. N. Jephcott (New York: Verso, 1989), 54.

63. William Faulkner, Nobel Prize Speech, December 10, 1950, William Faulkner on the Web, www.mcsr.olemiss.edu/~egjbp/faulkner/lib_nobel.html.

64. Jünger, "Total Mobilization," 139.

65. Walter Benjamin, "The Work of Art in the Age of Its Technological Reproducibility (Third Version)," in *Walter Benjamin: Selected Writings*, vol. 4, 1938–1940, ed. Howard Eiland and Michael W. Jennings (Cambridge, MA: Harvard University Press, 2003), 270.

66. Thomas Pynchon, *Gravity's Rainbow* (New York: Viking, 1973), 521.

67. On *Gravity's Rainbow* as an experiment in filmic language see Scott Simon, "Beyond the Theater of War: *Gravity's Rainbow* as Film," *Literature/Film Quarterly* 6 (1978): 347–63; and Hanjo Berressem, *Pynchon's Poetics: Interfacing Theory and Text* (Chicago: University of Illinois Press, 1993), esp. 151–90.

68. Pynchon, *Gravity's Rainbow*, 760.

69. Ibid.

70. Ibid.

71. Benjamin, "Work of Art," 269.

72. Ibid., 270.

Conclusion

1. "Soldier's Cell Phone Records Sounds of Battle," Associated Press, May 6, 2008, www.katu.com/news/18700614.html.

2. The soldier survived the engagement unharmed. The audio recording of the call was quickly available on American news websites, and the soldier's brother posted it on YouTube.

3. We might ask what the "story" really is here. Is what is remarkable that the phone was touched in the right way at the right time to establish a remote link between family members at a potentially crucial or even fatal moment in a young man's life? Or is it rather that while devices for the transmission of audio-visual data have changed radically over the past two centuries, tales of the ironic vicissitudes of happenstance that plague battlefields and their on-lookers have been routine since the dawn of the Napoleonic era?

4. See Joan Vennochi, "We're in a War—Where Are the Media?" *Boston Globe*, May 4, 2008; Brian Stelter, "TV News Winds Down Operations on Iraq War," *New York Times*, December 29, 2008; Alessandra Stanley, "Bob Hope's Spirit, but No Cheesecake," *New York Times*, June 12, 2009; and Joe Garofoli, "Iraq War Is Hell on the Bottom Line at the Box Office," *San Francisco Chronicle*, November 23, 2007. Recent research has detailed the tiny fraction of news reports devoted to Afghanistan, irrespective of spikes in U.S. casualties. See the Pew Research Center's Project for Excellence in Journalism, "America's Longest War Fights for Media Attention," www.journalism.org/numbers_report/Americas_longest_war_fights_for_attention.

5. Garofoli, "Iraq War Is Hell on the Bottom Line."

6. Thomas Doherty, *Projections of War: Hollywood, American Culture, and World War II*, rev. ed. (New York: Columbia University Press, 1999), 5.

7. Describing the "almost industrial-scale counterterrorism killing machine" currently in operation in Afghanistan, Jeff Stein has argued that "the real counterinsurgency lessons from Malaya and Vietnam are that operations must be hidden from cameras and reporters. This kind of killing is just too vicious for current tastes." "Beyond the Hero Syndrome," *Bookforum* 18(2) (Summer 2011): 7.

8. Stelter, "TV News Winds Down Operations."

9. Fredric Jameson has recently called attention to the surprisingly repetitive nature of war narratives: "One often has the feeling that all war novels (and warfilms) are pretty much the same and have few enough surprises for us, even though their situations may vary." "War and Representation," *PMLA* 124(5) (October 2009): 1533.

10. Nicholas Mirzoeff, *Watching Babylon: The War in Iraq and Global Visual Culture* (New York: Routledge, 2005), 67.

11. Ibid., 70.

12. The often-voiced concern that many military operations now take place in the absence of clearly defined policy goals could be a symptom of the fact that, like war, politics as nineteenth-century political leaders understood it is no longer wedded to a state form. On this question see Herfried Münkler, *The New Wars*, trans. Patrick Camiller (Malden, MA: Polity, 2005), 33–34.

13. John Mueller, *The Remnants of War* (Ithaca, NY: Cornell University Press, 2004), 1. In 1989 Mueller argued that "major war—war among developed countries—has gradually moved toward terminal disrepute because of its perceived repulsiveness and futility." *Retreat from Doomsday* (New York: Basic Books, 1989), 4. From a historical perspective, Mueller's position is not novel. As Barbara Ehrenreich observes, "The conviction that war is passé, or soon to become so, has a venerable history of its own." *Blood Rites: Origins and History of the Passions of War* (New York: Holt, 1997), 225.

14. This perceived shift in praxis has been registered by changes in terminology. Whereas wars were once "conventional" or "unconventional," the military brass now envision future struggles as "irregular," and at West Point the "irregular-warfare-specialty track" has become the most popular concentration for cadets. William Safire, "On Language Column: Beyond the Unconventional," *New York Times Magazine*, June 8, 2008, 22. Unsurprisingly, irregularities plague the use of the term *irregular* since, as historian William Thomas Allison observes, "No one has agreed on a definition. Irregular warfare is used interchangeably with partisan warfare, rebellion, fourth-generation warfare, insurgency and of course guerrilla warfare" (ibid.).

15. The argument that liberal democratic regimes are less likely to go to war with one another than with nondemocratic regimes was advanced by Michael W. Doyle, "Kant, Liberal Legacies, and Foreign Affairs (Parts 1 and 2)," *Philosophy and Public Affairs* 12(3–4) (Summer–Fall 1983): 205–54, 323–53. This theory quickly became influential in the academy and among foreign policy makers, some going a step further to argue that democracies are more likely to win wars when fighting against nondemocratic governments. For a critique of this "democratic triumphalism" see Michael C. Desch, *Power and Military Effectiveness: The Fallacy of Democratic Triumphalism* (Baltimore: Johns Hopkins University Press, 2008).

16. Michael Hardt and Antonio Negri suggest that "each local war should not be viewed in isolation . . . but seen as part of a grand constellation, linked in varying degrees both to other war zones and to areas not presently at war." *Multitude: War and Democracy in the Age of Empire* (New York: Penguin, 2004), 4.

17. Herfried Münkler has argued that "the Thirty Years' War took place when the statization of the social-political order was not yet complete, so that it

involved the conflict and cooperation among state, semi-state and private play-ers which is also typical of the new wars today." *The New Wars*, 49.

18. See Ulrich Beck, *The Cosmopolitan Vision*, trans. Ciaran Cronin (Mal-den, MA: Polity, 2006), esp. 132ff.

19. Steven Pinker, *The Better Angels of Our Nature: Why Violence Has De-clined* (New York: Viking, 2011), xxi. Pinker describes a "Long Peace," a marked decline of warfare between the major nation-states since 1945, and a "New Peace," an abatement of organized conflict of all kinds since 1989 (ibid., xxiv).

20. Numerous academic debates have addressed the question that now titles a famous exchange that took place between Sigmund Freud and Albert Ein-stein more than half a century ago: Why war? What forces conspire to permit—encourage, or necessitate—human beings to destroy one another on a mass scale? From the social sciences and the humanities to biology and cognitive psychology, these questions have prompted a host of diagnoses, although no etiological paradigm has managed to achieve a persuasive force that would al-low it to assume priority over others. Although studies by archeologists, psy-chologists, and animal behaviorists have concluded that *Homo sapiens* is an in-trinsically aggressive creature, such arguments have been accused of confirming existing cultural values rather than elucidating scientific facts. Some natural scientists and physical anthropologists have directly taken issue with the notion that warfare's storied history is a product of biological compulsions driven by genetic forces and have emphasized that, statistically, human beings cooperate far more often than they fight. The error of war studies would thus be that it focuses exclusively on violence while forgetting that it is the exception, not the rule. See, for example, Douglas P. Fry, *Beyond War: The Human Potential for Peace* (New York: Oxford University Press, 2007). From a different perspective it has been argued that societies emerge as a response to war (i.e., as an antidote to *bellum omnium contra omnes*), and conversely, it has been maintained that it is the inherently bellicose quality of sociability itself that ensures that orga-nized strife will never be a thing of the past.

21. Susan Sontag offers an example of this tendency when she discusses tele-vision broadcasts:

> Images shown on television are by definition images of which, sooner or later, one tires. What looks like callousness has its origin in the instability of atten-tion that television is organized to arouse and to satiate by its surfeit of images. Image-glut keeps attention light, mobile, relatively indifferent to content. . . . The whole point of television is that one can switch channels, that it is normal to switch channels, to become restless, bored. (*Regarding the Pain of Others* [New York: Farrar, Straus and Giroux, 2002], 105–6)

22. Michel Foucault, *Discipline and Punish: The Birth of the Prison*, trans. Alan Sheridan (New York: Random House, 1979), 169.

23. Carl Boggs writes that "there can be little doubt that warfare motifs, discourses, and priorities increasingly shape all phases of social life, impacting everything from language, media representations, and popular culture to the workplace, forms of consumption, and politics." *Imperial Delusions: American Militarism and Endless War* (New York: Rowman and Littlefield, 2005), ix. For another characterization of these dynamics see David Harvey, *The New Imperialism* (New York: Oxford University Press, 2003).

24. W. G. Sebald, *On the Natural History of Destruction*, trans. Anthea Bell (New York: Random House, 2003), 41.

25. Ibid., 5.

26. Ibid., 24. Sebald further underscores the traumatic dimensions of these dynamics when he quotes Alexander Kluge's claim that the survivors of the air raids "lost the psychic power of accurate memory" (ibid.).

27. Ibid., 10.

28. Ibid., ix.

29. Ibid., x.

30. Sebald seems to be registering the fact that advances in the ethics of coming to terms with the past have not kept pace with advances in trauma theory.

31. Sebald, *On the Natural History of Destruction*, 24–25.

32. For an important collection of essays in contemporary trauma studies that challenge many of our assumptions about the field, see *Trauma: Explorations in Memory*, ed. Cathy Caruth (Baltimore: Johns Hopkins University Press, 1995), 4–5.

33. Over the last decade, the possibility that people who followed live broadcasts of the destruction of the World Trade Center could now have posttraumatic stress disorder has been hotly debated: "Some experts have been skeptical of studies finding that people suffered [PTSD] from watching television coverage of the Sept. 11 attacks. (Congress effectively excluded TV watchers from its treatment program by requiring that victims had lived or worked within certain geographic boundaries.)" Anemona Hartocollis, "10 Years and a Diagnosis Later, 9/11 Demons Haunt Thousands," *New York Times*, August 9, 2011, www .nytimes.com/2011/08/10/nyregion/post-traumatic-stress-disorder-from-911still -haunts.html?hp.

34. As early as the mid-nineteenth century, the potency of the mass media's war reporting was regarded as a threat to the public's mental health. Writing at the start of the American Civil War, the physician and medical reformer Oliver Wendell Holmes Sr. argued as follows:

When any startling piece of war-news comes, it keeps repeating itself in our minds in spite of all we can do. The same trains of thought go tramping round in a circle through the brain, like the supernumeraries that make up the grand army of a stage-show. Now, if a thought goes round through the brain a thousand times in a day, it will have worn as deep a track as one which has passed through it once a week for twenty years. This accounts for the ages we seem to have lived since the twelfth of April last. ("Bread and the Newspaper," *Atlantic Monthly* 8 [1861]: 347; quoted in Eliza Richards, "Correspondent Lines: Poetry, Journalism, and the U.S. Civil War," *ESQ: A Journal of the American Renaissance* 54[1–4] [2008]: 145–70)

35. Geoffrey Winthrop-Young, "Drill and Distraction in the Yellow Submarine: On the Dominance of War in Friedrich Kittler's Media Theory," *Critical Inquiry* 28 (Summer 2002): 834–35.

36. Carl von Clausewitz, *On War*, ed. and trans. Michael Howard and Peter Paret (Princeton, NJ: Princeton University Press, 1989), 87.

37. Jean Baudrillard, *The Gulf War Did Not Take Place* (Bloomington: Indiana University Press, 1995), 30; and Paul Virilio and Sylvère Lotringer, *Pure War*, trans. Mark Polizotti (New York: Semiotext(e), 1983), 84.

38. Michael Walzer, *Arguing About War* (New Haven, CT: Yale University Press, 2004), ix.

39. Gilles Deleuze and Felix Guattari, *A Thousand Plateaus: Capitalism and Schizophrenia*, trans. Brian Massumi (Minneapolis: University of Minnesota Press, 1987), 421.

40. See Michel Foucault, *"Society Must Be Defended": Lectures at the Collège de France 1975–1976*, trans. David Macey (New York: Picador, 2003), 47–48.

41. Foucault asks: "If we look beneath peace, order, wealth, and authority, beneath the calm order of subordinations, beneath the State and State apparatuses, beneath the laws, and so on, will we hear and discover a sort of primitive and permanent war?" (ibid., 46–47).

42. Ibid., 48. Foucault argues that in trying to understand the emergence of the claim that "politics is the continuation of war" one has to proceed in both directions, as it were, asking who "saw war just beneath the surface of peace" and who found "in the mud of battles, the principle that allows us to understand order, the State, its institutions, and its history?" (ibid., 47). Foucault does not clarify why this dynamic of surface and depth, veiling and unveiling, came into existence in the first place.

43. Michel Foucault, *The History of Sexuality*, trans. Robert Hurley (New York: Random House, 1978), 93.

44. Hardt and Negri, *Multitude*, 12.

45. Ibid., 13.

46. Ibid., 4.
47. Ibid., 13.
48. Ibid., 14.
49. Ibid.; emphasis added.
50. Hannah Arendt, *On Revolution* (New York: Penguin, 1990 [1963]), 18–19.
51. Hannah Arendt, *On Violence* (New York: Harcourt Brace, 1970), 5.
52. Ibid., 46–47.

Index

Note: *Italicized* page numbers refer to photographs. Page numbers followed by n or nn indicate notes.